Sir Georg Solti

OTHER BOOKS BY PAUL E. ROBINSON

The Art of the Conductor: Karajan (1st edition 1975)

The Art of the Conductor: Stokowski (1st edition 1977)

The Art of the Conductor: Solti (1st edition 1979)

The Art of the Conductor: Bernstein (1st edition 1982)

Sir Georg Solti

✦

His Life and Music

The Art of the Conductor Volume 1

Paul E. Robinson

iUniverse, Inc.
New York Lincoln Shanghai

Sir Georg Solti
His Life and Music

Copyright © 2006 by Paul E. Robinson

All rights reserved. No part of this book may be used or reproduced by any means, graphic, electronic, or mechanical, including photocopying, recording, taping or by any information storage retrieval system without the written permission of the publisher except in the case of brief quotations embodied in critical articles and reviews.

iUniverse books may be ordered through booksellers or by contacting:

iUniverse
2021 Pine Lake Road, Suite 100
Lincoln, NE 68512
www.iuniverse.com
1-800-Authors (1-800-288-4677)

ISBN-13: 978-0-595-39953-6 (pbk)
ISBN-13: 978-0-595-84341-1 (ebk)
ISBN-10: 0-595-39953-3 (pbk)
ISBN-10: 0-595-84341-7 (ebk)

Printed in the United States of America

Contents

Preface vii
Introduction ix
CHAPTER 1   The Making of a Maestro 1
CHAPTER 2   The Maestro Becomes Sir Georg 16
CHAPTER 3   The Maestro at the Summit 30
CHAPTER 4   Forging Decca's Ring 50
CHAPTER 5   The Beethoven Nine in Chicago 64
CHAPTER 6   Mahler with Many Orchestras 82
CHAPTER 7   The Interpreter in the Opera House 104
CHAPTER 8   The Interpreter on the Concert Platform 117
CHAPTER 9   A Summing Up 132
SELECTED BIBLIOGRAPHY 139
DISCOGRAPHY 141
VIDEOGRAPHY 191
Index 201

Preface

This book set out on its initial journey more than twenty-five years ago. It was part of a series of books on conductors which began with *Karajan* in 1975, and continued with *Stokowski* in 1977. *Solti* came next in 1979, and the final volume was *Bernstein* in 1982. Each of these books was based on radio programs I had done for CJRT-FM in Toronto. The response to the broadcasts was positive enough that the Toronto publisher Lester and Orpen thought there might be a wider audience if the programs were put into book form. Two co-publishers were found almost immediately in Vanguard Press in the United States and Macdonald and Janes in the U.K. When the books were published in English a number of foreign publishers became interested and before long there were German, Japanese and Russian editions.

Inevitably, all of these editions have passed out of print, and other books on these conductors have been published. However, I have been surprised by how few of them offer what I set out to do in my original series. My books were never intended to be comprehensive biographies, but rather, as I stated in the original Preface to *Solti*,

> a short reference tool containing the basic facts of a conductor's life to date and a fair assessment of his work in opera and concert and on recordings, based on a cross-section of published opinion as well as on my own observations. The discography at the end of each book is another useful compendium of information about the conductor's work.

It seems to me that there is still a need for books of this kind. My long-term goal would be to produce books on at least a dozen or so prominent conductors but an easier goal to attain would be the updating of those I had already done. After more than twenty-five years since the original publication, it is obvious that something more than minor tinkering is required. In the case of Solti, for example, when the original *Solti* was published in 1979 he was very much in his prime as music director of the Chicago Symphony. He was to remain active for another eighteen years. In revising *Solti* I have tried to improve on and polish what I had written in 1979 but also cover the missing biographical ground between 1979 and 1997. Moreover, some of Solti's finest recordings were made in this later period of his career and they deserved some attention too. And since we are now looking back at a complete career, an overall consideration is required. Speaking of completeness, the Discography too has been updated and includes virtually all known Solti recordings. I am grateful to Raymond McGill of Decca Records for his invaluable assistance in improving the Solti Discography. Completely new for this edition is a Videography listing all of Solti's many films and DVDs of operas and concerts.

Since this book can trace its origin back to broadcasts over CJRT-FM I must once again express my appreciation to technician Ron Hughes for putting up with my conductorial obsessions on a weekly basis, and to station manager Cam Finley for giving me the opportunity to make the whole project possible. Others who gave invaluable help in the original research or in the more recent revisions included Bruce Surtees, James Creighton of the Recordings Archive, University of Toronto, Norman Pelligrini, Ray Nordstrand, Lois Baum and Tony Judge of WFMT in Chicago, Victor Marshall of the Dallas Symphony, Frank Villella of the Rosenthal Archives of the Chicago Symphony, and Raymond McGill of the Decca Record Company.

With the publication of *Sir Georg Solti: His Life and Music,* my series *The Art of the Conductor* is off and running for a new generation of music-lovers. It will be followed shortly by revised editions of my books on Karajan, Stokowski and Bernstein. In time there may even be some entirely new titles. To keep readers abreast of my new publications, recordings and other activities, I have created a website: www.theartoftheconductor.com

Introduction

There are many ways of measuring success in the world of music. Good reviews from the New York critics are universally acceptable; so too are high fees. But Georg Solti achieved these plateaus and much more. He enjoyed more special recognition in the form of a knighthood in 1971 and an honorary degree from Oxford the following year. The supreme accolade, however, was awarded him in 1977. That was the year he received a distinction few, if any other, musicians have had conferred upon them; his picture was featured on the cover of the Chicago telephone directory. In all seriousness, it would be hard to discover more conclusive proof of the impact Solti had on the city of Chicago. During a period in which the Chicago Black Hawks, the Chicago Bears, the Chicago Cubs and the Chicago White Sox failed to win any kind of glory, the Chicago Symphony was acclaimed the world over for its greatness, and Georg Solti was its music director and conductor.

In recognition and appreciation of the orchestra's international renown, its' members were greeted as conquering heroes when they returned from the 1971 European tour: they were given a parade down State Street and declared "Chicagoans of the Year." The praise has continued to pour in year after year, with ten-minute ovations for the annual New York concerts and showers of awards for the orchestra's recordings. Solti gave the people of Chicago a new and prestigious place in the sun and they loved him for it. It was only appropriate that his picture be in every Chicago home, courtesy of the Illinois Bell Telephone Company.

Who was the man behind this famous face? He was, above all, the music director of the Chicago Symphony from 1969 to 1991, but even during that period he was also tremendously active in Europe. In fact, he was usually only in Chicago about three months a year. He also maintained a residence in London, where he appeared regularly at the Royal Opera House and with the London Philharmonic. A third home for Solti, his wife Valerie and their children was in Italy, where they nearly always spent the summer, completely away from the concert circuit. From September to May, Solti was rehearsing, conducting and recording almost non-stop. During the summer months he insisted on setting aside time to reflect and prepare for the following season.

Solti was born in Budapest in 1912 and began his musical career as a pianist, and a very good one. He went on to apprenticeships at various opera houses before rising to the top as music director of the Bavarian State Opera in Munich, then artistic director of the Frankfurt Opera. Next came the music directorship of the Royal Opera House, Covent Garden, and then the Chicago Symphony. After his retirement from the Chicago Symphony in 1991, at the age of 79, he remained active as a guest conductor until his death in 1997. Throughout his career he was a major recording artist and for only one company, Decca. He made his first recording in 1947—Beethoven's *Egmont* overture with the Zürich Tonhalle Orchestra—and went on to record over 40 operas and a total of 250 separate albums primarily with the Chicago Symphony, the Vienna Philharmonic, and the London Philharmonic. Perhaps his most significant recording achievement was the first complete studio recording of Wagner's *Ring* cycle with the Vienna Philharmonic and with John Culshaw as producer.

By nature Solti was restless and intense. He was born with these qualities and to a great extent they made him the kind of conductor he was. Compare Solti with his contemporary Herbert von Karajan (1908-1989), conductor-for-life of the Berlin Philharmonic, and often mentioned as Solti's only peer. When Karajan stood on the podium, there was scarcely an unnecessary movement. His feet were stationary; his arms were perpetually extended in a smoothly flowing series of graceful gestures; his eyes were often closed and his face almost immobile. His body was not without tension but the movements were restrained. Or, consider Sir Adrian Boult (1889-1983), a former student of Artur Nikisch and an exponent of his mentor's famously minimalist conducting style. Often Boult was a picture of near immobility bordering on nonchalance. However, like the great Russian conductor Eugene Mravinsky or the German maestro Otto Klemperer, this desultory appearance frequently produced remarkable results.

And then there was Solti:

> Solti is the least graceful conductor since Dimitri Mitropoulos. His motions are jittery; his whole body is in motion; his shoulders as well as his hands are responding to the rhythm; his beat is a series of jabs, and he looks as though he is shadowboxing. (Harold C. Schonberg, *New York Times,* November 28, 1976)

Solti, it seems, could not keep still. Even when the music was quiet and slow moving, he had a tendency to give it a working-over with largely superfluous gestures, so that these more subdued passages emerged with an undercurrent of tension, although sometimes they were simply robbed of repose. Solti's elaborate movements were essential to him. They were the only means through which he felt he could adequately express himself, even though so many of them were impossible for an orchestra to interpret literally. One might have suspected Solti of trying to impress the audience, except for the fact that his gestures did little to flatter him. And, by and large, they were effective. The players might have disagreed with what Solti was doing or they might have preferred a more straightforward set of signals, but they found him impossible to resist. While Karajan concentrated by going into a sort of trance, Solti's concentration took the form of total physical involvement, where every part of the body was brought into play. The blazing eyes and the facial expressions—mostly deeply serious and intense, yet also dreamy on occasion—were other vital parts of his technique.

Another aspect of Solti's "everything up front" character was his outspokenness off the concert platform. His remarks to the press about the inadequacies of the Orchestre de Paris caused an almighty row. Nor did he hesitate to criticize the New York Philharmonic or tenor Jon Vickers. Even the good burghers of Chicago felt the lash of his tongue, as when he threatened to do away with the Friday afternoon subscription concerts because the dowagers were so inattentive and noisy in their chatter. Solti was certainly no shrinking violet, but there was a softer side to him too. He was also the maestro who so visibly mellowed after becoming a father late in life, and he was the Hungarian-born musician who was so deeply touched by the honor of a British knighthood for his role in bringing Covent Garden to international standards, that he preferred ever after to be called "Sir Georg" (pronounced George) Solti."

Although his performances rarely displayed much of a sense of humor, he was capable of entering into the spirit of an event. In his adopted country he formed a fond attachment for former Prime Minister Heath—himself an excellent musician and a sometime conductor—and on the occasion of Heath's birthday in 1973 Solti made a special contribution to the festivities. At that time, Solti was in London recording Mozart's opera *Così fan tutte*. He arranged for a recording of the sextet "Alla bella Despinetta" to be played at the party. To everyone's delight the final words had been altered to "Happy Birthday, Ted." The label of this unusual (private) recording read "with harpsichord accompaniment by G. Solti."

In spite of Solti's great love for England, he was a still a Hungarian, and his surname was still to be pronounced in the Hungarian manner, as "Sholti." One of his greatest triumphs late in his career was his first concert in Hungary since he fled the country just ahead of the Nazis in 1938. Forty years later, in March of 1978, he returned leading the Vienna Philharmonic. It was an unsettling experience for Solti to go back to his homeland—still not free after all this time and solidly behind the Iron Curtain—to see Budapest, city of his youth and to visit the graves of both parents and a sister. Before he would agree to this trip, Solti stipulated that his fee should be used to enable two young Hungarian conductors to further their studies in the West—a touching personal and political gesture from a man better known for his egocentrism and for his musical achievements. Solti lived long enough to see Hungary freed at last from the yoke of communism and the Soviet Union. Fittingly, his last recording made in Budapest the year he died (1997) was an album of music by Hungarian composers—all of them Solti's former teachers—with the Budapest Festival Orchestra.

1

The Making of a Maestro

At one time, it seemed that Hungary was the world's leading producer of first-class conductors. What other country could boast a list of living maestros which included Fritz Reiner, George Szell, Eugene Ormandy, Antal Dorati, Ferenc Fricsay, Istvan Kertesz and Georg Solti? Just why this should be so will have to be left to the sociologists. In Solti's case, it was a matter of being blessed with enormous musical gifts and being encouraged to use them.

Solti's father, Mores, grew up in the tiny village of Balatonfökajár, but moved to the capital Budapest to work first in the grain business and later in real estate. György (later changed to Georg), was born there October 21, 1912. When he was five years old his parents discovered that he had perfect pitch, and although they were far from wealthy they saw the need to develop his natural abilities. They bought an old piano and sent the boy for lessons. Solti took to this new activity with ferocious intensity, quickly demonstrating a precocious talent for the instrument. By the time he was twelve he was giving public recitals.

The following year, Solti enrolled in the Franz Liszt Academy of Music, Hungary's leading music school, for a broader training in music. During his five years there he was fortunate enough to be able to count among his teachers the country's greatest musical figures: Ernst von Dohnányi, Zoltán Kodály and Béla Bartók. It was no wonder, then, that Solti went on to become the most authoritative living interpreter of the music of these composers.

At some stage during his musical education, Solti was bitten with the conducting bug. He himself said it happened at age fourteen when he saw Erich Kleiber (1890-1956) conduct. At that time the Austrian-born Kleiber was head of the Berlin State Opera and a frequent guest conductor in Budapest. Kleiber was autocratic, intense and charismatic and he made a strong impression on the young Solti. By the time Solti graduated from the Liszt Academy in 1930, he was positive that conducting was what he wanted to do more than anything else. The problem was how to begin? Up to this point in his life, he had never conducted an orchestra.

How does any eager young musician become a conductor? For European musicians the answer—regardless of the difficulties it may present in North America with far fewer opera companies—is and was invariably the same: become a coach in an opera house. In fact, nearly all the great conductors, including Kleiber, were opera coaches at the outset of their careers due to the fact that the job offers practical training. After all, how does a conductor gain experience? He is never allowed in front of an orchestra because he does not know how to conduct. But he cannot conduct because he is unable to practice. Without an orchestra at his constant disposal, he is like a violinist without an instrument. In an opera house the budding conductor acts as vocal coach, accompanying singers at the piano to prepare them for their roles. He also rehearses the chorus, perhaps even conducting the offstage chorus for performances. After a few years, when he is asked to lead a performance from the pit, he knows entire operas inside and out; not only every note of the score but all the pitfalls. He knows too how to coordinate all the different forces under his command and how to correct mistakes when they occur. He may turn out to be mediocre in his ability to interpret a score or control an orchestra, but at least he comes to the podium prepared.

This is also the reason so many of the leading conductors are pianists. If one takes the opera house route to conducting, it is an essential skill. Like Karajan, Szell, Leinsdorf, Klemperer, Walter and so many others, this was the route that Solti followed too. In 1930, at age eighteen, he emerged from the Liszt Academy in Budapest and took his first job in music, as a coach at the Budapest Opera. He was on his way as a conductor, although it was to be some years before he got near an orchestra.

While working in Budapest, Solti spent several summers at the Salzburg Festival serving as an opera coach with Arturo Toscanini (1867-1957). Solti even played the glockenspiel in some Toscanini performances of Mozart's opera, the *Magic Flute*. His prowess on this instrument can be examined today on a live recording of one of the 1937 Salzburg performances (Naxos Historical 8.110828-29).

Solti was absolutely spellbound by Toscanini, his total dedication, his precision and his drive. It must be said, however, that throughout most of Solti's career perhaps he was overly influenced by the eminent Italian conductor in matters of speed and rigidity of tempi, not to mention emotional intensity. Solti himself admitted as much in a conversation with William Mann in 1974, recorded and released as part of the English edition of the Beethoven symphonies.

At Salzburg during the 1930's, Toscanini and Wilhelm Furtwängler were the towering figures among conductors, although very different from each other in their methods and interpretations. It must have been extremely difficult for a young conductor to simultaneously appreciate the good qualities of both men. For reasons of prior training and temperament, Solti emulated Toscanini at the expense of Furtwängler, deploring the latter's apparent carelessness in matters of precision, tempo and rhythm. As far as Solti was concerned, Furtwängler was completely beyond the pale as a conductor, although Solti later revised this view, recognizing the German maestro's considerable ability after all. The mature Solti said himself that he sought to combine the best of both Furtwängler and Toscanini (*Memoirs,* p. 74).

Solti served an eight-year apprenticeship at the Budapest Opera before he got his first opportunity to mount the podium as a maestro. It was March 11, 1938 and the opera was Mozart's *Marriage of Figaro*. After long years of working, waiting and hoping, Solti was about to prove whether or not he had it in him to be a conductor. If he made a mess of it, he might be denied another chance for years to come, perhaps for good. One can imagine the pressure Solti was under. At twenty-six years of age, determined to be a conductor, impatient that he should have had to wait so long before even beginning, he was at last taking his bows in front of a vast audience and turning to impose his will on orchestra and singers. Would they help him through this terrible initiation or would they delight in showing how green and inexperienced he was?

Unfortunately, it is not possible to report that the young lion emerged triumphant at the end, hailed as "the greatest conductor to appear at the Budapest Opera in the past twenty years." This is the accolade one might expect to find in the biographies of all the great conductors, but it is not in Solti's because history intervened.

March 11, 1938 was a special day not only for Solti, but for Hungary, Austria and the world. While Solti conducted Mozart's most inspired comic creation, word spread through the house like wildfire that Hitler was only 130 miles away, marching into Vienna. This awful news utterly destroyed concentration both on the stage and in the audience, and Solti's debut became a monumental irrelevancy.

> That was quite a night. All my friends left at intermission. The news came through that Hitler had marched into Vienna, and everybody ran home thinking he was going to continue the march to Budapest. This was a damp ending to my debut. There was not even a celebration after the performance. (*New York Times* interview with Harold C. Schonberg, March 24, 1957)

A Nazi invasion of Hungary was imminent and everyone knew what that could mean for Jews living there. Solti was Jewish and needed no further warning to recognize the need to get out of Hungary. He applied for a visa to go to the United States but was turned down and went to Switzerland instead, where he spent the rest of the war years.

His career as a conductor had already begun late; now it seemed as if it would go no further than an ill-fated debut at the Budapest Opera. From that night it was to be another four years before Solti conducted again. It was only in 1942 that Solti was invited to conduct two performances of Massenet's *Werther* in Geneva. Unfortunately, the performances were nearly a fiasco and the experience did little to build confidence in the young conductor.

But Solti was by no means idle in Switzerland. For two years he lived in Zürich, in the home of tenor Max Hirzel. Solti had met Hirzel in Budapest a few years earlier and Hirzel had very kindly left an open invitation to Solti to call if he ever came to Zürich. Solti was in Lucerne at that time working with Toscanini, and Solti's parents called him to warn him not to return to Hungary. Solti had neither money nor friends in Switzerland but recalled Hirzel's offer. Hirzel had an important career at the time and his wife was a vocal coach. In return for free lodging Solti helped Hirzel in the preparation of new roles and also coached some of his wife's more advanced vocal students. Solti also practiced the piano like a madman. In fact, he practiced so hard the neighbors complained—to the police! But the practicing paid off. Solti won first prize at a 1942 international piano competition in Geneva.

Another benefit of his piano playing and coaching activities in Zürich, was that he fell in love with a young Swiss pianist who came to study with him. Sadly, she married someone else but Solti recalled that "our love kept me alive, intellectually and psychologically." (*Memoirs*, p. 60) Two years later, Solti was in love again with another Swiss girl, this time it was Hedi Oechsli, his future wife. Solti credits her with giving him a sophistication and worldliness he sorely lacked:

> I was a late developer, really quite backward, and in some respects neither intelligent nor well educated…Hedi gave me a little grace and taught me how to behave—although she never *completely* succeeded in this." (*Memoirs, p. 61*)

In the years immediately following the war Solti continued to practice and to perform publicly as a pianist, and most notably as a sonata partner for German violinist Georg Kulenkampf in a memorable series of recordings (See Discography). Solti's playing in sonatas by Mozart, Beethoven and Brahms is impeccable, and altogether worthy of his, at that time, much more distinguished collaborator. Kulenkampff, nearing the end of his career, was Germany's leading violinist. He died in 1948.

It is commonplace today for conductors to rise to fame overnight. It happens so often that those who do not are dismissed as being demonstrably ungifted. In 1943, at the age of twenty-five, Leonard Bernstein made the front page of the *New York Times,* stepping in for an ailing Bruno Walter, and emerging victorious. Zubin Mehta was jetting between Montreal and Los Angeles as music director of both cities' orchestras before he was thirty. At the same age, Seiji Ozawa was head of the Toronto Symphony and about to take over the San Francisco Symphony on his way to the Boston Symphony within a very few years. Yet Solti, a major talent as things turned out, was not even given a chance to conduct regularly until he was in his mid-thirties.

Had it not been for the war, Solti's career almost certainly would have moved ahead a lot faster. With his talent, he would have become a star of the Budapest Opera and before long, in demand at the more prestigious European opera houses. On the other hand, the war's end unexpectedly benefited Solti. In 1945 there was a dearth of conductors in the German-speaking world. Many of the great ones, such as Walter, Klemperer, Busch, Szell and Reiner, had fled before the war. Those who had stayed, Furtwängler, Karajan, Böhm and Knappertsbusch among them, were suspected of collaboration and prohibited from conducting until they had been interrogated by de-nazification tribunals. In the areas of Germany occupied by American forces, music control officers were appointed in an effort to get the opera houses and concert life back to normal. It happened that the officer in charge of the Bavarian section was Edward Kilenyi, an American pianist who had been a classmate of Solti's in Budapest during the 1920's. Either Kilenyi was desperate for a conductor or Solti had made a remarkable impression on him; whatever the explanation, Solti was appointed music director of the Munich State Opera.

In normal times such a post would have been out of the question for a man of Solti's inexperience. One of Germany's leading opera houses was not likely to choose as its head a conductor with exactly one opera performance to his credit, and that single performance seven years before! But these were not normal times. In 1945 the Munich State Opera was a pale shadow of its former self. The house had been destroyed by Allied bombing, first-rate singers as well as conductors were in short supply, and there was no money. Music Director Solti lived in one small room in a bombed-out house with no roof.

However, these overwhelming problems were simply minor details in the eyes of the ambitious and energetic Solti. For here at last was the chance to conduct and to conduct regularly; it was just the learning experience he needed. He developed an enormous repertoire in Munich, including German, Italian and Russian operas and even a number of new works. For example, in the 1949-50 season he conducted *Tobias Wunderlich,* a new opera by Joseph Haas, a pupil of Max Reger's, and in his seventieth year at the time of the premiere. The same season Solti conducted Mussorgsky's *Boris Godunov* in the Rimsky-Korsakov arrangement and orchestration, Verdi's *Rigoletto* with tenor Hans Hopf as the Duke of Mantua and Wagner's *Tannhäuser.*

A curious feature of the repertoire of German opera houses at that time was the paucity of Wagner operas. Since Wagner's works had been favored by the Nazis, their performance was not encouraged by the occupying authorities. Thus, while Solti later became renowned for his Wagner, he was able to conduct very little of it in Munich. *Götterdämmerung* was presented there in 1951—the first presentation of the work in Germany since the war—but the conductor was Hans Knappertsbusch. The entire *Ring* cycle did not see the light of day in Munich until many years later.

The most prestigious event at the State Opera was always the Munich Festival, in which the *Bayerisches Staatsoper* put its best productions on show for the international press and public. The English critic William Mann was particularly impressed by a *Salome* he saw there in 1950:

> The most consistently breathtaking of the five Festival performances I saw was without doubt that of *Salome*...Solti's reading brought the clarity of chamber music to this vastly orchestral score, but without losing an iota of the power and polychromatics with which we generally connect it. (*Opera*, 1950)

The following year at the Festival, Solti was again featured in operas by Richard Strauss, leading performances of *Ariadne auf Naxos* with Maria Reining and Wilma Lipp, and *Der Rosenkavalier* with Reining and Sena Jurinac.

It was also in 1951 that Solti was invited for the first time to the Salzburg Festival. This was during a period when the festival was dominated by Furtwängler who conducted nearly all the operas and many of the concerts himself. Solti was assigned a Mozart opera Furtwängler never cared to conduct: *Idomeneo*. The work is exceedingly difficult to bring off either dramatically or musically. It is written in a more consistently serious style than any of the famous Mozart operas and lacks memorable arias save the brilliant "Parto, parto!" with clarinet obbligato. When one considers that Furtwängler probably appropriated most of the rehearsal time and the best players for his own productions, it is not surprising that one observer had this to say of Solti's performance:

> The orchestral playing was poor. Solti, the conductor, was either fighting a losing battle with tired performers or else not fighting the right battle, and the Italian accents of the singers (apart from Güden) were so execrable as seriously to distort the music. (The Earl of Harewood, *Opera*, November, 1951)

It did not help either that Lord Harewood had just seen an extremely successful production of *Idomeneo* at the Glyndebourne Festival. Nonetheless, it was something of a coup for Solti to be invited to Salzburg in the company of many of the leading conductors of the day including, besides Furtwängler, Jochum, Böhm, Stokowski, Kubelik and Edwin Fischer. It must have given Solti great personal satisfaction to return to Salzburg as a full-fledged maestro fourteen years after having served as a coach with Toscanini.

Solti next appeared at the Festival in 1955, conducting Mozart's *Magic Flute*, a work Furtwängler had always reserved for himself at Salzburg. It was given to Solti only after Furtwängler's death in the fall of 1954. Solti had a fine cast to work with, headed by Elisabeth Grümmer, Erika Köth, Christa Ludwig and Gottlob Frick. The stage director was Gunther Rennert and sets were designed by no less an artist than Oskar Kokoschka. The production received generally good notices, although Solti himself drew some negative comments:

> Musically, the opera received a routine performance. Georg Solti did not seem always to have the orchestra under control and though his tempi were more orthodox than those of his *Don Giovanni*, he did not elicit an unusually distinguished performance. (Christopher Raeburn, *Opera*, October, 1955)

On the other hand, when Solti conducted the same work at Frankfurt a few months later, another critic, Andrew Porter, was extravagant in his praise:

> The musical direction of Georg Solti, one of the best of all Mozart conductors, was the triple pillar of the performance: tempi exactly judged, phrasing flexible but firm and a bewitching balance within the orchestral parts, (*Opera*, December, 1955)

The Salzburg invitations were by no means the only ones extended to Solti during his sojourn in Munich. He was signed to a recording contract by Decca and made his first orchestral recording in Zürich in 1947: Beethoven's *Egmont* Overture with the Zürich Tonhalle Orchestra. In 1949, Solti recorded Haydn's Symphony No. 103 (*Drumroll*), with the London Philharmonic. In the early 1950's he made more recordings in London for Decca. These recordings with the London Symphony and the London Philharmonic of works by Suppé, Bartók, Kodály and Mozart, set him apart as a conductor of enormous energy and drive, with extraordinary ability to get the best out of an orchestra, and the recordings helped build his international reputation. In the summer of 1952 he appeared at the Edinburgh Festival conducting Mozart's *Magic Flute* with the touring Hamburg Opera.

In 1952, after six seasons at the *Bayerisches Staatsoper*, Solti resigned and accepted a similar post at Frankfurt, where he stayed for a decade. Since Munich was at that time, and still is today, the more prestigious house, it is puzzling that Solti should have made this move. It could be, however, that the decision was not his alone. By 1952 Munich could once more attract the most celebrated names in opera and had perhaps outgrown its need for Solti. Yet even though Frankfurt was not a great leap forward in Solti's career, it did not exactly inhibit his growth either. He continued to expand his repertoire and to mature as a conductor, and his guest conducting elsewhere in the world became more frequent. It was in Frankfurt, moreover, that Solti was noticed by Decca producer John Culshaw and invited to work on the historic *Ring* cycle with the Vienna Philharmonic.

Although Solti did not take over as *Generalmusikdirektor* until the fall of 1952, his first appearances in Frankfurt were in the spring of that year, conducting Bizet's *Carmen* with Rosl Zapf in the title role. One of the great triumphs of Solti's first season was the premiere performance in Germany of the revised version of Paul Hindemith's opera *Cardillac,* produced by Rennert. It caused a sensation when it was taken to the Berlin Festival in November, 1953, earning fulsome praise both for the Frankfurt Opera company and its new chief:

> It is not considered one of Germany's leading companies and in sheer resources it is clearly inferior to Berlin. But the performances it gave of the new version of *Cardillac* had a unity of style, a sense of musical excitement and a rhythmic vitality that were lacking in most Berlin performances. These qualities were due in the first place to the remarkably fine conducting of Georg Solti. Hindemith's wonderful score is complex—notably in the vast contrapuntal choruses that open and close the work—yet he was clearly the master of every detail, and continued to convey this mastery to his singers and players so that the whole performance shone in what I can only inadequately describe as an intense intellectual and musical luminosity, compara-

ble, perhaps to the effect the Brahms symphonies made under Toscanini. (Peter Heyworth, *Opera,* November, 1953)

Just a month later, however, Solti was involved in a controversial production of Mozart's *Così fan tutte* in Frankfurt. This sublime, eighteenth century comedy of manners was updated to the 1840s, much to the chagrin of many observers, and Solti did not escape unscathed when he decided to conduct the modernized version:

> The efficient, though rather rigid direction of Georg Solti could not redeem this frivolous maltreatment of a masterpiece. (*Opera,* December, 1953)

But by 1958, at least one critic had noticed a significant improvement in Solti's conducting of this same opera in Frankfurt:

> His interpretation of *Così fan tutte* in 1958 was characterized as usual by agility, vitality and springy tempos, but whereas his finely balanced sensibility had in the past occasionally lapsed into an overnervy fluctuation of mood and expression, he had now achieved a moment of utter tranquillity which was lacking in his 1954 performances of the same opera. (Ernst Thomas, *Opera,* August, 1961)

Yet even in his first years in Frankfurt, there were many who were impressed by Solti's Mozart, particularly his *Don Giovanni,* which was often singled out for praise along with his *Otello.* Both operas seemed to bring out the best in Solti: an almost fanatical attention to rhythmic exactitude coupled with unflagging energy.

> Both performances were conspicuous for their musical discipline which was responsible for the fact, not always to be taken for granted these days, that singers and orchestra were meticulously together. This discipline of Solti's has in it nothing of rigidity. He has the right amount of *Musizierfreudigkeit* to make *Otello* and *Don Giovanni* sound almost as if they were easy to perform. The problematic choral scenes of the first *Otello* act were not only of flawless precision but also completely transparent. The orchestra played very well indeed and eagerly followed Solti's exacting Mozart demands. (Curt Preauer, *Opera,* April, 1953)

Solti also began earning an enviable reputation for his Strauss, Wagner and Verdi. His conducting of *Don Carlos* in 1957 was immensely satisfying to Ruth Uebel:

> Georg Solti certainly belongs to the top rank Verdi conductors of the day. His reading was as exciting as usual, and the brilliant dramatic climaxes never overshadowed those lyrical portions of the score which were lovingly conducted. (*Opera,* December, 1957)

And in his review of a new production of *La Forza del Destino* in 1956, Ralf Steyer heaped the highest possible praise on Solti:

> The tender *cantabile* of Verdi's melody, the dramatic impulse, the vigor of the accents—all this was realized through his understanding of the basic coherence of the drama, in an ideal manner that one knows only from Toscanini and de Sabata. Unfortunately, the stage let him down completely. (*Opera,* December, 1956)

But the same critic was quite capable of recognizing Solti's weaknesses, which he thought were particularly glaring in a production of Johann Strauss' *Die Fledermaus* a few months later:

> Solti blew the music away at a jet-propelled tempo so that not merely was the detail not affectionate and clear, but it simply could not be perceived. In addition the orchestra played without delicacy and there were discrepancies on the stage and in the pit...the grand occasion to which we had been looking forward did not come off. It was a pity. There was friendly applause, but not the amount that Solti used to receive. (*Opera,* March, 1957)

While Frankfurt was not then counted among the leading opera houses in Europe or even in Germany, Solti considerably enhanced its stature both at home and on tour. In addition to the sensational appearance of the company in Berlin in 1953, there was a visit to Paris in 1956 during which Solti conducted Gluck's *Orfeo* and Strauss' *Der Rosenkavalier,* the latter with an excellent cast headed by Maria Reining, Christa Ludwig, Hanny Steffek and Kurt Böhme.

Meanwhile, Solti's personal reputation was growing by leaps and bounds on the international scene. Spring 1953 saw his opera debut in England conducting

Mozart's *Don Giovanni* at the prestigious and exclusive Glyndebourne Festival, where he received a favorable critical reaction:

> One enjoyed the drive, virility, and seriousness of purpose which characterized Georg Solti's reading of the score, yet one was less happy about the stage, where with the exception of Jurinac's superb Elvira, and to a lesser degree Harshaw's Anna, no one else seemed well cast. (Cecil Smith, *Opera*, September, 1953)

Another debut, this time in North America at the San Francisco Opera, took place later that same year. It was one of the most significant events of Solti's career. He conducted both opera and concerts and, moreover, he appeared with the San Francisco Symphony as a candidate for the post of permanent conductor, succeeding Pierre Monteux. The list of possible successors included some of the biggest international names, among them Stokowski, Leinsdorf, Münchinger, Steinberg and Fricsay. Solti conducted the orchestra for three weeks, beginning with a program comprising Haydn's Symphony No. 103, Strauss' *Don Juan* and Beethoven's Symphony No. 5. He failed to win the post, even though he was well-received by both public and press. The job ultimately went to a flamboyant but all but unknown Spaniard named Enrique Jordá, and his selection turned out to be a disaster.

Solti's opera conducting in San Francisco was also praised:

> The high point of the German repertory to date was the sensationally tense not to say overwhelming, *Elektra*, with Inge Borkh as the heroine, Margarete Klose as an incomparably hag-ridden Klytemnestra, and Georg Solti presiding. Solti is the first guest conductor to be engaged both by the San Francisco Opera and the San Francisco Symphony Orchestra and his interpretations of *Elektra* and *Tristan* fully justified this innovation. (Alfred Frankenstein, *Opera*, December, 1953)

An interesting footnote to Solti's North American debut is that it was not intended to take place in San Francisco at all. He had been invited to conduct the Chicago Symphony at the Ravinia Festival in July of 1953. However, when he applied for a visa at the American consulate in his home base of Frankfurt, it was not forthcoming. The reason given was that Solti's name appeared on a list of members of the "German-Soviet Society", a well-known communist organization in Munich. In 1953 communists were not welcome in the United States. Solti was quick to declare his innocence in a statement issued to the press:

> The list is forged. I testified under oath that I have never been a member of this society, but the consulate officials told me this was not sufficient. The consul believes too that the list is forged, but he said that the matter must be cleared up before I get a visa. (*New York Times,* July 12, 1953)

Solti flew to Munich to get to the bottom of the matter in co-operation with officials of the West German government. Although he was quickly given a clean bill of health by all concerned, his visa was not actually granted until August and he was forced to cancel his Ravinia appearances. Solti's official debut in the United States, therefore, took place September 13, 1953 in San Francisco rather than a month earlier in Chicago. Solti finally got to Ravinia in the summer of 1954, for his first concert with the Chicago Symphony and the beginning of a beautiful friendship.

After San Francisco, Solti began to make annual visits to the United States. His most important engagements were at the Chicago Lyric Opera in 1956. The previous season, Music Director Nicola Rescigno had resigned and the company's financial affairs were in a colossal mess. Miraculously, the chaos was sorted out in time for the next season with an outstanding roster of new conductors, including Solti and Mitropoulos, and the best singers available anywhere, among them Renata Tebaldi, Jussi Björling, Birgit Nilsson and Richard Tucker. Up until this point in his career as an opera conductor, Solti had never had the opportunity to work with such a galaxy of stars and they must have been a large part of the attraction for him in Chicago that season. He conducted Wagner's *Die Walküre* with Nilsson, Paul Schöffler and Christa Ludwig, *Salome* with Inge Borkh, *La Forza del Destino* with Tebaldi, Tucker, Giulietta Simionato and Ettore Bastianini, and *Don Giovanni* with Nicola Rossi-Lemeni as the rake and Leopold Simoneau as Don Ottavio. Solti was consistently criticized for his fast tempos in most of the operas and for tolerating long cuts in *Die Walküre*. His greatest success was with the Verdi:

> This was a performance to be remembered and treasured. Mr. Solti redeemed himself by his judicious choice of tempi and by his ability to keep the huge choral ensembles together. (Howard Talley, *Opera,* January, 1957)

The following season Solti was back in Chicago for more Verdi (*Don Carlos* and *Un Ballo in Maschera,* both with Jussi Björling), and Mozart's *Le Nozze di Figaro.*

Like Solti's North American debut, his long-awaited New York debut did not take place as originally planned. In April of 1957 he was engaged to appear with the Symphony of the Air. This was the remnant of Toscanini's old orchestra, the NBC Symphony, struggling to survive on its own under a new name. It believed, quite rightly, that it had scored a major public relations coup in presenting a leading conductor's New York debut, and before its arch-rival, the New York Philharmonic. But with the death of Guido Cantelli in a plane crash, the Philharmonic found it had some weeks to fill in the middle of the season. Solti could not ignore the fact that the New York Philharmonic was the better and more prestigious orchestra when he was asked to be Cantelli's replacement for two weeks in March, and he immediately accepted the Philharmonic's offer. The Symphony of the Air was furious that Solti's New York debut should be taken from them, and said so to the press. Not surprisingly under the circumstances, Solti's appearance with the Symphony of the Air was cancelled. It seems that the ambitious Solti was not one to allow a good opportunity to pass him by, no matter what prior obligations he might have.

The press coverage for Solti's New York debut could hardly have been more triumphant had he written the reviews himself. Four different critics from the *New York Times* were effusive in their praise. Howard Taubman called Solti's debut "an impressive affair," and remarked that the Hungarian conductor "has a gift for leadership and a mature musical point of view." (March 15, 1957) A few days later, at another concert, a second critic was equally impressed:

> Mr. Solti had made a strong impression at his debut with the Philharmonic on Thursday night. He greatly reinforced that impression yesterday with the drive and intensity of his conducting. He had not got halfway through the Weber Overture (*Oberon*) before it was clear that he was one of those rare musicians to whom there is no such thing as an indifferent phrase. Each note sounded alive with meaning. (E.D., *New York Times,* March 18, 1957)

The following week, Harold C. Schonberg was more restrained but both approving and precise in his remarks. His comments on Solti ring true even long after Solti's death:

> He has very direct notions about music, especially full-blooded music, which is where his inclinations seem to lie. He is not over-subtle, nor does he seek fancy effects. His music-making has a straight, clear line. (*New York Times,* March 22, 1957)

Finally, from a fourth *Times* critic, we have another favorable review, as well as a useful description of Solti's movements on the podium during this period:

> Mr. Solti keeps to a minimum the head-shakings and arm-wavings whereby innocent bystanders suppose conductors to be interpreting the music…His beat was precise but inconspicuous; cues, although infrequent, conveyed the conductor's intentions with graphic vividness. (J.B., March 25, 1957)

For his part, Solti praised the New York Philharmonic and his first experience of a great American orchestra:

> The technique is remarkable here. With many European orchestras you have to rehearse many passages to get them just right. Here they know those passages perfectly. And so with very little work you can get the same musical results as with European orchestras, and in addition, you generally have a higher technical standard. (Interview with Harold C. Schonberg, *New York Times,* March 24, 1957)

While Solti was involved in the important and concentrated work with the New York Philharmonic—eight concerts during a two-week period with all the attendant rehearsals—it says something for the man's energy and broad interests that he also managed to attend some plays. He was particularly struck by *My Fair Lady* and *Long Day's Journey Into Night*.

Solti's career was characterized by steady and dogged steps rather than by rapid progress. It is not surprising, therefore, that his arrival at the Metropolitan Opera—the absolute summit for opera singers and conductors alike—should not occur until 1960, seven years after his American debut in San Francisco. By 1960, Solti was well-established as music director of the Frankfurt Opera, celebrated for his *Ring* recordings on Decca, and known to at least a segment of the American public for his appearances in San Francisco, Chicago, and New York. He conducted four performances of Wagner's *Tannhäuser,* at the Met, beginning December 17, 1960 with a cast which included Jerome Hines, Hans Hopf, Leonie Rysanek and Hermann Prey who was also making his Met debut. At a time when the opera house was being criticized for its dearth of first-rate conductors, Solti's debut was much appreciated:

> Solti's conception of the score, as might be expected, was spacious, imaginative and poignant, and the orchestra under his tutelage was consistently first-rate. (Richard Repass, *Opera,* April, 1961)

The pattern of Solti's life in the late 1950's and early 1960's was to spend a few months each year in the United States, several months guest conducting in Europe, and the rest of the time at his home base in Frankfurt. The wonder is that with the increasing demand for his services, he stayed so long in Frankfurt. But he always preferred to plant roots when he accepted a permanent appointment. He was a conductor concerned with building and preserving, and he was highly successful in doing just that in most of his appointments: Munich, Frankfurt, and later London and Chicago. In 1960, however, the pressure finally became too much and Solti resigned from the Frankfurt Opera to become music director of the Royal Opera House, Covent Garden, beginning in the fall of 1961. This appointment signaled the arrival of Georg Solti as one of the most eminent and powerful conductors of the day. Covent Garden was already among the select handful of leading opera houses in the world, and during the ten years of Solti's tenure there, its international stature was enhanced even further.

Solti's farewell production in Frankfurt was Verdi's *Falstaff*, with sets by Caspar Neher and stage direction by Erich Witte. It was lauded as one of the best productions in years with Solti's humorous and poetical conception receiving special praise. His last evening was June 19, 1961. The next day he was in London giving his first press conference as music director of Covent Garden.

2

The Maestro Becomes Sir Georg

When Solti was named the new music director of the Royal Opera House, Covent Garden, he had also recently accepted the same title with the Los Angeles Philharmonic. Both appointments were announced within a few months of each other and would take effect in the fall of 1961. This meant that for the first time in his career Solti would be simultaneously the head of a major orchestra and a major opera house. The third crucial ingredient in Solti's musical life at this time, albeit a less time-consuming one, was the first-ever complete recording of Wagner's *Ring* cycle. *Das Rheingold* was recorded in 1958, and the other three parts of the *Ring* were completed by late 1965—a seven-year project that did a great deal to enhance Solti's reputation. It was on the strength of these almost universally-acclaimed recordings that critics began to refer to him as "the greatest Wagner conductor alive." Thus, Vienna (for the *Ring* recordings), London and Los Angeles were seen to be the three points of Solti's compass for the foreseeable future. As we shall see, Los Angeles very quickly and unexpectedly dropped out but this apparent setback had little effect on Solti's growing American presence.

When Solti was appointed music director of the Los Angeles Philharmonic he actually had very little experience as a symphony conductor and was far better known for his work in the opera house. As mentioned earlier, he had made some recordings in London, (music by Mozart, Kodàly and Bartòk), several with the Vienna Philharmonic (Beethoven symphonies 3, 5 and 7), and a few with other orchestras. He had also done some guest conducting with orchestras in New York and Chicago. So the Los Angeles appointment was a major boost to Solti's career, and he was determined to take the post even if it meant making a grueling commute between London and Los Angeles with fairly frequent side trips to Vienna thrown in for good measure. As things turned out, Solti did not get a chance to test the viability of his Los Angeles connection.

Before his first season in Los Angeles had begun, a crisis erupted which forced his resignation. The position of assistant conductor of the Los Angeles Philharmonic was vacant and Solti supervised auditions to find a suitable young conductor to fill it. He chose the twenty-three year old Zubin Mehta. But without consulting Solti, the president of the board, Mrs. Norman B. Chandler, had taken it upon herself to decide that Mehta would substitute for an ailing Fritz Reiner as guest conductor. More than that, Chandler also named Mehta as principal guest conductor. Solti was horrified:

> I had nothing at all against Mehta, who was an outstandingly talented young conductor, but the fact that the chairman of my new orchestra's board had engaged a chief guest conductor without asking my opinion was intolerable. Mrs. Chandler had the reputation of interfering. I knew that if I accepted her intrusion in this matter, she would try to interfere in all other artistic decisions and would undermine my authority. I cabled back to say that under these conditions, I was unable to honor my contract in Los Angeles. (*Memoirs,* pp. 120-121)

Solti did not even get the courtesy of a reply from Mrs. Chandler and his new position in Los Angeles had disappeared before it had even started.

Not surprisingly for a conductor of Solti's energy and ambition, the elimination of Los Angeles from his life did not free up any more of his time for the Royal Opera House. He simply filled in the gaps in his schedule with guest conducting stints elsewhere. He even took on a major responsibility with another American orchestra, the Dallas Symphony.

Paul Kletzki suddenly withdrew for personal reasons as music director of the Dallas Symphony in 1961. Solti was asked to be "senior conductor" until a permanent music director could be found. In the 1961-62 season Solti made two extended visits conducting a total of twenty-one concerts. His repertoire in Dallas was challenging and uncompromising. His concerts included an all-Stravinsky program, Beethoven's *Missa Solemnis* and works by Bartók, Berg and Janáček. But Solti had set his sights higher; the Dallas Symphony was, in Solti's words, "an excellent provincial American orchestra," (*Memoirs,* p. 129). A member of the orchestra at that time, flutist Harvey Boatright, recalls that Solti's "whole musical sense was so grand and clear that it was a great pleasure to work under him." (*Dallas Morning News,* June 3, 2000) But Boatright felt that Solti was somewhat frustrated with the orchestra:

> He realized we were not going to respond like he wanted a great orchestra to respond. I got the impression that we were a kind of disappointment to him. But he went ahead and did what he could, and we played some grand concerts.

Dorothea Kelley played viola in the Dallas Symphony for 24 years and she remembers Solti with great affection and admiration:

> We all thought he was the greatest, almost everybody there did. He just took over and it was just perfect, the very first concert. And when he did [Beethoven's] Fifth Symphony, it was a different piece—I'd never heard it before. It was just entirely different the way he went at it.
>
> Solti was very kind. If the trumpet came in late because he had car trouble, he was kind about it; he didn't blow his top. Now our dear, darling Kletzki, who was just a doll—we all loved him—what a temper he had! If something didn't go right—Wow! Wow! But then he'd be over it in a minute and he'd be back saying, "Excuse me. I wasn't feeling well." (Interview with Olin Chism, *Dallas Morning News,* June 15, 1998)

Unlike his experience with the Los Angeles Philharmonic, Solti actually got to conduct some concerts with the Dallas Symphony but the "marriage" lasted only one season. Solti was not interested in putting down roots in Dallas. Years later it was hard enough to get him to spend time in Chicago. Solti returned to the Dallas Symphony just once more, for two concerts in March of 1964.

More than 20 years later Solti came back to Dallas at the helm of the Chicago Symphony in February, 1987. Solti delighted the audience at the Music Hall with a program of works by Wagner, Corigliano and Beethoven, and then left them applauding wildly after what critic John Ardoin called a "rip-roaring performance" of Sousa's *Stars and Stripes Forever* (*Dallas Morning News,* Feb. 17, 1987). As it happened, Solti was scheduled to conduct the Dallas Symphony in a special concert in the new Meyerson Symphony Center, Nov. 1, 1997, but he did not live to fulfill that engagement. Solti died on September 5.

During the course of his ten seasons at Covent Garden, Solti played a vital role as music director but he conducted relatively few performances. In his most active year, 1969-70, he conducted twenty-seven performances, but sometimes as few as twenty as in the 1963-64 and 1968-69 seasons. In his last season he conducted only fifteen. When Solti first came to Covent Garden as music director in 1961 he made sure that his duties would not prevent him from pursuing opportunities elsewhere, particularly as a concert conductor. It was a sign of the times that Solti's successor, Colin Davis, conducted about the same number of performances while he was music director at Covent Garden.

Solti had first appeared at Covent Garden in December, 1959 conducting *Der Rosenkavalier.* He had been warmly praised:

> Georg Solti made a welcome Covent Garden debut and drew some magnificent playing from the orchestra. There were some wonderful sonorities, rather lacking in recent Strauss performances here, and some very sensuous playing. What one missed was tenderness, but that was a quality lacking in the performance as a whole, except when the divine Jurinac was on stage. (Harold Rosenthal, *Opera,* January, 1960)

So it followed that when Rafael Kubelik resigned as music director of Covent Garden, Solti, one of the few first-rate opera conductors available at that time as well as one who had already made a good impression in the house, was offered the job by Lord Drogheda, chairman of the Royal Opera board. Solti declined at first saying that he had had enough opera for the time being. He was about to resign his post in Frankfurt and go to Los Angeles. However, Sir David Webster, Covent Garden's managing director, pursued Solti to Luxembourg for further negotiations. By then Solti was more interested, but before making up his mind he asked the advice of Bruno Walter. When Walter advised him to accept, Solti gave in and signed a three-year contract.

Solti made his next appearance in the pit at Covent Garden early in 1961 directing a recently composed British opera, Benjamin Britten's *A Midsummer Night's Dream.* At this point, Solti had been announced as the new music director although he did not take charge until the fall of that year. But it was a shrewd move to have him direct a British opera in a house becoming increasingly sensitive to the question of foreign domination of repertoire, artists and conductors. The board of Covent Garden made it very clear to Solti that British composers must be encouraged and that British performers were to be used whenever possible.

At his first press conference in June of 1961, Solti was reassuring on all counts as he laid out his plans for future seasons. He announced that he intended to make the house "the best in the world." Further, he promised to use and develop British artists and said that he was planning a revival of Britten's *Billy Budd* as well as new productions of Tippett's *King Priam* and Walton's *Troilus and*

Cressida. He was in favor of performing certain operas—comic, Slavic and modern works—in English rather than in the original language. In terms of non-British repertoire he specifically mentioned operas such as Schoenberg's *Erwartung* and *Moses und Aaron*. The completion of both a Mozart cycle and a *Ring* cycle was also in his plans. And Solti was obviously not merely dreaming. During the course of his ten-year regime at Covent Garden only two operas on his original list—*Faust* and *Lulu*—were not performed.

The first new production in the Solti era was an offbeat choice: Gluck's *Iphigénie en Tauride,* a rarely performed opera, well out of the mainstream. Solti conducted performances at the Edinburgh Festival in the fall of 1961, and then brought the production to London where it received mixed reviews. A more important assignment came a few weeks later when Solti entered the pit to conduct his first Wagner at Covent Garden: *Die Walküre*. On the strength of his recorded *Ring* cycle, as yet only partially completed but nonetheless widely acclaimed, and his work in Munich and Frankfurt, Solti was already highly regarded as a Wagner conductor, and much was expected of this new *Die Walküre*. The producer was the experienced and admired Wagnerian bass Hans Hotter who also sang Wotan in the production. His contribution as producer was generally thought to be traditional and often dull. The sets by Herbert Kern made even less of an impression; in fact, reaction was so negative that Kern was dismissed and another designer engaged to take over the rest of the *Ring* cycle. So it was left to Solti and the singers to carry the day. With a cast featuring Jon Vickers, Hotter, Rita Gorr and a solid group of British singers including Claire Watson and Michael Langdon—and the splendid Josephine Veasey among the Valkyries—there was little to fault on the musical side, and Solti himself won plaudits for the intensity and drive of his conception, and for the wonderful playing of the orchestra. At least musically, it was an auspicious beginning for the new *Ring* cycle.

On a less positive note, this series of *Die Walküre* performances turned out to be the last collaboration between Vickers and Solti at Covent Garden. Such was the tension that developed between them at rehearsals that Vickers refused to sing henceforth in any productions conducted by Solti. The Canadian tenor thought that Solti bullied him. For his part, the conductor complained that Vickers was uncooperative, and said as much in a letter to Vickers:

> I feel I must say first of all that I am very disappointed with our collaboration in *Walküre* especially as I felt that your cooperation was somewhat lacking. I regret this very much because I feel strongly that each individual vocal part must fit into the whole scheme in order to make a homogeneous perfor-

mance…I felt that I met with a rejection of almost every suggestion. (M. Haltrecht, *The Quiet Showman*, 1975)

Solti and Covent Garden had hoped to have Vickers for *La Forza del Destino* and *Otello* in the near future, but Vickers would agree to sing only if Solti were not in the pit. Solti himself took the initiative in trying to lure Vickers back, particularly for the revival of *Die Walküre* as part of the complete *Ring* cycle in 1964; still the tenor could not be persuaded. Solti's *Ring* cycle would have to proceed without the greatest Siegmund of the day. Vickers never sang again with Solti, and the conflict between them was one of Solti's greatest frustrations during his tenure at Covent Garden.

Later in his first season, Solti was in charge of an unusual triple bill produced by Peter Ustinov, which included Schoenberg's *Erwartung*, Ravel's *L'Heure Espagnole* and Puccini's *Gianni Schicchi*:

> In all three there were the hallmarks we have come to recognize in all Solti performances: excitement, tension, beautiful orchestral tone and the revelation of details in the score hitherto unheard. (Harold Rosenthal, *Opera*, August, 1962)

At the end of the 1961-62 season, critics were generally pleased with what Solti had achieved, and were inclined to be tolerant where there was room for improvement. But in the second season the gloves were off. Even Solti's Wagner was no longer regarded as sacrosanct. In fact, the editor of *Opera*, Harold Rosenthal, began a persistent series of attacks on Solti's Wagner which continued throughout the conductor's tenure as music director. Reviewing the 1962 *Siegfried*, Rosenthal began the assault:

> It is also inclined to be loud, and thrilled as I was to hear great surges of orchestral sound, I felt a trifle battered by the beginning of Act 3. What I did find missing was tenderness and poetry. (October, 1962)

But the unmitigated disaster of Solti's second season was without doubt a new production of Verdi's *La Forza del Destino*. The trouble began when producer Sam Wanamaker quarreled with the designer, Renato Guttoso. Guttoso quit and Wanamaker ended up designing the sets himself, but not to the satisfaction of Sir David Webster who thought them too sparse for grand opera. Wanamaker also chose to stage the work *à la* Brecht at the expense of Verdi's intentions, and to the absolute bewilderment of the singers. Carlo Bergonzi, an outstanding Italian tenor but never much of an actor, was the leading man, and his female counterpart was not the scheduled Leontyne Price but the vocally insecure Floriana Cavalli. The results were vividly recalled by Montague Haltrecht:

> At the first night the duel scene had elements rather of Chaplin than of Brecht, Bergonzi first losing his sword, and then suffering further embarrassment when his visor dropped…Cavalli sang disastrously flat and more or less without voice. The huge aria of the final act was awaited with dread, and as the poor thread of a voice uncertainly emitted an approximation of the last notes, another voice from the gallery hissed out, charged with venom—"This is disgusting! Where's Shuard?" The unfortunate Cavalli came out before the curtain at the end of the evening, and as her body bent in a bow it seemed as though she was being broken by the weight of booing. (*The Quiet Showman*)

In his last appearances of the season, conducting Mozart's *Le Nozze di Figaro*, Solti fared no better, being accused by the *Times* of "skating over the score." Unfortunately, by the end of this nightmare of a season Solti's contract was up for renewal and there was no question as to what his decision would be. He had been persuaded to come to Covent Garden in the first place only after much hesitation, and now, with all the abuse from the press, Solti's first inclination was simply to get out while the going was good. He had never before encountered such criticism in his career and it hurt him. But Sir David Webster and the board of the Royal Opera had become strong believers in Solti and did everything they could to persuade him to stay. Solti was a stubborn man and eventually he resolved to dig in his heels and carry on. This decision also had much to do with the fact that Solti had never conducted a complete *Ring* cycle in the opera house, and it mattered to him that he remain long enough to do so.

In his third season Solti conducted the postponed *Billy Budd* and *Götterdämmerung*, the final part of the *Ring*, although the complete cycle would not be given until the following season. With *Billy Budd*, Solti scored a major personal triumph, demonstrating once again his affinity for the music of Britten:

> Georg Solti's handling of the score was one of his best achievements. Sometimes he pressed the music forward too urgently: the most serious case in point was at the F major chordal arch, which had almost intolerable vividness in Britten's own graver yet more sharply colored handling. But he seemed to catch all the score's flying brilliance and mighty groundswell, and steered his elaborate forces with a certain hand. (John Warrack, *Opera*, March, 1964)

Although not British by birth, the music director of Covent Garden had championed the country's leading opera composer, just as his successor Colin Davis would do for Michael Tippett. Solti's belief in Britten helped to affirm that operas by living British composers were welcome at Covent Garden, even if the repertoire was otherwise rather reactionary in character. When Britten died in 1976, Solti spoke of him with affection and added a personal recollection of their work together on *Billy Budd:*

> I felt that the *piano* marking for an *espressivo* passage did not give enough sound, so I asked Ben if it could be changed to *forte*. We played it through changing the *piano* to *forte*—"I like it," he said. "Let's keep the Solti version." But in the end I was sorry I had made the suggestion as I truly preferred the original *piano* marking! He was always most encouraging and at the same time highly critical but in a constructive rather than negative sense. I adored working with him. Britten was an operatic genius. His departure has left an enormous emptiness in the world of music and in the lives of his friends. (*Opera,* February, 1977)

Solti's biggest success that season, however, was not with Britten or Wagner, but with Verdi. Harold Rosenthal went out of his way to praise Solti's conducting of *Otello:*

> I am quite convinced that this *Otello* is the finest thing Solti has so far done at Covent Garden. This is *his* opera beyond any doubt, and I wonder if there is a finer *Otello* conductor anywhere in the world? Solti combines the nervousness of a Beecham with the burning incandescence of a de Sabata, to which he added his own special gifts of virility and the ability to judge and calculate orchestral sonorities. One would perhaps welcome a little more expansiveness, especially over the more lyrical moments of the score. (*Opera,* June, 1964)

But when Solti's eagerly awaited *Ring* cycle appeared the following autumn, Rosenthal was even more annoyed by Solti's Wagner than he had been by the conductor's *Siegfried* two years before:

> I wish I could have seen a musical and dramatic shape in it…Mr. Solti's climaxes do not seem to be related one to the other, and themes, leading-motives, call them what you will—are often played in quite different ways…the Forest Murmurs was almost devoid of poetry…the Rhine Jour-

ney was far too fast…and the noise of the Funeral March was almost vulgar. (*Opera,* November, 1967)

John Greenhalgh, writing in *Music and Musicians,* was equally critical:

> They [brilliant orchestral sound and exciting climaxes] are no compensations for failing to sustain the whole work, despite its length. Under Solti the music of the *Ring* has been more a series of fragmented episodes, as he has moved from one climax to another, the threatening *longueur* in Wagner's music thereby kept at bay. (March, 1971)

In spite of this strongly negative reaction to Solti's *Ring* from some observers, the production of the entire work was a major achievement for Covent Garden. And with Solti's recorded cycle nearing completion to a crescendo of favorable comment, it was a coup for this opera house that such a celebrated Wagner conductor should do his first complete live *Ring* with them.

If the new Solti *Ring* drew a mixed reaction in the 1964-65 season, so too did *Moses und Aaron* on an even grander scale. The work is so difficult to play and sing and the problems for the producer so complex, that it had been staged only twice before, in Zurich and Berlin. Solti was one of the instigators of the project for Covent Garden even though he was advised by friends not to do it; they said it was impossible. Yet Solti was convinced that the work was magnificent and went ahead anyway. The producer was Peter Hall, managing director of the Royal Shakespeare Company but a new face at the Royal Opera House. His wry comment was: "Any director likes to be challenged by the impossible."

There are those who dismiss *Moses und Aaron* for its dissonant, tuneless score, and call it a scenic oratorio because of its biblical text and lack of action. Schoenberg wrote the libretto himself and often his stage directions seem meant for some "opera house of the mind," as Peter Hall put it, rather than for anything as temporal as the Royal Opera House, Covent Garden. Here is an example from a scene in Act 2:

> The priests embrace and kiss the maidens. Behind each pair a girl stands with a long knife and a jug for catching the blood in her hands—the girls hand the priests the knives. The priests seize the virgins' throats and thrust the knives into their hearts. (Scene 3)

The opera deals with the problem of finding faith and of communicating religion to the masses without corrupting the message. The most spectacular scene in the work and the one which attracted the most attention in the press following the London performances was "The Golden Calf and the Altar," an orgy on a lavish scale. In previous productions little attempt had been made to depict the debauchery on stage, but Hall insisted on making the scene as realistic as possible. "If you do the orgy stylized I don't think the horror would be unleashed." (BBC interview) To achieve his purpose, Hall covered the entire stage with naked couples in the act of copulation. Audience reaction ranged from "shocking" and "vulgar" to "boring" but the customers came. All performances were sold out, with scalpers getting as much as twenty-five guineas a ticket. Apart from the orgy, the audience was treated to a spectacle involving a chorus of 130, forty-five actors, twenty children, fifteen dancers, thirty extras, and a veritable zoo which included six goats, a bullock, a horse and two donkeys and, in Peter Hall's words, "a very large orchestra spattered in blood (from the activity on stage) in the pit."

Seven weeks of intensive rehearsals went into the production, and the hard work paid off. Solti and Hall received most of the praise; Solti for making the abrasive score as clear and as exciting as it could possibly be, and Hall for his extraordinary conception. Hall's participation was undeniably crucial to the entire project and helped erase memories of *La Forza del Destino*. Particularly unforgettable were his richly detailed crowd scenes. But *Moses und Aaron* was very much a team effort which did a great deal for Covent Garden's prestige. The opera house had demonstrated that it could attract some of the best talent in the country and be innovative on a very high level.

Peter Hall collaborated with Solti on no fewer than eight productions and he recalls they were among his most intense theatrical experiences:

> I suppose *Moses* was my most exhilarating experience with him. But we did a thrilling *Tristan und Isolde,* and he taught me something I shall never forget: an understanding of Wagner's time. It is not like the time of other mortals. Everything in Wagner's world takes longer because it is more intense. His music exists in a hallucinatory, slowed-up tempo—the kind that comes upon us when we are in acute crisis, as when the car moves with dreadful inevitability towards the crash. In the *Ring* there are long, long scenes in slow motion; then, in two minutes flat, the world turns upside down. The feelings are eternal; but the action when it comes is quick and apocalyptic. (*Making an Exhibition of Myself,* pp. 230-231)

Solti's faith in the score of *Moses und Aaron* led him to conduct it again at the Paris Opera and with the Chicago Symphony in a concert version.

The same season which saw the production of *Moses und Aaron* and an entire *Ring* cycle also contained Solti's first Covent Garden performances of a Richard

Strauss opera. The work he chose was *Arabella,* which he had recorded in Vienna a few years before. Here again production standards were very high, with Rudolf Hartmann directing and Peter Rice designing the sets. The cast was headed by Dietrich Fischer-Dieskau and Lisa Della Casa. With Solti in the pit, it was an *Arabella* of a lifetime for those who saw it.

The following season (1965-66) Solti repeated his *Ring* cycle and *Moses und Aaron,* added another Wagner opera—*Der fliegende Holländer*—revived *Der Rosenkavalier* which had brought him such success at his Covent Garden debut, and continued the ongoing Mozart cycle with *Die Zauberflöte.* It was his fifth season as music director and he was now comfortable in the role. He was respected for his recent achievements with Wagner, Strauss and Schönberg, and, in fact, there was a general feeling emerging that Solti was one of the best things to ever happen to Covent Garden. The London house could now boast more performances of a consistently high standard musically, dramatically and visually, than its opposite numbers in Milan, Vienna, Munich and New York. Even the troubled Harold Rosenthal admitted that perhaps Solti had achieved the goal he had set himself at his first press conference: to make Covent Garden "the best opera house in the world." But in a conversation with the conductor in 1968, Rosenthal pursued one of his favorite themes, that Covent Garden was still not doing enough to develop British artists. Solti's answer was the same as it had been in 1964 when Rosenthal had first brought up the topic:

> Covent Garden is an international house, and we are not really the training ground for young artists. They grow up and develop at Sadler's Wells and with Scottish and Welsh Opera for the most part. (*Opera,* June, 1968)

At the height of his popularity at Covent Garden, Solti made a firm and publicly announced decision to leave at the end of his tenth season, 1970-71. It was time, he said, to set opera aside for a while and to conduct more concerts:

> I will have spent ten years here—a nice round period—and twenty-five or so years in opera. It's time for a change. I want to catch up on my concert career. But of course I will not give up conducting opera and I hope I'll be invited back to Covent Garden. (*Opera,* June, 1968)

Solti gave the board three years notice to find his successor before the fateful day, and within a matter of months of giving notice in London he took up the position that was to be the summit of his career, as music director of the Chicago Symphony. But he remained close to Covent Garden until the end of his life, averaging about one production a year.

In his last years as music director at Covent Garden there were more triumphs in store for Solti, particularly with Strauss—*Die Frau ohne Schatten* and *Salome*—and with Wagner—*Tristan und Isolde* (this last marking his farewell appearances as music director in the spring of 1971). Jess Thomas sang Tristan with Birgit Nilsson and Ludmilla Dvoráková alternating as Isolde. The producer was Peter Hall. The collaboration of conductor and producer recalled the success of *Moses und Aaron* a few seasons back in raising standards on the stage and in the pit to a uniformly high level:

> If there is a real major achievement in the production it is that Peter Hall has imposed a consistent acting style, to a greater extent than I have ever seen, on a largely established cast, and on international principals...such beautiful playing Solti drew from the orchestra that one was transported...sad goodbye to a Wagner conductor who really has reached maturity and greatness. (Tom Sutcliffe, *Opera,* August, 1971)

Even so, Harold Rosenthal expressed his usual reservations about Solti as a Wagner conductor:

> Solti is never at his best on first nights, and as so often in the past, I was rather disappointed in him as a Wagner conductor. The *Prelude,* taken very slowly, almost fell apart, and each act seemed to be treated as a separate entity with its own scale of dynamics, rather than as part of a whole...at the last night things went much better. (*Opera,* August, 1971)

The night of his final performance, all manner of tributes were paid to Solti including a KBE presented by Prime Minister Edward Heath, a great music-lover and sometime conductor himself. Solti was knighted shortly after he became a British citizen about a year later. He was enormously proud of his acceptance by the British people and chose henceforth to be called *Sir* Georg Solti.

During his ten years at Covent Garden, Solti had also become more British in the sense that he had divorced his first wife Hedi, whom he had met in Switzerland during the war, and married Valerie Pitts, a young reporter sent to interview him for BBC-TV. The affair began in 1964, and after both parties had obtained divorces they were married in 1966. According to people who knew the couple well, Valerie was responsible for transforming Solti from an arrogant and sometimes tempestuous maestro into a more relaxed and domesticated figure. Certainly his conducting did show signs of mellowing during the 1960's and Solti was seen to be spending much of his free time with his newborn first child, Gabrielle.

Summing up Solti's ten years at Covent Garden, Harold Rosenthal gave him credit for tremendous improvement in the general standard of performance in the house, and for bringing 'his own brand of electrical excitement into the theatre—a kind of glamour, which only existed on limited occasions previously." (*Opera,* October, 1971) But the critic took strong exception to Solti's own assessment of what he had done:

> When I arrived in London there was a beautifully kept semi-amateur opera house. Now it is fully professional. (Interview with John Higgins, *Times,* June 12, 1971)

This comment, in Rosenthal's view, exhibited a remarkable ignorance of the many exceptionally enjoyable evenings in the pre-Solti era, presided over by the likes of Kleiber, Beecham, Giulini, Kempe, Kubelik, etc. none of them noted for their "semi-amateur" affiliations.

Rosenthal also very much lamented Solti's failure to develop the nucleus of a true ensemble in the house, using British singers. But in Solti's defense, it must be said that there is today not a single major opera house in the world operating with such a system. What was possible in the European opera houses of the twenties and thirties was out of the question by the sixties. Costs were too high and audiences all too aware of the world's great voices on records; they insisted on hearing the stars and not the unknown local artists. No major opera house today could pay the bills with the sort of rep group that stayed together from opera to opera in the old days. Rosenthal castigated Solti for achieving only a series of "fine, festival-like productions with hand-picked casts," (*Opera,* October, 1971) when no music director anywhere could have done more. What a music director can do today in a major opera house is improve the quality of the orchestra and the chorus, the elements that must stay the same week in and week out, and that is what Karajan did at the Vienna *Staatsoper,* Levine at the Met and Solti at Covent Garden. But what they all did and what Levine continues to do as well is hand-pick the singers and directors to create world-class productions.

Rosenthal wanted to see more British singers in leading roles, more new British operas, and more British producers and designers working in the house. But when one considers that these were matters for which Solti was not solely responsible, his efforts on behalf of British nationalism were considerable under the circumstances. British singers of the stature of Gwyneth Jones, Peter Glossop and David Ward were used whenever possible; three Britten operas and two by Tippett were mounted as well as Walton's *Troilus and Cressida,* Bennett's *Victory,* and Searle's *Hamlet.* This was by no means a radical record, but it was well above the average in the ranks of major opera houses. Covent Garden, moreover, was no place for trying out the first efforts of unknown composers. There are other less costly venues for that.

As for producers, Solti was successful in attracting Peter Hall to work on *Moses und Aaron, Tristan und Isolde,* and the *Knot Garden,* and excellent work was also done by other producers of international stature including Visconti, Zeffirelli, Copley, Kaslik, Schlesinger and Hartmann.

After his retirement as music director in 1971, Solti returned regularly to Covent Garden to conduct major new productions including *Elektra* (October, 1972), *Carmen* (October, 1973), *Die Frau ohne Schatten* (June, 1975, repeated April, 1976), *Parsifal* (1979), and many more well into the 1990's. However, he did leave Covent Garden with the expressed intention to concentrate more on his concert career, and for the most part, he did just that, particularly in Chicago.

3

The Maestro at the Summit

The Chicago Symphony has a proud and illustrious history. It was founded in 1891 by Theodore Thomas, one of the most dynamic and influential conductors of any age. It is also due to Thomas that Orchestra Hall was built in 1904 especially to house the Chicago Symphony, the first auditorium in the United States ever constructed for the exclusive use of a symphony orchestra. When Thomas died in 1905 he was succeeded by Frederick Stock, who had been associate conductor under Thomas. During Stock's thirty-eight year tenure the Chicago Symphony gained world renown, especially through its recordings, the first of which were made in New York in 1917. On the orchestra's fiftieth birthday, in 1941, major composers, Stravinsky, Milhaud, Kodàly, Glière, Harris and Walton among them, were commissioned to write works for the occasion.

Stock was followed in fairly rapid succession by Désiré Defauw (1943-47), Artur Rodzinski (1947-48) and Rafael Kubelik (1950-53). Fritz Reiner began his ten-year sojourn as music director in 1953 and under his direction the orchestra became famous for its virtuosity and discipline (most notably in works by Richard Strauss, Wagner and Bartók), and for its quality of sound, which many observers felt combined the best of European and American orchestras. The recordings made by Reiner and the Chicago Symphony for RCA Victor at the beginning of the stereo era in the late 1950's still stand as being competitive with recordings being made today, more than fifty years later, both in terms of performance and sound quality.

The Reiner era ended with the conductor's death in 1963. He was succeeded by Jean Martinon, about whom argument continues to this day in Chicago. In some quarters Martinon is praised as a fine musician with particular expertise in contemporary music, who expanded the orchestra's repertoire. But others think he was pedantic in his treatment of the musicians and out of his depth in much of the bread and butter repertoire, i.e. German music, which the orchestra had learned to play so well under Reiner.

Martinon's ultimate downfall was caused by his failure to get along with too large a segment of the orchestra. The bad feeling which developed between the pro-and anti-Martinon factions of the orchestra continued long after his departure from his post in Chicago (in 1968) and even after his departure from this world (in 1976).

The principal thorn in Martinon's side was the long-time and universally-respected principal oboist Ray Still. He so disliked Martinon's behavior as man and conductor, and so often argued with him during rehearsals, that Martinon decided the troublesome oboist would have to go if he were to maintain his authority as music director. The crunch came in 1967:

> Martinon and I just didn't get along. I thought he was ruining the orchestra. He even accused me of playing wrong notes during a concert. A perfectionist like me! There were a lot of little things...Once I was reading a book in rehearsal, during a movement when I wasn't playing. He ordered me off the stage. I put the book away...Well, to make a long story short, I got fired. (Interview with Peter Gorner, *Chicago Tribune,* January 31, 1980)

Unfortunately for Martinon, Still dug in his heels and fought the firing through the orchestra, the union and the courts. In the end, after a great deal of bitterness, Still won his case to stay on with the symphony and Martinon was finished. Of the many players who took Martinon's side in the dispute, one was principal flautist Donald Peck. Still neither forgave Peck nor even spoke to him even though they sat beside each other day in and day out, year in and year out. When Solti took over he was apprised of the situation and tried to act as mediator for the two players, but Still refused to budge. Solti himself always ran a tight ship with the orchestras he conducted, making it clearly understood at the outset that he was boss and that he wasn't interested in introducing democratic procedures where musical decisions were concerned. Not surprisingly, he himself soon had a run-in with Still. In an interview some years later Solti described what happened:

> At a recording, a very good wind was displeased with the way he had played, and he stopped to redo it. However, I did not want to stop, knowing quite well the merits of what we were doing, and that eventually a small incident could be edited out. But he did not continue to play his part. Thus, I was forced to stop the performance, and I made a small scandal. This has been

the only time in five years, where I have had to remind someone that the decision to play or stop was mine only. (*Harmonie,* September, 1974)

Ray Still was obviously a very proud and difficult man but he was also one of the glories of the Chicago Symphony and the recording studio incident notwithstanding, he and Solti developed a relationship of mutual respect. And Still finally put his differences with Peck behind him too. In an interview with Peter Gorner in 1980 he acknowledged that he hadn't spoken to Peck for 10 years but that that state of affairs was a thing of the past:

> We're very friendly. After 10 years, I figured it was long enough. I think I've mellowed. I'm much happier now than I used to be. The orchestra is very healthy under Solti. He's one of the great musicians of the world, and he collaborates with an orchestra instead of conquering it. (*Chicago Tribune,* January 31, 1980)

Still and Solti went on to make beautiful music for many years. In fact, the great oboist was still in the orchestra even after Solti had retired. Still himself retired in 1993. Peck stayed even longer; he retired from the Chicago Symphony in 1999.

But we digress to follow the Ray Still story to its ultimately happy ending. How did Solti come to Chicago in the first place? With Martinon on his way out, the Orchestral Association of the Chicago Symphony set about to find a suitable replacement. The key figures involved in the search process were Louis Sudler, the chairman, and John Edwards, the executive vice-president and general manager. Sudler was a highly accomplished singer who had been active in the Chicago Civic Opera productions of the 1940's. When his vocal career came to a standstill he threw himself into his real estate business and amassed a very large fortune. He joined the board of the Chicago Symphony in 1964 and became president two years later. It was a bad time for the orchestra. In addition to the Martinon crisis, huge deficits were piling up and there did not seem to be much that could be done to rectify the situation. Moreover, the renovation of Orchestra Hall to provide better amenities for the players and the audience had succeeded in destroying the hall's much-praised acoustic excellence. Needless to say, none of this did much for the orchestra's morale or its fund-raising efforts. The future looked very grim indeed for the new president.

One of Sudler's initial priorities was to find a first-class manager for the orchestra—a man with the vast experience of orchestra management necessary to restore stability and help plan for the future. Through luck or persuasion, Sudler found the ideal person in John Edwards. Here was a man who had worked for half the leading orchestras in the United States and who knew the musical world like the back of his hand. With over thirty years experience behind him, Edwards was one of the most gifted and imaginative planners and problem-solvers around. At the time he was approached by Sudler, Edwards was quite contentedly managing the Pittsburg Symphony. He had already turned down the Chicago job once before, in 1964. The second time around, however, flattered at receiving so much attention from one of the so-called "Big Five" orchestras—Chicago, New York, Boston, Philadelphia and Cleveland—and excited by the chance to be in on the choice of a new conductor, he accepted the offer.

Sudler had decided that the Chicago Symphony was a great orchestra and deserved the finest conductor in the world. He believed, quite rightly, that if the musical end of things were healthy, corporations would be more inclined to contribute. The choice he and Edwards settled on was Herbert von Karajan, the most famous conductor alive and also the most expensive. Sudler put together what was apparently a very attractive offer to Karajan and it was presented to him by Michel Glotz and Ronald Wilford in Milan. (Osborne, p. 560) Glotz was Karajan's record producer and one of his closest confidantes and Wilford as President of Columbia Artists Management, was one of the most powerful men in the entire world of classical music. He had worked with Karajan and represented him for many years. Particularly in matters involving American orchestras Karajan paid careful attention to Wilford's opinion. The problem was that Karajan was conductor-for-life of the Berlin Philharmonic and almost totally disinterested in even guest conducting American orchestras let alone taking a permanent post with one of them. Two weeks with the notoriously difficult New York Philharmonic in 1957 had been enough. Karajan was also well aware that Furtwängler had been offered the Chicago Symphony in 1949 and could not accept in the face of a storm of opposition based on his wartime activities. It was unrealistic of Sudler and Edwards to think that they could lure Karajan to Chicago but it was a measure of their ambition and determination that they chased the Austrian maestro all over Europe seeking his acceptance. But apparently there was some ugliness and double-dealing involved in these negotiations too. According to Karajan's biographer Richard Osborne, while Sudler's offer was being presented to Karajan Edwards was actively pursuing Solti. And apparently Solti was actively involved in trying to convince Wilford that Karajan was all wrong for Chicago. (Osborne, p. 803).

When it became obvious that Karajan's indifference to the job was genuine, Sudler and Edwards began to seriously consider other conductors and to think about the real possibility that more than one man might be necessary for the job. With the orchestra now on a year-round schedule and star conductors unwilling to restrict themselves to one orchestra, there was a good chance that the Chicago Symphony might be unable to find the single conductor it wanted and deserved.

After Karajan, the most celebrated conductor at work in 1967, and young enough to take on a long-term appointment, was Solti. His *Ring* cycle recordings had made him a star and the standard of performance he had achieved at Covent Garden was the talk of the musical world. In fact, the Chicago Symphony had approached Solti before hiring Martinon in 1963, but Solti had declined the offer because it would have demanded too much of his time. Two years into Covent Garden this was an understandable response. But five years later Solti was feeling the need for a change, especially one that would allow him to spend more time on concert work and less on opera. However, as much as he wanted the Chicago post, he also wanted to leave himself relatively free for guest conducting in Europe. By this time, the new management of the orchestra had come to accept the fact that it could not expect more of a conductor of Solti's stature, and the two parties reached an agreement. Solti would assume his position in Chicago in the fall of 1969 conducting only twelve weeks each season plus several weeks of touring. The orchestra was to institute regular visits to New York and make its first-ever European tour in the very near future.

The initial approach to Solti by Sudler and Edwards had involved a breathtaking and ingenious scheme that would have seen Karajan as music director with Solti and Carlo Maria Giulini as associates or principal guest conductors. In the light of their temperamental and musical differences, one can scarcely imagine Karajan and Solti sharing the same orchestra, but what an exciting triumvirate that would have been.

Still, the actual outcome of Sudler and Edwards' negotiation was not unimpressive. Giulini readily agreed to serve as principal guest conductor with Solti as music director. Giulini was not an ambitious man and was happy to leave the administrative end of leading an orchestra to Solti (although to everyone's surprise Giulini later accepted the post of music director of the Los Angeles Philharmonic). For his part, Solti went out of his way to accommodate himself to Giulini with respect to choice of repertoire. Unfortunately, the plan broke down after a few seasons, with Giulini gradually withdrawing into the role of occasional rather than principal guest conductor. He remained long enough, however, to win the love of the orchestra and a vast and adoring audience in Chicago. Giulini was principal guest conductor from 1969 until 1972. In 1970 Henry Mazer was added to the conducting staff as associate conductor. Another international star was added to the team when Claudio Abbado became principal guest conductor (1982-85).

When Solti arrived as music director in Chicago he already had at least something of a track record in the city. He had conducted the Chicago Symphony at Ravinia in 1954 in a program which included Tchaikovsky's Symphony No. 5, and he had worked at the Lyric Opera in the 1950s. In December of 1965 he had appeared with the CSO for the first time downtown, at Orchestra Hall. When he took over as music director in 1969 he was still the music director at Covent Garden. Following his departure from Covent Garden two years later, many people thought he was intending to expand his activities in Chicago and conduct more than twelve weeks of concerts. By 1971 he had already had a considerable impact on the orchestra and after the CSO's first European tour in the fall of that year, audiences and press alike were ecstatic in praise of the remarkable chemistry between Solti and the great American orchestra. This was Solti's first full-time orchestral appointment and it had quickly added a new dimension to his reputation. But to nearly everyone's consternation, Solti did not increase his commitment to Chicago by a single week, nor did he ever do so. Instead, he took on new posts with other orchestras: first, the Orchestre de Paris and then the London Philharmonic. Solti was asked in 1980 if he was spending enough time in Chicago:

> This is a very difficult question! What is enough? On the one hand, one should be there ten months; on the other hand, there is no good to conducting too much because the public would get bored, and the musicians would get bored with you. I think a certain golden middle policy is right here, which I think I'm doing. I'm spending about four months there in a season, in two or three parts. (Chesterman, *Conductors in Conversation,* p. 44)

Ironically, Solti's involvement with the Orchestre de Paris was a short-lived and stormy affair which ended disastrously in 1975 largely because, as he himself admitted, he did not give the job enough of his time. Since Solti's task in Paris was to raise a second-class orchestra to the top rank, one wonders why, with a first-class orchestra in Chicago already clamoring for more of his time, he would be interested in trying. The same question could have been put to Herbert von Karajan when he took on the Orchestre de Paris before Solti, while continuing as chief of the Berlin Philharmonic. Nor were Karajan and Solti exceptional in this regard. One of the most extreme examples of this kind of multi-directorship occurred when Seiji Ozawa, not content with the Boston Symphony, decided to head up orchestras in San Francisco and Tokyo at the same time. More recently,

Charles Dutoit was simultaneously music director in Montreal, Paris and Tokyo, and somehow found time to take charge of the summer season of the Philadelphia Orchestra.

Why do so many conductors feel the need to take on more than one orchestra at a time? More specifically, why did Solti do it? Most conductors would give the same answer Solti did in 1978, that staying too long at a stretch in one place becomes boring to the audience and to the players. It also has something to do with the fact that there are simply not enough celebrity conductors to go around and every major orchestra wants one. The only solution is for orchestras to share them.

For Solti the reasons were both personal and professional. On the personal side, he did not particularly like Chicago. When he arrived in 1969 Solti's impression of Chicago was that it was "a sleeping beauty," or "a beloved but neglected piece of old furniture." (*Memoirs*, p. 164) His remarks to the press about the city's lack of cultural sophistication got him in hot water on several occasions. In particular, he was outspoken about the dreariness and inattentiveness of subscription audiences, especially the Friday afternoon dowager crowd: "I don't believe in one-sex audiences." He believed that Friday afternoon concerts were anachronistic and did away with them.

Solti also had problems putting down roots in Chicago. For most of his twenty-two years there as music director he and his family lived in a hotel, first the Drake and later the Mayfair Regent. Solti's children—Gabrielle and Claudia—were born during his early years in Chicago, and he and Valerie had to make some decisions about how they would be raised:

> If we made Chicago our permanent home, the girls would be left behind when we returned to Europe for concerts. They would be Anglo-Hungarian children living six months a year in the United States, without their parents. The alternative was to educate them in Switzerland or England, where their grandparents lived. For this reason, we finally settled in England; at least they wouldn't be as rootless as I am. (*Memoirs*, p. 170)

Solti admits that any solution would have been difficult for the family. He greatly regretted spending so much time away from home when the children were growing up.

But while Solti never lived in Chicago he maintained a formidable presence there. During his extended visits he threw himself into the life of the orchestra, conducting rehearsals, concerts, recordings and auditions and taking care of the administrative work. He and Valerie entertained frequently and they also appeared regularly at social functions. Solti eagerly participated in the annual fund-raising marathons for the CSO on WFMT radio and Valerie often participated in activities of the orchestra. She took part in several of the Petite Promenades given for second and third grade students, including a *Carnival of the Animals,* and a puppet version of Humperdinck's opera *Hänsel und Gretel* for which she provided the narration.

While England was home for the Solti family from the time of his Covent Garden directorship, he also established a summer home in Italy. Nearly every year Solti and family went to the Italian village of Roccamare, 125 miles north of Rome. Each summer, while the Chicago Symphony was grinding out three concerts a week at the Ravinia Festival in Chicago's northern suburbs, Solti was recharging his batteries at his Tuscan retreat. Roccamare and his time there became almost sacred to Solti and it was almost impossible to make him go anywhere else in the summer months. One notable exception was his first and only appearances at the Bayreuth Festival in 1983 to conduct the *Ring* cycle.

When Solti agreed to come to Chicago for the fall of 1969, one of his conditions was that the orchestra expand its touring. It was an expensive proviso but Solti thought it was a necessary investment to raise the Chicago Symphony's profile. If New York and Europe could hear the orchestra they would surely be impressed, and glowing reviews and tumultuous ovations would improve both playing and fund-raising. The orchestra had been to New York before, under both Reiner and Martinon, and in 1959, during the Reiner era, a European tour had been scheduled but canceled at the last moment due to the conductor's illness. It was not until Solti took over the orchestra that it had the opportunity to travel extensively. In 1971, Solti and the CSO presented twenty-five concerts in fifteen cities in Europe, including London, Berlin and Vienna. The stop in Vienna even included recording sessions for Mahler's Eighth Symphony. This work required several extra choruses and they could be found much more cheaply in Vienna than in Chicago. The orchestra was received everywhere with almost boundless enthusiasm. European audiences and critics had heard fine American orchestras before—Chicago was the last of the Big Five to cross the ocean—but after so many good reports, so many distinguished recordings, and above all after such a long wait, it must have been a special thrill to see and hear the Chicago Symphony.

Three years later the orchestra returned to Europe to even greater acclaim, except in Paris. Solti was, at that time, also head of the Orchestre de Paris and had made some rather harsh comments about the orchestra's ability. He brought the Chicago Symphony to Paris to demonstrate exactly what the French musicians lacked. Predictably, some critics regarded this as a challenge to their national pride. They attacked the American orchestra for its cold, military precision and said they much preferred the freedom of their own orchestras.

In 1978 Solti and the Chicago Symphony were back in Europe a third time, giving concerts at the leading festivals in Edinburgh, Lucerne, Berlin and Salzburg. Solti was a highly competitive man and proud of his achievements. It must have given him special pleasure to appear with his own orchestra at Salzburg where his sole rival, Karajan, was king, and where the Vienna Philharmonic and the Berlin Philharmonic were resident orchestras year after year. Salzburg was one of the musical summits and Solti had reached it at last with his own orchestra.

Another important foreign tour was the 1977 visit to Japan. As might be expected, audiences and critics were stunned:

> No orchestra in Japan can produce the combination of resources of this one...Japanese critical reviews always tend to be harsh on American orchestras. But the Chicago Symphony, for the first time, produced a richness and dimension of sound that made my skin crawl and that will never be reproduced, no matter how advanced audio products become. (Junichiro Kawazuka, *Nihon Keizai Shimbun*)

After the first European tour the CSO toured every year. There were annual visits to New York, run-outs within a 100-mile radius of Chicago and usually a more extensive U.S. tour every year. During Solti's tenure he led the CSO on five European tours, three Japanese tours and one Australian tour in 1988.

Perhaps the annual New York visits did more than any other tours to enhance the image and reputation of the orchestra and its music director. It certainly helped that Solti often presented blockbusters there that would have been too expensive to take on an extended tour. New York was given the best that Solti and the CSO had to offer. It was costly but it got attention and accolades. In addition to massive Mahler and Bruckner symphonies Solti gave New York a complete concert performance of *Das Rheingold,* and Act III from *Götterdämmerung.* New York concertgoers and critics alike were constantly reaching for superlatives. It certainly helped that the other Big Five orchestras were not offering much competition. When Solti and the CSO started to make their annual visits to New York in the early 1970's the Boston Symphony and the New York Philharmonic were struggling with conductors, the Cleveland Orchestra had faded with the death of George Szell in 1970 and Ormandy and the Philadelphia Orchestra had become admired more for their durability than for their excitement. The CSO under Solti became something special and almost in a class of its own. After a performance of the Mahler Fifth. Winthrop Sargeant made this observation in the *New Yorker* and it was typical:

> The conclusion of the final *Allegro* was the occasion for the longest ovation I have ever seen any conductor receive (except possibly Herbert von Karajan) since the time of Toscanini. It would probably have gone on all night but for the fact that Mr. Solti led his concertmaster off the stage.

The New York critics have a reputation for being rather tough, but for Solti and his orchestra from the Midwest they generally went along with the ecstatic audiences. Harold Schonberg was especially effusive after a performance of Wagner's *Das Rheingold* in 1971:

> The climax of the New York orchestral season came tonight in Carnegie Hall, courtesy of Georg Solti and the Chicago Symphony Orchestra…The performance was completely sold out. Everybody went wild, and for good reason. It was an evening of greatness…a great opera played by a great orchestra under a great conductor. (*New York Times*)

After a performance of Brahms' *A German Requiem* in the spring of 1978, Raymond Ericson of the *New York Times* pronounced it "the best performance this writer has ever heard…Mr. Solti, with a superb orchestra and chorus at his command, seemed to do everything exactly right." (May 14, 1978)

New York was and still is the place where all the world's ranking orchestras feel compelled to appear regularly to prove to the folks back home that they are as good as they keep saying they are. For this reason, a New York concert can be a nerve-shattering experience. To fail in New York is to be demonstrably put in one's place in the scheme of things. But to succeed as splendidly as Solti and his orchestra had done, was to know that one was not only good but the best.

While the extra effort that goes into New York concerts undeniably makes for special performances, a few listeners and even some members of the orchestra felt that the competitiveness and the ovations got in the way of an honest assessment of what the orchestra could do. One Chicago Symphony player expressed this sentiment in a letter to the *Chicago Tribune* in 1974:

> When an orchestra can bring down the house at Carnegie Hall with a program of Mozart or Haydn, we can then be convinced of our success. Instead, the Chicago Symphony Orchestra is sounding more and more like the brass band at the half-time show of Maestro Solti's football game.

Perhaps this player had in mind the standard set by George Szell and the Cleveland Orchestra in the previous decade. They were acclaimed as the best around on the strength of their Mozart, Haydn and Beethoven performances, not for their Mahler and Wagner concerts.

Solti too was well aware of the pressures and liabilities of performing in New York:

> The orchestra still suffers a lot from that "second city" complex. Carnegie Hall is still the magic name, and we are so obsessed with conquering Carnegie, I have to tell the players, "Don't look at the crowds, try to relax, it's just another concert." But it never works. In New York the orchestra plays with a tension that surprises even me. I constantly have to make them play softer than they do at home. (*New York*, September 20, 1976)

Unfortunately, the Chicago Symphony's regular fall and spring visits to New York had to be reduced to a single series each season. Even for superheroes, frequent trips to New York became almost prohibitively expensive. Even sold-out houses and rave reviews were not enough. There was still a deficit on every visit.

Although touring is extremely important for the reputation of the orchestra and its conductor, it is expensive. Many people believe that in order to foster good will and to demonstrate American cultural sophistication, the U.S. State Department routinely sponsored foreign tours by symphony orchestras, including the Chicago Symphony. In fact, with so many orchestras demanding the chance to travel funds have always been scarce, and ambitious orchestras have always had to find other ways to finance such ventures. For the Chicago Symphony's 1978 European tour, the City of Chicago put up $150,000, believing the orchestra's exposure abroad would be good for the city's image. After all, even today in some countries where reruns of *The Untouchables* on television is still popular fare, it is still believed that gangsters run wild in the streets of Chicago. For this same tour the orchestra also received a substantial contribution from the Continental Illinois Bank. In return, the bank used one of the orchestra's London concerts as a kind of gala party for the opening of its new London branch. Obviously, such helpful financing must be the result of hard work by the orchestra's board members. At the same time, fund-raising would not stand a chance if the product were not superlative. By 1978 Solti and the Chicago Symphony were universally acknowledged as being not merely superlative, but in nearly every respect in which orchestras and conductors are evaluated, unbeatable.

Back home, Chicago audiences and press enthusiastically endorsed the superstar status granted Solti and the CSO in New York. The one glaring exception was Claudia Cassidy, the notorious critic who single-handedly forced Rafael Kubelik from his post with the orchestra in 1953. Of an opera performance conducted by Solti she observed that the maestro was smiling when the ensemble was so bad he should have been cutting his throat. Being the hyper-sensitive man that he was, Solti never forgot that review: "I really have a hate for that woman. I wouldn't be in Chicago today if she were still writing." (*New Yorker,* May 27, 1974) But with the departure of Cassidy from the daily press in Chicago Solti had little to fear. Robert C. Marsh of the *Chicago Sun-Times* was the most influential critic during much of Solti's tenure and he was lavish in his praise of Solti from the beginning. In Solti's first season he described a performance of Stravinsky's *Le Sacre du Printemps* as "the most perfect realization of this music I have ever encountered." (February 27, 1970)

It should be noted that Marsh was a Toscanini admirer of many decades standing, and that he approvingly set Solti squarely in that tradition. The more rhapsodic Giulini he related to Toscanini's old nemesis Wilhelm Furtwängler. Not surprisingly, then, Marsh was not especially complimentary in his reviews of Giulini's Chicago concerts.

Thomas Willis, music critic of the *Chicago Tribune* until 1977 and later a member of the Faculty of Music at Northwestern University, was also a strong Solti supporter, although both Willis and Marsh were critical of Solti's frequent and extended departures from Chicago, or, as Willis put it, his "absentee landlordism." (*The Chicago Guide,* May, 1971) Another Chicago critic, Karen Monson, formerly of the *Daily News* and an early Solti enthusiast, held the conductor in something approaching awe. She was the only American journalist to accompany Solti on his historic return to Hungary with the Vienna Philharmonic in the spring of 1978, and she sent back detailed reports on the conductor's every word.

Solti was often criticized in Chicago for his long absences and for the conservatism of his repertoire, but as far as his conducting was concerned he was among friends. Nearly all observers agreed that this was a golden age for the Chicago Symphony and that Solti was responsible for it. Solti himself was well aware of what he had achieved. On one occasion he responded to the suggestion that he ought to show more gratitude to Chicago by declaring that "the city should erect a statue to me. Eight years ago when I came, the orchestra was virtually unknown, nationally and internationally. We accomplished a small miracle."

In spite of Solti's unbecoming immodesty, he was right, as most members of the orchestra readily agreed. Many of them might have preferred other conductors in this or that piece, or even in general, but they respected the standards Solti imposed on them and the new acclaim. They also appreciated the substantial increase in their paychecks. In 1973 the starting salary for a member of the Chicago Symphony was $320 a week. Five years later it was $500. And the majority of the players negotiated salaries far beyond that. Moreover, recording fees accounted for another $3,000-$5,000 annually per musician. Under Martinon, the orchestra's recording career was at its lowest ebb. Its records did not sell and no company would risk making more. With the upsurge of the orchestra's reputation under Solti, record producers now came begging. In the late 1970's the CSO was recording regularly with Solti for Decca, with Levine for RCA, Barenboim and Abbado for DG and Previn for Angel. For a time Giulini was also recording with the CSO for Angel and DG but starting in 1978 he could no longer do so under the terms of his new contract when he moved to the Los Angeles Philharmonic.

It was also due to Solti that the orchestra returned to regular radio broadcasting after a long silence. At one time more than 300 stations were broadcasting CSO concerts, and for the players this meant about $2,000 more each season. The broadcasts were made possible not from earned income on the sale of the programs—most classical radio stations are public stations and historically can afford to pay little or nothing for programming—but by a grant from Standard Oil of Indiana which donated $500,000 annually. Standard Oil certainly could find other uses for its money were it not for the orchestra's current prestige. Add to that the earnings ($1,000 per player) from a series of television tapings for Unitel and it was not surprising that the musicians were all smiles on the subject of Solti. Not only were the musicians being showered with praise from audiences and reviewers, but they were also making more money than ever before. The lowliest member of the CSO was making in excess of $32,000 a season in the late 1970's, and more than twice that when Solti retired in 1991.

When he arrived in Chicago in 1969 Solti expressed concern about the average age of the members of the orchestra. The implication was that many of the older players would soon be fired. This comment caused understandable fear and anxiety in the orchestra but Solti had no intention of making wholesale and arbitrary changes. He took his time and filled vacancies as they occurred. But he also took steps to do something about the general scarcity of gifted young players in the 1970s. He encouraged the CSO's own training orchestra for young professionals—the Civic Orchestra of Chicago—and many of these young players have graduated into the parent orchestra. By the late 1970s nearly fifty per cent of the musicians in the Chicago Symphony were alumni of the Civic Orchestra. With the increase in salaries and other income, the CSO was also able to attract some of the best musicians in the world. It is a tribute to Solti that many of these great players came to Chicago in the first place; it is an even greater tribute that they didn't want to leave. Principal flutist Donald Peck and principal oboist Ray Still have already been mentioned as staying in their positions more than forty years. The legendary principal trumpet Adolph "Bud" Herseth retired in 2001 after holding the position for more than fifty years! Solti himself served a mere twenty-two years as the CSO's music director, and at his death he was just weeks away from conducting his 1,000th concert with the orchestra.

Among Solti's greatest achievements in Chicago have been the recordings. There were complete cycles of the Beethoven, Brahms, Bruckner and Mahler symphonies as well as major choral works by Bach, Beethoven, Berlioz, Brahms and Verdi, all with the much-admired Chicago Symphony Chorus trained and led in the Solti years by Margaret Hillis. And there were complete operas too, among them Wagner's *Der fliegende Holländer* and Schoenberg's *Moses und Aron*. For his grand finale as music director in Chicago, Solti conducted Verdi's *Otello* with a cast headed by Pavarotti and Kiri Te Kanawa. It was recorded live by Decca. The recordings were not only good; they were often judged to be the best, winning Grammy Awards from the National Academy of Recording Arts and Sciences year after year. The CSO's recordings have won a total of fifty-eight Grammy Awards.

Solti was often criticized for the conservatism of his repertoire in Chicago and for performing too little music by contemporary composers. There is certainly some truth in this criticism, but it should not be overstated. What made the CSO under Solti so successful in New York and elsewhere were performances of music by Wagner, Mahler, Bruckner, Richard Strauss and other mainstream European composers. Solti was expert in this repertoire and was able to work with the CSO to give the best possible performances of this music. This was his specialty and it became their specialty as a team. Only the critics were demanding more contemporary music. It can be argued that major orchestras have an obligation to play music by living composers, and that American orchestras should support their own composers. But it is not necessarily the job of the music director to conduct that music himself. He should make sure, however, that it is given a hearing. It is up to the management, in this case John Edwards or Henry Fogel, Edwards' successor, and Solti, to hire the right guest conductors and request that they play the best music they can find by living and by American composers. And to a great extent, that is exactly what was done in Chicago during the Solti era. For the record, Solti himself conducted several important contemporary works, including David Del Tredici's *Final Alice,* John Corigliano's Clarinet Concerto, Sir

Michael Tippett's Symphony No. 4, Gunther Schuller's Flute Concerto and *Seven Studies on Themes of Paul Klee,* and Lutoslawski's Symphony No. 3.

No music director of an organization as large as the Chicago Symphony can take charge of the entire organization, no matter how dictatorial his methods and that was certainly not the case during Solti's years in Chicago. It takes a very large administration to take care of business for a major symphony orchestra, to raise the money, sell the tickets and keep financial affairs in order. When Solti arrived in 1969, the manager of the CSO was John Edwards. While Solti liked to take much of the credit for the orchestra's success under his leadership, a fair share must be given to Edwards. It was Edwards not Solti who ran the day to day operations and who found the money to meet the payrolls week in and week out. It was Edwards who supervised the nearly two hundred people it took to put on Chicago Symphony concerts. And remember that Solti was only in Chicago about twelve weeks out of the year and when he was away he was busy conducting concerts or making recordings somewhere else. Like Solti, Edwards had worked his way up through a network of smaller organizations and by the time he arrived in Chicago he had become just about the best manager in the business. He was a manager's manager, a wise man in the business, constantly in demand for advice to colleagues. Solti and Edwards worked well as a team for about fifteen years, until Edwards's death in 1984. Edwards's successor was Henry Fogel, manager of the National Symphony in Washington, D.C. The Solti-Fogel relationship was far less successful than the Solti-Edwards relationship had been, and Solti did not mince words on the subject in his memoirs. Solti had been warned by Rostropovich, the National Symphony's conductor, that Fogel would probably try to do what he had done in Washington, that is,

> replace the entire management personnel with his own people, so that he could hold total control. In the end, the Chicago Symphony's board of directors hired Fogel, who did exactly as Slava had predicted. (*Memoirs,* p. 179)

Solti was appalled by how many people in the administration had been let go and how much larger the Fogel administration staff was than the old one. Solti sensed that Fogel had his own vision of what the Chicago Symphony should be and that he, Solti, was not part of it. Solti decided it was time to leave, and he did. When Solti decided it was time to step down he did not make a complete break. He became conductor laureate and returned to Chicago every season from 1991 to 1997 for several weeks of concerts and recordings.

Naturally, there was tremendous excitement over the succession but the race was quickly narrowed to just two candidates: Claudio Abbado and Daniel Barenboim. Although Norman Lebrecht claimed that Solti was backing Abbado (*The Maestro Myth,* p. 255) and that Barenboim had "won the orchestral vote narrowly ahead of Abbado," Solti had a different recollection:

> I had no personal preference, as they both seemed good to me; but when the players took a vote, they rejected Abbado, on the grounds that he rehearsed details in a fussy way, without giving the orchestra an overall vision of each work. By seventy votes to thirty, they chose Barenboim over Abbado, and their preference matched Fogel's. (*Memoirs,* p. 180)

Barenboim was indeed chosen to lead the Chicago Symphony. He had been a regular guest conductor and appeared often with the orchestra as a piano soloist too. He was much admired for his remarkable musicianship. But just three years later Barenboim had discovered just how hard it would be to succeed a legend:

> Sir Georg stepped aside in 1991, yielding the post of music director to Daniel Barenboim after 22 years, and a cloud of complaints has hovered over Orchestra Hall ever since. Critics have howled about the orchestra's sound and Mr. Barenboim's interpretive inconsistencies; patrons have complained about repetitious programming and the presentation of work by contemporary mediocrities, singers of the Chicago Symphony Chorus have grumbled that Mr. Barenboim's tempos vary so much from moment to moment that they can never gauge how much breath they will need; and players have voiced displeasure over changes in seating onstage and the presence of empty seats in the house. (Sarah Bryan Miller, *New York Times,* May 8, 1994)

More than ten years later (2006), however, Daniel Barenboim was still the music director of the Chicago Symphony, although he had recently announced his resignation. Neither his concerts nor his recordings with the Chicago Symphony have come close to rivaling the success of his predecessor. Rather ominously the CSO reported its first deficits in many years and acknowledged that its concerts are not the guaranteed sell-outs they used to be either on tour or in Chicago. Fogel stepped down in the face of increasing financial problems at the CSO. The Solti years are looking better than ever in the history of the CSO.

What was it about the combination of Solti and the Chicago Symphony that bowled over music-lovers everywhere? Granted, he made the orchestra play well, but surely they had enough ability and pride to do that anyway. Exactly what did he get out of them that seemed to suggest he had powers bordering on the magical?

Solti said once that to be a conductor one must have imagination and also the power to make an orchestra play what one imagines; a straightforward comment, but also a shrewd one. By way of example, Solti often cited one of his teachers in Budapest, Ernst von Dohnányi. One of the great pianists of all time, he could give an overwhelming recital one day, and then conduct the worst orchestral concert the next. He had no talent for conveying his enormous insight to an orchestra. Say what you will about Solti, he knew what he wanted and knew how to get it. However, this is true of all successful conductors and one must go further to explain how Solti obtained what *he* wanted.

Energy is crucial. It is exhausting keeping after an orchestra day in and day out, always insisting on perfection, and always demanding the players' undivided attention. And Solti had this energy in abundance. In addition, a conductor must be resourceful and diplomatic. It is not enough to repeat over and over, "That's not right. Do it again." The players only become tired, frustrated and ultimately antagonized. Rather, a good conductor must be absolutely precise about what is wrong—is the passage too loud, too soft, too slow, too penetrating, too expressive? He must isolate the problem by having the offending instruments play alone and perhaps more slowly. If the strings are at fault, perhaps a change in bowing will help. Again, Solti was good at this aspect of his job.

It is also of the utmost importance that the conductor have something to offer at the concert beyond time-beating competence. Some conductors put all their energy into rehearsal and then rely totally on the orchestra's memory during performance. But Solti's painstaking vigilance never abated. It was partly the way he set himself on the podium, tense and poised like a runner at the starting-line. It was also his eyes and facial muscles, both of which imparted an infectious alertness. Regardless of how tired the players may have been and whatever their domestic problems, Solti's presence was so compelling it was difficult for the musicians to do otherwise than give him 100 per cent. This unique ability to project the authority of his personality accounted in large measure for Solti's tremendous success in communicating his vision of the music to an orchestra. He convinced the musicians by means of his persuasive presence and also by means of the previous experiences they had had with him that he was fully prepared, that he was deeply committed to the music, and that he would lead them safely through the score.

Interestingly, Solti's methods were not always so successful with orchestras other than his own. The frequently-voiced criticism from players about Solti when he guest conducted was that "he came on too strong," or that he "bullied them," not rudely but persistently. During his early years in England, his often overwrought and very un-British approach earned him the nickname "The Screaming Skull." Players who didn't know Solti often shut him out, doing what they were told but without any enthusiasm. Some players simply detested him. But given time, Solti often earned respect and admiration:

> Solti often appeared to the audience to be over-conducting, and laboring mightily to bring forth very little. Generally speaking, players who got to know Solti better, learned to appreciate his formidable musicianship and total involvement, and came to enjoy working with him. (letter from Owen Toller, *Gramophone,* Awards Issue, 2002).

The rapport between the members of the Chicago Symphony and Solti owed something as well to the cumulative influences of Reiner and Martinon on the orchestra. It is obvious from the pre-Solti CSO recordings that the brass section was at once enormously strong, clear and well-balanced. The playing of the brass in the Reiner Wagner and Strauss recordings is remarkable for its agility and security of attack and intonation. But the sound also has a darkness more commonly found in European than in American orchestras. The same comments could be made about the winds and strings. Under Reiner and Martinon the CSO was also a spectacularly precise orchestra. Again, the recordings bear witness. Solti always preferred a big sound and an opulent sound. At the same time, he was fanatical in his concern for rhythmic clarity. No wonder he found the Chicago Symphony so much to his liking, and why he could build on what he found when he first arrived. By contrast, the Vienna Philharmonic, for all its fabled power and richness, was often a problem for Solti. To his ears, the musicians were sloppy about rhythmic matters, moving far too sluggishly from note to note. Solti recalled a typical experience working with the Vienna Philharmonic on *Walküre* in 1957:

> The difficulties began immediately, with the famous "Ride of the Valkyries," which opens the third act of the Wagner opera. The brass played the main motif sloppily, making the dotted eighth note too short and the sixteenth note too long. Their attitude was: When it comes, it comes. I insisted that they play the rhythm correctly—and they hated me for it. They hated me because I knew what I wanted and made specific demands of them. Whenever we differed on a point of interpretation, they automatically assumed that I was wrong. Among other things, I demanded that opening chords be

played precisely together, whereas they felt that a chord that isn't precisely together sounds "warmer." To me, it is slovenly. (*Memoirs,* p. 108)

In Chicago, Solti found something like the strong, lush sound of the Vienna Philharmonic, although not the distinctive instrumental timbres of that orchestra, coupled with the most sophisticated rhythmic sense he could ask for. It is no wonder he reveled in the playing of the Chicago Symphony.

It is instructive to compare recordings of the same works—Beethoven's Third, Fifth and Seventh symphonies, and some Wagner overtures—made by Solti with both the Vienna Philharmonic and the Chicago Symphony. The Beethoven symphony recordings are not the best examples, however, because the later Chicago versions are uncharacteristically dull in performance and recording. The Wagner overtures are more illuminating. Solti's old versions with the VPO are excitingly played and recorded, but the newer CSO recordings are even better in terms of intonation and precision, while no less gripping. For some conductors, the Vienna Philharmonic would be enough. For Solti, with his never-to-be-forgotten exposure to Toscanini's criteria, the Chicago Symphony was able to provide more of what he heard when he studied a score. In the CSO, Solti found the ideal instrument for the realization of his musical ideas. And the players responded as readily as they did because he did not need to ask them to change their style of playing. The "Solti Sound" was essentially the same as the "Reiner Sound." In each case, one is not talking about an approach that personalizes the music in the manner of, say, a Stokowski or a Beecham. Rather, it was an approach based on adherence to an ideal of a careful rendering of what the composer wrote, in the Toscanini tradition. But in Solti's case it was more than fidelity to the score that he learned from Toscanini. It was also a total commitment to the job at hand that manifested itself in music-making of extraordinary intensity. This approach could be hard on the players, especially those who preferred a more businesslike conductor, but for Toscanini and Solti and musicians who cooperated with them, it could be tremendously inspiring. Orchestra musicians are a notoriously disgruntled breed and rarely acknowledge that the person standing on a box in front of them has any right to be there. But the members of the Chicago Symphony had no doubt that in Solti they had one of a kind. On the occasion of his

75th birthday, October 21, 1987 they sent him a greeting the like of which few music directors have ever received from their players:

> With admiration for your vigor and enthusiasm, with appreciation for your musical integrity, with pride that you are our colleague, with pleasure that you are our friend.

4

Forging Decca's Ring

In 1958, when the *Ring* project was set in motion by Decca Records, Solti was still largely unknown outside Germany. By the time this mammoth enterprise was completed, in 1965, he was a figure of international stature. These recordings established him as being, beyond any doubt, an important conductor.

It is hard to believe now that there was a time when no complete recording of Wagner's *Ring* cycle existed. The four operas, or music dramas as Wagner preferred to call them, comprise one of the undisputed masterpieces in the history of music. Yet half a century passed before they attracted the active attention of any record company. There are five or six complete *Ring* recordings on the market today, but in 1958 there was not even one. The work is huge both in terms of the forces involved—sixteen harps plus batteries of anvils are added to an already immense orchestra in *Das Rheingold*—and in terms of sheer length, in the LP era a recording of the *Ring* required four large boxed sets containing from three to six LPs each. No company had attempted anything on this scale before, and was especially reluctant to do so when there was no hard evidence that a market existed anyway. In addition, casting was a problem. Critics had been complaining for years about the dearth of real Wagnerian voices. Where were the *heldentenors*, *heldenbaritones* and leather-lunged Brünnhildes to be found?

Nonetheless, at the urging of producer John Culshaw, Decca decided to take the plunge in 1957. Or at least it decided to take the first step. *Die Walküre* was the most popular of the *Ring* music dramas and had been recorded once already by another company. Decca now planned to produce its own *Walküre* and, if sales were encouraging, to go on to do the other three parts of the *Ring*. In order to guarantee the success of the recording, Decca intended to use the universally acclaimed Queen of Wagnerian sopranos, Norwegian-born Kirsten Flagstad. Unfortunately, Flagstad was unwilling to take on the entire role of Brünnhilde at that late stage in her career and, in any case, wanted to sing the part of Sieglinde too. After many months of negotiation, the company was forced either to accept Flagstad on her own terms or to do without her. Having committed itself to some sort of start on the *Ring,* and still believing that the project was doomed without Flagstad, Decca went ahead with an impossible mixture: Act I of *Walküre* with Flagstad as Sieglinde and Hans Knappertsbusch conducting; scenes from Act II with Flagstad as Brünnhilde and again with Knappertsbusch; and the whole of Act III with Flagstad as Brünnhilde and Solti conducting. The only participants common to all three parts were producer John Culshaw and the Vienna Philharmonic Orchestra. With this kind of hodgepodge and with an incomplete *Walküre* emerging as a result, the notion of recording the entire *Ring* seemed far-fetched indeed.

But Culshaw and his superiors at Decca were undaunted. The *Walküre* experience had taught them a great deal about how to handle such projects. More importantly, market response was sufficient to indicate a widespread interest in large chunks of Wagner on records. Culshaw therefore suggested going on to *Das Rheingold* which, unlike *Walküre,* had never been recorded before. Also in *Rheingold's* favor was the fact that it had neither a soprano nor a heldentenor problem and that it was the shortest of the *Ring* dramas. Decca's management still believed the magic of the Flagstad name was an essential ingredient in the production, and as there was no major role for her in *Rheingold,* Culshaw managed to persuade her to undertake the part of Fricka. In his published account of Decca's *Ring* recording, *Ring Resounding,* Culshaw explained why he devoted so much of his time to dealing with the sensitive and unpredictable Flagstad:

> In retrospect it may seem that we paid an inordinate amount of attention to persuading Flagstad to sing what is, after all, a small role. There were two main reasons, and the first was commercial. In 1958 the name Flagstad was still a very powerful draw for the Wagner audience, and nobody at that stage could possibly predict whether *Rheingold* was going to be an expensive success or an expensive flop. Anything which might contribute to its sales potential was of importance to those who were investing money in such an unknown starter. Had she refused, we would have gone ahead without her because by then it was too late to withdraw. The other reason was that those of us who dreamed that *Rheingold* might be the beginning of the first recorded *Ring* wanted above all that Flagstad should be a part of it, no matter how modest, for we sensed that time was running out for her.

In fact, Flagstad died in 1962 just after the completion of Decca's *Siegfried,* the third part of the *Ring,* and the first of its' *Ring* recordings in which she was not involved. By that time, though, after the extraordinary success of *Rheingold*, the participation of a Flagstad was no longer crucial.

How did Solti become involved in such an historic project? Surely Decca, in its concern for commercial viability, would have wanted a conductor possessing both an international reputation and a recognized affinity for Wagner. In 1958 Solti was all but unknown to the record-buying public. However, Culshaw had seen Solti conduct *Walküre* in Munich in 1950:

> It affected me more than any other Wagner performance I have ever heard. It was not the best I had heard, but it was the most unified; it was a conception; and it was theatre. (*Ring Resounding*)

And Culshaw was not the only one at Decca impressed by Solti. In the mid-forties, Maurice Rosengarten, the head of the company, had spotted Solti and signed him to a contract. By the mid-fifties, Decca had recorded Solti in a fairly sizable number of symphonic pieces, even though the conductor was best-known for his work in the opera house. It seemed only a matter of time before Solti would record some opera for Decca. Moreover, it appeared likely that the opera would be by Wagner, in view of Solti's growing reputation with the composer's works. The Vienna Philharmonic was under contract to the record company as well, and there was never any doubt that the *Ring* would be made with this world-renowned orchestra which was, and still is, the pit orchestra for the Vienna *Staatsoper*. The combination of Solti and the Vienna Philharmonic appeared inevitable.

But the conductor Decca had in mind for the *Ring* project was Hans Knappertsbusch. His *Parsifal* performances at Bayreuth had become legend, and he was equally respected for his interpretations of the other Wagner music dramas. However, like many conductors, Knappertsbusch, who could be a spellbinder in the opera house or the concert hall, was a boring *Kapellmeister* in the studio. Also, if Culshaw is to be believed, Knappertsbusch really disliked making recordings. He hated rehearsing and he hated retakes:

> The truth is that Knappertsbusch took very badly to recording conditions, and no matter what we did, the genius which he so certainly revealed in the theatre refused to come alive in the studio…We tried to drag him, kicking and screaming, into the twentieth century of the gramophone record, the era of the listener at home who hears without any visual aid and without the community of the theatre. It was an alien world for him. (*Ring Resounding*)

By contrast, Solti's work with Culshaw on Act III of *Walküre* had been immensely satisfying. Solti was exactly the sort of man who could exploit the potential of the recording process. A tireless ball of energy and a perfectionist, he worked quickly and responded well to requests for retakes. No matter how many times he went over a passage, it never became routine or dull. Culshaw wanted his *Ring* cycle to have all the electricity of a first-class, live performance; he wanted it to be a theatrical experience. With Solti as conductor he was assured of the realization of these ideals. The excitement of those recording sessions and Solti's pivotal role in them has been preserved for posterity in a remarkable 1965 BBC film called *The Golden Ring*, now available on DVD.

While the ultimate artistic and commercial success of Decca's *Ring* project confirmed the wisdom of the choice of Solti as conductor, it was still a calculated risk in 1958. Solti was largely inexperienced in conducting *Rheingold*, and when he came to record *Siegfried* and *Götterdämmerung*, he had yet to conduct live performances of either work.

It makes far greater sense to record a work immediately after a series of public performances. This procedure saves on costly rehearsal time and ensures that the conductor has a firm conception of a piece as a complete entity when he comes into the studio. When one considers that Herbert von Karajan was then head of the Vienna *Staatsoper*, that he was a very experienced *Ring* conductor and an established recording star, and that he was currently mounting a production of the *Ring* at the *Staatsoper* with many of the same singers Decca had in mind for their recorded *Ring*, it seems strange that Karajan was not chosen for Decca's *Ring* project. After Knappertsbusch, he was the logical choice both artistically and commercially for any *Ring* cycle to be made in Vienna beginning in 1958. Furthermore, Culshaw was later to embark on a series of opera recordings for Decca, including *Aïda*, *Otello*, *Die Fledermaus* and *Carmen*, all with Karajan and the Vienna Philharmonic. Culshaw offered the following explanation:

> The decision to record the *Ring* was taken after the huge success of the Solti Flagstad *Walküre* Act III which was made in 1957. At that time Karajan was under exclusive contract to EMI, and did not come to Decca until either 1958 or 1959. (His first Decca recording was *Zarathustra*). But Solti was a front-runner in any case because—quite apart from artistic considerations—he was developing a truly international name. (Letter to the author, November 20, 1978)

Karajan did record the *Ring* later, for Deutsche Grammophon, in connection with performances given at the Salzburg Easter Festival in the late 1960s.

Even on the eve of recording *Rheingold*, there were those who thought the whole idea was ridiculous. One such skeptic was Walter Legge, Culshaw's opposite number at EMI. Culshaw and Solti have both told the story of Legge's doubts with enormous pleasure, although Culshaw identified Legge only as "a very distinguished colleague." Here is Solti's account:

> I remember meeting him at the bar of the Imperial Hotel in Vienna on the eve of the recording of *Das Rheingold*. "Well, what are you doing here?" he asked. "We start recording *Das Rheingold* tomorrow morning." "*Das Rheingold*..." He was astonished, "it is a very beautiful opera, but you won't sell a single record!" Since 1958 we sold more than 300,000 sets! For him this was impossible to imagine. This great discoverer of talent had Furtwängler and Flagstad under contract and it never occurred to him to record the Tetralogy with them. He was convinced that such a recording would not sell: *Die Walküre* or *Tristan* maybe (he in fact recorded these) but *Das Rheingold*, *Siegfried* and *Götterdämmerung* were to him synonymous to financial disaster. (*Le Point*, No. 133, April 7, 1975)

Decca's *Das Rheingold* was a sensation when it was finally released. Its commercial and artistic success proved that a market existed for Wagner operas on record. This was in the early days of stereo recording, when companies were rushing into the market with the most spectacular effects they could devise. The dynamic range, the immediacy of sound, the timbral accuracy of each instrument and the overall realism in the *Rheingold* recording appealed not only to Wagner buffs and opera fans, but to a new breed altogether, which was just beginning to have an impact on the record industry. These were the audiophiles or hi-fi nuts. *Rheingold* became the favorite demonstration record to show off expensive amplifiers and speakers.

Die Walküre is the second of the four *Ring* music dramas, and one might have expected Decca to have tackled it next. But since the company already had generous excerpts from *Walküre* on the market, it decided to leave *Walküre* until later and to proceed with *Siegfried* instead. Yet four more years were to elapse before *Siegfried* was finally recorded. Other opera projects in more advanced stages of production had to be given priority, and Decca had to deal with an almost insuperable problem of casting the title role. Although Wolfgang Windgassen was ultimately to make the recording, Culshaw was against him initially and explored every other possibility. At one stage, Culshaw decided to take a chance on a promising but inexperienced young tenor. The voice was right for the part, and while the man had never sung the role, he agreed to learn it with Decca's coaches under Solti's supervision.

The recording sessions were scheduled for May of 1962, but as late as mid-April Decca's budding heldentenor did not yet know the part. Still, the company persisted with its novice until three sessions with the orchestra forced everyone concerned to admit defeat. Siegfried would have to be replaced. All the material recorded thus far was useless, of course, and with no Siegfried in sight the entire project seemed doomed. The only way out was to get hold of the only tenor currently singing the title role on a regular basis in 1962: Wolfgang Windgassen. Windgassen knew that Culshaw had passed him over, and he was further aware of Culshaw's casting fiasco. Was the tenor likely to want to help Culshaw salvage the *Siegfried* project? As it happened, Windgassen was more than willing to step in, but his agent insisted on making the most of Decca's plight. The fee demanded was so high Culshaw was again convinced that there would never be a *Siegfried* recording. Frantic contract negotiations continued right into the recording session in which Windgassen was scheduled to appear. Finally, the lure of being the first-recorded Siegfried won Windgassen over, and he overruled his agent.

Siegfried turned out to be as fine an achievement as *Rheingold* had been. Windgassen may not be the Siegfried of one's dreams—the world of opera is still waiting for that—but he is competent, and the Act III duet with Birgit Nilsson is electrifying. Overall, the casting is superb with Hans Hotter as Wotan, Gustav Neidlinger as Alberich and Gerhard Stolze as Mime. For many years Stolze was one of the greatest singing actors on the operatic scene. Although his voice was not beautiful in a conventional sense, his powers of characterization were amazing. More amazing still is that he recorded the part of the dwarf while still receiving treatment for a devastating attack of polio.

Two years after *Siegfried,* Culshaw and his crew returned to the *Sofiensaal* in Vienna to record *Götterdämmerung.* Before the sessions, Decca decided to provide optimum studio conditions and installed a great deal of new recording gear, within a newly-constructed control room. How strange that in old Vienna, a city where some of the best concert halls in the world may be found, the ideal recording location should turn out to be a dance hall! The fact is that engineers can capture the sound of the Vienna Philharmonic far better in the *Sofiensaal* than in any concert hall, including the orchestra's home, the legendary *Musikverein.* The numerous outstanding recordings made in the *Sofiensaal* certainly bear this out.

The casting for *Siegfried* was carried over into *Götterdämmerung,* with Windgassen as Siegfried, Nilsson as Brünnhilde, Neidlinger as Alberich and, of course,

Solti conducting. Outstanding additions to the ensemble were Dietrich Fischer-Dieskau as an unusually sympathetic Gunther, and Gottlob Frick, as black and menacing a bass voice as one could ever hope to hear, as the evil Hagen. By this time, Nilsson had become the indispensable component Flagstad had been when the *Ring* project was first discussed. In the roles of Brünnhilde and Isolde, Nilsson, with her power, beauty of tone and endurance, was matchless. No one could soar over a Wagner orchestra in full cry as she could. One of the great liabilities of the long-awaited Karajan *Ring* cycle for DG recorded just a few years later is that it attempts to do without Nilsson. The substitutes, Régine Crespin in *Walküre* and Helge Dernesch in *Siegfried* and *Götterdämmerung,* for all their subtleties of interpretation, sound woefully overtaxed in comparison to Nilsson.

Solti's conducting is on an even higher level of achievement than it was for *Siegfried.* As Edward Greenfield observed, one finds, in *Götterdämmerung,* a Solti

> revealing a warmth, a consideration for the singers' needs as well as the orchestra's which was not there before…now Solti builds his climaxes far more subtly, with—it now seems—more love than before, without losing the excitement that has always marked his Wagner conducting. (*High Fidelity/Musical America,* December, 1965)

Following the completion of the first recorded *Götterdämmerung,* Decca had only to retrace its steps and do an entire *Walküre.* With the end of the cycle in sight, the record company lost no time, returning to the studios in Vienna only a little more than a year after *Götterdämmerung.* Birgit Nilsson was again Brünnhilde and once more at the top of her form. But Hans Hotter as Wotan was in the last stages of his career and the supercharged, large-scale concept of the performance severely taxed him. The choice of James King as Siegmund was also an unhappy one. King did not sing badly; it is just that he sang with no particular distinction. The ranking Siegmund in 1965 was Jon Vickers, and he was soon to record the role with Karajan. Vickers combination of musical insight and dramatic power was in a class all its own.

The completion of the first recorded *Ring* cycle was just cause for celebration. All those who participated in the project felt that they had reached the end of an important journey. And indeed they had. The recordings received all the appropriate accolades in terms of reviews, prizes and sales figures, and they still stand today as one of the greatest achievements of the gramophone. While much of the credit must go to Solti and the Vienna Philharmonic, and to vocal stars of the magnitude of Birgit Nilsson, George London and Hans Hotter, it was John Culshaw and Gordon Parry and their colleagues in the Decca recording team who were ultimately responsible for the amazing sound of the recordings. Culshaw encouraged his forces to give their best and to master the many difficult passages in these works. The notoriously difficult *Rheingold* Prelude, for example, can sound bad enough in the opera house, even though it is quiet music and disasters in performance are often partially covered by the noise of chattering and late arrivals. Culshaw's problem was to get all eight horns to play their successive solo entries perfectly in the same long take. The overlapping entries did not allow for editing.

While Culshaw's influence in the *Ring* recordings was extensive, it was not unusually so. It was in the nature of the recording medium in the second half of the twentieth century that the producer should have considerable input. He may have months of difficult work to do both before and after the sessions, and he often makes artistic decisions which one might expect to be the conductor's prerogative. It was Culshaw who sought out and auditioned the right kind of steerhorn for *Götterdämmerung,* and it was Culshaw too who called Bayreuth to try to resolve a textual ambiguity in the score of *Walküre.*

Because the Decca *Ring* recordings began at a time when Solti was just beginning to conduct performances of the cycle in the opera house, it might be argued that Culshaw was taking advantage of Solti's inexperience. No doubt there were matters Solti could have had more say in or dispatched more quickly had he been a more seasoned conductor of Wagner's music. On the other hand, the Decca *Ring* was not a live performance. It was a recording. And in matters concerning recorded sound Culshaw, not Solti, was the expert. The same distinction would have applied even if Toscanini or Karajan had been the conductor. Solti was an autocrat by nature when it came to musical matters but he recognized that when it came to recordings he was part of a team, and in this case, an unusually gifted one:

> Culshaw was an enthusiast and a man of musical vision and taste, but not a technician. The technical mastermind behind the recordings was Gordon Parry, a highly talented engineer. I was lucky to have with me, in my early recording career, these two remarkable men, who gathered around them an outstanding team. Although we inevitably had some differences of opinion, together we created an artistic combination that produced highly successful and interesting records. (*Memoirs*, p. 110)

Since the *Ring* project stretched over a period of seven years, stylistic developments were evident in the work of certain performers. This was especially true of Solti, as many critics were quick to note, for he was the only one involved at every stage of the cycle. And since *Walküre* was the last of the recordings to be made, the most dramatic comparisons concern it and the 1957 excerpted version. Reviewing the complete *Walküre* in *High Fidelity,* Conrad L. Osborne was critical of Culshaw's elaborate special effects, but commented at length on Solti's improvement as a Wagner conductor. He found Solti less nervous and more controlled. Osborne also suggested that the new, improved Solti had become a better Wagner than a Verdi conductor:

> It is not my favorite kind of Wagner conducting, but to me it sounds involved, dramatically aware, in a way that his Verdi, for example, does not. (November, 1966)

Other critics have been less favorably impressed by Solti's Wagner. Samuel Lipman, in a 1978 article entitled "Performing the *Ring*," compared extensively all the complete recorded *Ring* cycles, from Solti through Karajan, Böhm, Furtwängler and Goodall, and he had some detailed critical comments about Solti's conducting:

> He seems to have concentrated upon the exaggeration of short-range effects, and in particular, upon giving more prominence to the brass than has any other conductor. Many of these effects are startling, as are his frequent changes of tempo in excess of Wagner's indications. Regardless of the individual excellences of many passages, his *Ring* lacks an overall conception, whether musical or perhaps philosophical, that would go beyond the separate characters and their scenes to the question of the wider image of the entire work. (*Commentary,* January, 1978)

In an article published in 1971, John Greenhalgh made similar observations, not about the Decca *Ring* but about Solti's Covent Garden performances of the cycle:

> It is to the conducting of Solti that some of the most adverse criticism of the *Ring* of the sixties must attach itself. Serious reservations must be made of Solti's overall interpretation. If one takes the *Ring* as a whole and excludes individual performances, it has been basically disappointing. The *Ring* has not been heard as a single phrase of music lasting fourteen to fifteen hours in playing time. Yet it is as vital for a conductor to comprehend the *Ring* so, to hear it as a unity, and not to conduct it as four different operas, as it is for Brünnhilde to sing "Heil dir Sonne" in one breath. Covent Garden's recent *Rings* have contained orchestral sound of unsurpassed brilliance and climaxes

of tremendous excitement. These and other merits of Solti's conducting are acknowledged and valued, but they are not what is required, first and foremost, when conducting the *Ring* in the opera house. There are no compensations for failing to sustain the whole work, despite its length. Under Solti the music of the *Ring* has been more a series of fragmented episodes, as he has moved from one climax to another, the threatening *longeurs* in Wagner's music thereby kept at bay. (*Music and Musicians,* March, 1971)

Later in the article, Greenhalgh suggested that Solti's problems with the *Ring* in the opera house can be traced to his earlier experience recording the work; that is, the stop-start studio approach prevented Solti from realizing the work as a total entity in the opera house.

It could be, however, that Lipman and Greenhalgh and several others, while putting their fingers on one feature of Solti's conducting, failed to interpret it correctly. From Solti's obvious obsession with detail they generalized that he had no view of the entire cycle. They further buttressed this argument by pointing out that because the recording sessions for the Decca *Ring* stretched over a period of many years, the set could not possibly project a unified view of the work. But what view of the whole can one expect to find, and how does it manifest itself? Wagner too labored on the parts of the *Ring* for many years and there are stylistic disparities in the music that attest to his development as a composer. Furthermore, there are differences in the orchestral textures appropriate to each of the *Ring* music dramas.

The story of the *Ring* and the music that Wagner created to tell the story is complex, sometimes confused and difficult to interpret. Solti's problem was not that he hadn't grasped the unity of this manifold work; rather, it was that his conception often entailed interruption of the long line in the music, and this is a quite different criticism. Solti appeared to have a very clear, firm idea of how the music should be played. He was totally in command of his orchestra and singers, from the first bar of *Rheingold* to the last bar of *Götterdämmerung*. He insisted on accuracy of rhythm and intonation, yet his reading is by no means merely literal. On the contrary, it is highly dramatic. Lipman's and Greenhalgh's criticisms imply that Solti not only broke the work up into sections for recording purposes, but that his interpretation was fragmented as well. This would suggest that there was a frequent loss of tension. Where does this occur? One can certainly point to many instances where it might be felt that the volume is too loud, the tempo too fast or the phrasing rather bland; still, these objections do not mean that the conductor lacked an overall conception. They mean only that one is in disagreement with that conception. Solti himself attempted to provide a clearer understanding of his ideas concerning the *Ring* in an interview he gave for a French magazine in 1975:

> My concept of the Tetralogy was not a "Germanic" concept, in the sense that it was taken at that time. The *Ring* was conceived then as an enormous gloomy sonority—somber, without rhythm, oceanic. According to what one called "tradition" it had to be misty, hazy. My concept was the opposite. I love clarity, rhythm, precision. It is in that spirit that I recorded the *Ring,* and I don't have the feeling at all that I maltreated the arrangement. Wagner's works are full of rhythm! It goes without saying that other interpretations are just as acceptable! Take, for example, four recordings of *Walküre:* one of Karajan, one of Furtwängler, one of Böhm, and mine. It is almost unbelievable that such a work could sound so completely different each time, while remaining so beautiful and moving! (*Le Point,* April 7, 1975)

This was a fair, although somewhat misleading assessment. Solti does explicitly reject the "Germanic tradition;" however, he was by no means radical—he was simply more precise in execution than most. The presence of the Vienna Philharmonic guaranteed an authentic Wagner sound, with a tremendous weight when necessary and lovely tonal coloration, particularly in the strings. The orchestra was also capable of expressing the poetry of the music, but not often enough under Solti. In eliminating the gloom, he frequently did away with the poetry as well. This becomes especially obvious when one compares his recordings to those of Karajan and Furtwängler. In addition, both conductors maintain the flow of the music more consistently than does Solti. Unlike Solti, they "play across the bar lines." The forfeiting of Wagner's mystical side was the price Solti willingly paid to do the *Ring* his way, but it was a valid way that paid dividends in matters of precision.

Solti admitted that he once found the *Ring* cycle abhorrent because of its Nazi associations, but later changed his mind, even about that blond, blue-eyed Nazi prototype, Siegfried:

> I sympathize with Siegfried. He is abused by the dwarf but he loves animals. Through the bird he learns about the miracle of a woman. He didn't want the gold. He didn't want to fight. He is a superman but not a Nazi superman. You can of course read everything that way, but I think even in Shakespeare you can find supermen. And Wotan, he is killing the thing he loves. He is stupid. You cannot defend that either. (BBC interview, 1965)

Forging Decca's Ring 61

In spite of any changes or improvements Solti might have made in his *Ring* performances in later years, his *Ring* cycle for Decca remains a milestone in the history of recorded sound, and it is also one of his greatest achievements as a conductor. It faithfully reflects his musical attitude at a certain time in his career, and it is an attitude which commands respect and admiration.

There were indications that as Solti grew older he was mellowing in his approach to certain works. Unfortunately, he never had an opportunity to record any part of the *Ring* a second time. In the opera house he returned to the *Ring* in 1976 when he did *Rheingold* and *Walküre* at the Paris Opera. It was intended to be a complete cycle but it didn't work out that way. Solti was unhappy with the directors, Peter Stein for *Rheingold* and Klaus Michael Gruber for *Walküre*. But the biggest problem was the orchestra:

> For me, the last straw was the dress rehearsal of *Die Walküre*. When I walked into the pit, I discovered that the first trombonist and the bass trumpet had not taken part in any of the previous rehearsals. Because these two instruments play the *leitmotifs* all the time, they are essential in *The Ring*. The results were terrible, and the production was my swan song at the *Opéra*. (*Memoirs*, p. 176)

Solti returned to the *Ring* one last time when he was invited to conduct the complete cycle at Bayreuth in 1983, in the festival theater created by Wagner. Wolfgang Wagner, grandson of the composer and now the general manager of the festival, had the great idea to invite Solti, one of the outstanding Wagner conductors of the day to preside over a new *Ring* in Bayreuth. Instead of being a career highlight for Solti, it turned out to be an unhappy experience. Frederic Spotts in his book *Bayreuth: a History of the Wagner Festival,* called it one of the festival's "most magnificent flops." Solti had invited his long-time Covent Garden colleague to direct and much of the blame was heaped on him. Friedelind Wagner was quoted as declaring "this is the worst amateur show I have ever seen in a theatre. Peter Hall has no idea of the *Ring,* nor of directing…This is the downfall of Bayreuth." (*Abendzeitung, Munich, May, 1984,* quoted in Spotts, *op. cit.)*

The debacle was documented in agonizing detail in Stephen Fay's book *The Ring: Anatomy of an Opera.* As recounted by Fay, Hall and designer William Dudley found the *Ring* experience at Bayreuth a nightmare and one or both were on the verge of packing it in on numerous occasions during the preparation for the performances. While Hall and Solti got along fine as they always had, Hall had terrible problems with Wolfgang Wagner. Wagner seemed to have legitimate issues with designs being late, and demands for complicated stage machinery including a huge tank filled with water. These and other problems ultimately put the production well over budget. It didn't help that Hall spoke no German and went out of his way to avoid confrontation while Wagner spoke no English and seemed to relish shouting at the top of his lungs at the slightest provocation.

As in Paris, one of the biggest problems was the orchestra. It was second-rate. Solti also found the famous covered pit in Bayreuth an exceedingly difficult place to work. The heat nearly did him in but more importantly he could not hear or see what was going on:

> If anybody had told me when I was at music school that I would one day be in a pit where I couldn't hear anything or see all the players, I would have become a doctor. (Fay, *op. cit.,* p. 106)

But an even bigger problem was the quality of the singers. As late as the dress rehearsal for *Siegfried,* major casting was very much in doubt. In fact, the dress went so badly the tenor cast as Siegfried (Reiner Goldberg) had to be replaced. For Solti it was a case of *déjà* vu: he had had the same experience in recording the *Ring* for Decca in the 1960s. In spite of Hildegard Behrens's great success as Brunnhilde in this production, Solti came to the conclusion that there were simply not enough capable singers around to cast the *Ring*:

> there are no dramatic sopranos capable of singing Brünnhilde, no *Heldentenors* capable of singing Siegfried, and no Wagner bass-baritones capable of singing Wotan as the parts should be sung." (*Memoirs,* p. 178)

The tradition in Bayreuth is to gradually develop a new production over a period of several years. But neither Hall nor Solti wanted anything more to do with Bayreuth. Solti begged off for 'medical reasons.' Wolfgang Wagner was outraged:

> Peter Hall and Georg Solti left us with a ruin. Neither had the courage to stand by their work and bring it to completion. (*Financial Times*)

In his autobiography, Hall defended himself by arguing that Bayreuth should not be attempting to mount an entire *Ring* cycle all at once, in the same season. Hall says that he and Solti only agreed to do so against their better judgment. There was never enough rehearsal time and no chance to properly experiment with design ideas. No wonder there was conflict and chaos. As for the charge made by several German critics that he had no concept of the *Ring,* Hall argued that he was reacting against the then-current fascination with politicizing the work. Hall was trying to get back to what Wagner intended:

> My concept was...to try to reveal the corruption of power and of wealth, and the purity of regeneration, with natural forces as the important corrective to human faults. But this was considered altogether too contradictory and too ambiguous. What did I *mean?* the critics cried. (*Making an Exhibition of Myself,* p. 255)

Solti came to the conclusion that major changes were in order for Bayreuth. Instead of persisting in the notion that Bayreuth should be kept as a perpetual shrine for Wagner's major operas, the festival should bring in works by other composers from Weber to Henze. "The Wagner Festival as such has outlived its time, and new thinking is needed." (*Memoirs,* p. 179)

5

The Beethoven Nine in Chicago

Beethoven's nine symphonies, taken as a unit, stand as one of the monuments of symphonic thought. If Haydn invented the symphony as a work for orchestra in four movements, Beethoven gave the form an unparalleled capacity to express the deepest and the subtlest of feelings. Moreover, Beethoven used symphonic form with infinite resourcefulness. Each of the nine symphonies is a unique entity, different from the others both musically and emotionally. In each, Beethoven set himself new problems and then solved them in new ways.

Consequently, the Beethoven symphonies are an essential part of any conductor's repertoire. He generally learns the works during his student days and wrestles with them throughout his career. But he is one of the elite indeed if he emerges from the struggle with glory. During the past half-century, although many conductors have played and recorded these pieces time and again, by general consensus, only the performances of Toscanini, Weingartner, Furtwängler, Mengelberg, Klemperer, Szell and Karajan have stood the test of time. While one or two others might be added to the list depending on personal bias, these men are the most widely heralded interpreters of the complete cycle. They are also, of course, among the most celebrated conductors generally. In other words, almost all of the conductors we call "great" have made their mark with the Beethoven Nine. The exceptions—Stokowski, Beecham and Koussevitsky come to mind—are few.

Solti himself readily pointed out that he came to the conducting of the Beethoven symphonies rather late in his career, and really did not have much concentrated experience with them until he took over the Chicago Symphony in 1969, at the age of fifty-seven. The first Beethoven symphony he conducted was the Seventh, in Munich, in 1946. In the course of his tenure there at the Bavarian State Opera he performed all the symphonies except the Ninth. His chance to do that work came finally in Frankfurt during the 1950's when he was music director of the Opera. Solti's concert work while he was at Covent Garden was intermittent and never focused on Beethoven. Finally, in Chicago he got the opportunity not only to play but also to record all nine.

Solti had made a recording of the Fourth with the London Philharmonic in 1950, and went on to record the Third, Fifth and Seventh with the Vienna Philharmonic in 1958-59, but a complete cycle for posterity was a special occasion. In a recorded conversation with music critic William Mann included as part of the complete set when it was first issued in the U.K. on LPs, Solti remarked that every conductor should record the nine symphonies three times in his career: first, when he is young, about thirty—"*Sturm und Drang*" performances very likely, according to Solti; second, when he is in the middle of his career, around fifty years old; and finally, if he has time, when he is about seventy. Solti recorded nearly half the symphonies fairly early in his late-blooming career and they are very much in the *Sturm und Drang* style characteristic of the young Solti. But he was into his sixties before the chance came to do a complete cycle, between 1972 and 1974. Fortunately, he was able to record a second complete cycle, again with the Chicago Symphony, very late in his career (1986-90). Among his contemporaries, Herbert von Karajan had the rare opportunity to revisit the Beethoven Nine as a complete cycle on records, four times over the course of his career.

Solti's early Beethoven recordings—tremendously vigorous, loud, fast and exciting performances with some wonderful playing on the Vienna Philharmonic recordings—are aptly characterized as *Sturm und Drang*. By contrast, the later recordings with the Chicago Symphony are still energetic, but for the most part slower, quieter and generally the work of a more mature conductor.

In his conversation with William Mann, Solti singles out Toscanini as the most important influence on his approach to conducting Beethoven. Above all, he says, it was Toscanini's "desperate seriousness" which impressed him. Toscanini was always working, always pouring over the score, while Solti was at that time, in his own words, "lazy and easy-going." In his younger days, Solti supported Toscanini's view that the Beethoven symphonies should be played fast, in accordance with the metronome markings, with great power and with a single tempo maintained throughout whole movements. Only much later did Solti seriously consider Furtwängler's much more flexible and personal approach to Beethoven.

When he came to record all the symphonies in Chicago starting in 1972, Solti felt that the "truth for Beethoven" lay somewhere between the conceptions of these two conductors, and he tried to find that middle way. In fact, the predominantly moderate tempi of the first Chicago Symphony Beethoven cycle (1972-

74) are departures from the Toscanini ideal, although they still retain something of the Italian conductor's obsession with precision and intensity. But it could hardly be said that these performances represent a move towards the Furtwängler approach. Furtwängler's Beethoven was characterized, above all, by freedom of tempo; it was also notable for its spiritual and poetic qualities rather than for its precision. Also, Furtwängler's best performances exhibited a delightful inevitability and spontaneity. The music seemed to be advancing according to an irresistible logic while at the same time sounding fresh and alive. Such descriptions do not readily come to mind when listening to Solti's Beethoven. Even in conversation about the symphonies, Solti seemed primarily concerned with technical problems.

Nevertheless, Solti's CSO Beethoven cycles have their own fine qualities. Above all, a wonderful authority is evident throughout; here is a master conductor who knows exactly what he wants and who has sufficient force of personality to persuade the musicians to give it to him. Furthermore, Solti frequently achieves first-rate ensemble playing, particularly in matters of rhythm. Rhythmic figures, which often cause problems in performances even by good conductors and orchestras, are never carelessly rendered by Solti's players. Solti's honest interpretation—his strict obedience to the letter of the score—is equally admirable. Every repeat in every movement is observed; all *sforzandi* are played with the same intensity; even traditional alterations to the score are cast aside in favor of the original.

But these performances do have their shortcomings. The first cycle was recorded over a period of about two years in three different locations: first, the Ninth Symphony at the Krannert Center in Chicago; next, the Sixth and Seventh Symphonies in the *Sofiensaal*, Vienna; and then the rest in the Medinah Temple, Chicago. The Medinah Temple recordings are the worst: there is little resonance with the result that the strings sound as if they are forcing their tone almost constantly, and the woodwinds lose their individual colors. This ambience is particularly unfortunate because it reinforces what is least admirable in Solti's conducting.

In determining where to lay the blame for the poor sound, one must take into consideration a number of factors: 1) the sound of the hall as it affects the performance being recorded, 2) the sound of the hall as it affects the performance we hear, 3) the sound produced by the engineers (including the sound of the hall, microphone placement, mixing, pressing, etc.) as it affects the performance we hear, and 4) the sound intended by the conductor. If the Medinah Temple recordings are compared to the recordings by the same orchestra at the *Sofiensaal* in Vienna, the superiority of the latter is undeniable: the orchestra has a much warmer sound, the strings are forcing far less and the winds have color and individuality.

The Krannert Center recordings are also much better than the Medinah in these respects. One might be led to conclude, then, that the inferior sound of the Medinah recordings is either the fault of the hall or the engineers. Yet, throughout all these performances there remains, to a greater or lesser degree, a characteristic aggressiveness in Solti's conducting, sometimes appropriate and sometimes not. For this reason one cannot indiscriminately attribute the particular quality of these recordings, or any recordings for that matter, to either the hall, the engineers, the conductor or the members of the orchestra who might not be able to cope with the acoustics of the hall. It is a complex matter, which must be constantly borne in mind. As far as the Medinah performances are concerned, the sound would be a great impediment to anyone's Beethoven, and must certainly color an appreciation of Solti's.

In any case, and for whatever reasons, while he aims at a middle road between Toscanini and Furtwängler, Solti fails to offer the kind of insight and excitement achieved by either conductor. He is vigorous and intense, but the result is often far from exciting. There is a heaviness of rhythmic accentuation that destroys both continuity and forward motion. One has the feeling that Solti is trying too hard to keep his impetuosity in check, as if to prove how mature he has become. He seems to be saying to himself, "no more headlong tempi, and no more bombastic outbursts." And yet *Sturm und Drang* is part of his nature. To restrain himself as stringently as he does in his first CSO Beethoven cycle is to destroy the lifeblood of the music.

The second cycle, recorded more than ten years later, between 1986 and 1990, again uses more than one venue, and one—Orchestra Hall, the CSO's home concert hall—which wasn't used at all in the first cycle. In the second cycle Orchestra Hall was used for all the symphonies except 5 and 9, which were recorded in Medinah Temple. Frankly, it is difficult to tell the difference between Orchestra Hall and Medinah Temple in these recordings, and that might have to do with the fact that by the time of the second cycle a new recording technology had emerged. The digital age had begun in the early 1980's, and it quickly became the standard in the industry for making recordings. Shortly afterwards, the compact disc rapidly emerged as the preferred delivery system to the consumer.

But controversy developed almost immediately as to whether the new technology was all is was hyped to be by the record companies. Many listeners complained about a brittle, artificial quality that seemed to be characteristic of digital recordings and claimed that the old analogue techniques had greater warmth and depth. Some of the first digital recordings were certainly disappointing if not downright awful, but the engineers soon learned to refine the technology and within a few years there was no looking back. Digital technology and compact discs meant among other things that tape hiss and surface noise were gone forever. Also, it became much easier than ever before to edit. By the late 1980s we were in a new age of recorded sound and Solti's second Beethoven cycle was one of the earliest beneficiaries. In fact, the new technology was probably the most compelling reason for Decca to undertake the new cycle.

Orchestra Hall in Chicago has never been considered one of the world's great concert halls. It has often been criticized for its lack of warmth and presence. Some tinkering has been done over the years but orchestra Hall is still only serviceable at best. As a recording venue for the CSO it was avoided for many years in favor of more resonant facilities such as Medinah Temple, a vast barn of a place often used to present traveling circuses. And Decca certainly jumped at the chance to record the CSO at the *Sofiensaal* whenever the orchestra visited Vienna. For the second CSO Beethoven cycle the new digital technology provided some improvement but it could not entirely overcome the deficiencies of the venue, in most cases, Orchestra Hall. The Chicago Symphony was one of the world's great orchestras and it could certainly play with warmth and refinement but much of that is lost when the orchestra is recorded in Orchestra Hall.

As for Solti, the truth is that his ideas about the music had not really changed much since the first cycle. His general approach is the same, which is to say that in terms of tempi and other parameters of interpretation, he is still middle of the road. Admittedly, some of the tempi are a little faster, reflecting Solti's considered opinion that many of Beethoven's controversial metronome markings are, after all, quite playable, and should be respected wherever possible. But faster is not always better in music and certainly not in Beethoven. A conductor has important decisions to make about tempi but it is at least as important to capture the drama and poetry of the music. This is solid, highly professional music-making, but without much imagination, insight, involvement or personality.

Let me now deal with each of the symphonies in turn. My comments are largely based on the first CSO cycle but where there are significant differences between the two versions they are noted.

Symphony No. 1 in C major Op. 21

Beethoven's First Symphony is often treated as an early work: more "Mozartean" or "Haydnesque" than "Beethovenian." It is generally felt that the real Beethoven does not emerge until the *Eroica* wherein one can recognize the fire, the pathos and the epic proportions lacking in the earlier symphonies. It is necessary, therefore, for a conductor preparing a performance of the First Symphony to consider it in relation to the remaining eight. The Beethoven of the C major was not yet the man who composed the others, either emotionally or musically, and the danger is that the conductor will blow up the slender proportions of this symphony to somehow speak the language of the *Eroica,* the Fifth or the Ninth. In fact, the C major is clearly modeled after the symphonies of the classical masters; it uses the standard Mozart-Haydn orchestra—while Mozart and Haydn enjoyed big orchestras when they had them available, the norm was an ensemble of 20-35 players—and the forms of its movements are almost textbook examples.

In his conversation with William Mann, Solti pointed to two features of the First to refute the claim that the composition is "Haydnesque:" the seventh chords, which open the work, and the fragmentary statement of the main theme at the beginning of the last movement. These are indeed unprecedented features for a classical symphony, but so too were numerous others like them in many of Haydn's symphonies; for instance, beginning with a timpani roll in No. 103, and using extra percussion in No. 100. Such innovations have nothing whatever to do with the essential style of the piece. In practical terms this means that Beethoven's First Symphony will not respond well to the extremes of tempo and dynamics, which can be convincingly applied to his Third or Fifth Symphonies.

If, for example, a conductor uses a large string section appropriate to Wagner and Strauss, he obliterates the handful of woodwinds called for in the C major. Doubling the winds by way of compensation, as is often done today, only compounds the original mistake by creating much too big a sound. And if the *sforzato* accents are played in a violent manner appropriate to the Seventh, the modest proportions of the work are utterly destroyed. Beethoven's First Symphony is neither profound in expression nor revolutionary in technique, but it is often misunderstood by conductors overawed by the spirit of the later Beethoven.

Solti's performance is a compelling one. He is wonderfully attentive to rhythmic detail, and scrupulously careful about every marking in the score. One hears no unmarked *ritardandi* or *accelerandi* here. Nothing is added to personalize the music or to make it superficially exciting. Nevertheless, his realization is not necessarily successful. Rejecting the notion that the C major is "Haydnesque," Solti uses what sounds like a very large string section. Coupled with a tendency to stress downbeats, the result is a relentless heaviness, even in quick passages. The first themes in the *Allegro* sections of the first and last movements are absolutely classical in character, and when played with the appropriate lightness can be delightfully bouncy and infectious. Under the weight of sound Solti applies to the music, however, the fragile textures are beaten to a pulp. Although accents are laudably observed throughout the performance, they are consistently overdone, in a style appropriate to the later Beethoven symphonies.

In the opening bars Solti achieves absolute unanimity of attack on the chords but the result is aggressive rather than noble or grand. When he comes to the second subject in the *Allegro* he maintains the tempo with implacable rigidity. No slowing up is marked at letter B but surely at least a feeling of relaxation is intended, and this is not achieved. The oboe solo sounds rushed and unbending. For all the clarity of Solti's rhythms, at bar 277 the main theme cannot be heard clearly at all in the first violins, basses, celli and bassoons because the rest of the orchestra is so loud.

The second movement is played in much the same way. The first beat of every bar is given a heavy accent, and so too is the eighth-note pick-up whenever it occurs. Within the framework of Solti's inflexible tempo the music sounds like a march. There ought to be suggestions of a march, to be sure, particularly when the timpani joins in with the dotted rhythm later in the movement, but one should not be given the impression that the whole movement *is* a march.

In the last movement the notes are rendered without much humor or excitement. There is little sense of mock drama in the slow introduction, in which the theme of the following allegro is introduced in tantalizing fragments. And when the *Allegro* does begin it is again elephantine when it should be light as a feather.

My impression is that a powerful and serious personality has organized and directed this performance. It is tough-minded, stiff and rhythmically exact to a fault. Chords are played like heels clicking together rather than like musical instruments sounding with each other. The result is a reading altogether too tough and severe for the nature of the music. The youthful innocence is lost.

The second version with the CSO from 1989 is somewhat faster and lighter and this is a definite improvement. However, the timpani lack definition in both versions. This is such a pervasive problem in Solti's Beethoven recordings one must conclude that it is not the fault of the hall or the engineers; Solti wants it that way.

Symphony No. 2 in D major Op. 36

Similar virtues and drawbacks may be found in Solti's performance of the Second Symphony. This is a more ambitious work than the First, but it is still essentially classical in style. It is not a piece given to heaven storming, let alone even a fleeting glimpse of tragedy, but rather finds its elements in a persistent feeling of joy and exuberance. Again, the conductor ought to aim at classical lightness in the textures and articulation in order to facilitate the essential flow of the music. He should also guard against introducing any suggestion of pomposity and aggressiveness. Solti, who encourages his orchestra to play with considerable heaviness, obviously has different ideas about the music. In the *Allegro* section of the first movement, for instance, the notes are hammered flat when they should be released quickly in order to spring forward to the next.

The slow movement is marked *Larghetto,* which is surely Beethoven's way of cautioning the conductor not to take the music too slowly. Solti ignores the warning in a performance devoid of grace and buoyancy. As in the First Symphony, he maintains one tempo throughout each movement, even for the *Trio* sections in the *Scherzos* (although the *Scherzo* of the First Symphony is called by the old name, *Menuetto).* While there is no indication in the score that a slower tempo should be taken here, it is traditional to do so—not always a good reason, to be sure—but the music does feel unyielding and hard-driven if there is not at least a slight relaxation in the tempo for the *Trios.*

Another unusual feature of Solti's recording of the Second Symphony is the absence of a single real *pianissimo.* In fact, the first one in the entire cycle does not occur until the beginning of the development section in the first movement of the *Eroica.* It is true that this is an effect Beethoven exploits more fully in his later works, and in no case should the *pianissimo* have the disembodied, dramatic quality essential to fine performances of the Fifth or the Ninth. Nonetheless, there is room for much quieter playing in the Second Symphony at bar 105 in the *Scherzo* and at bar 338 in the last movement, to take just two examples.

In Solti's re-recording of this symphony in 1990, many of the problems I complained about in the earlier recording were eliminated. For example, the dynamic range was greatly improved, allowing for some really soft playing. Solti also finds a better, more flowing tempo for the slow movement. But again, especially in the exciting coda of the last movement, a crisper contribution from the timpani would have been welcome in both recordings.

Symphony No. 3 in E flat major Op. 55 *(Eroica)*

Beethoven's Third Symphony is in many respects a new kind of symphony. This is true both of the emotions expressed and of the textures and orchestration—the numbers and kinds of instruments and how they are used—and the two are, of course, related. On the most superficial level, the *Eroica* is longer and louder, but it is also more wide-ranging in its expression and more complex structurally than either of his first two symphonies. While an orchestra of only medium size can very effectively play it, it is not inappropriate to use a larger orchestra. Still, the use of six horns instead of the three called for in the score—a not uncommon occurrence—is probably going too far. This touch certainly adds to the power of the big climax in the last movement but it also pushes Beethoven too far in the direction of Bruckner and Richard Strauss to be entirely convincing.

Solti's tempo for the first movement is quite moderate. More reminiscent of Klemperer than Toscanini, it is effective at least at the beginning. Concerning repeats in this and other Beethoven symphonies, Solti makes an interesting comment in his *Memoirs:*

> Although I observed the repeat of the exposition when I recorded the Third Symphony, I do not do so in live performance, because I feel that it makes the movement too long and that it spoils the proportions of the symphony; I do, however, observe all the other repeats in the Beethoven symphonies. (p. 214)

The heaviness of both sound and accentuation encountered in Solti's performances of the First and Second Symphonies is at last suited to the character of the music. There is tremendous authority through the exposition section, as Solti not only hammers every *sf* but also allows the solo winds time to phrase their successive *dolce* entrances. However, doubts about Solti's conception set in when he avoids any sense of climax at bars 275-279. What seems to be required here is a gradual buildup in tension, finally released after it becomes nearly unbearable. In Solti's hands, the sequence is quite uneventful. Further along, at the buildup beginning in the basses and celli (bar 341), the listener is jarred by the strength of the accents when the general marking is *piano*. These overdone *sf*'s are more appropriate to a *forte* passage and their effect here is to destroy a necessary feeling that something ominous is impending. At bar 408 there is an inconsistency between horn and flute concerning the rendering of the repeated quarter notes—the horn plays them *legato;* the flute distinctly separated.

Finally, at the *coda* of the movement, another instance of Solti's scrupulous adherence to the letter of the score crops up. The trumpets of Beethoven's day did not have available on their instruments all the notes called for in the theme at bar 655, so Beethoven had them begin to play the passage and let the woodwinds finish it alone. Since the modern trumpet can supply all the required notes, it now plays the entire theme in tonic and dominant in most *Eroica* performances, a practice undoubtedly more in line with Beethoven's intentions. To stick slavishly to the score, as Solti does in both of his Chicago recordings—and as Toscanini, Furtwängler and Karajan do not—is to do away with the overwhelming grandeur and excitement of this magnificent *coda*. Solti did follow modern practice in his first *Eroica* recording with the Vienna Philharmonic.

The second movement is once more lacking a sure sense of tension and release. It is accurately played but seems episodic and arbitrary. The trumpets surprise us by suddenly bursting forth at bar 96 where we expect to hear the *sempre più forte* Beethoven wrote; but where is their power when it is asked for at bar 76? Solti's treatment of the trumpets in such passages is as puzzling as it is unconvincing.

The third movement is played quite fast but, as is so often the case with Solti, too heavily for the character of the music. The heaviness is here accompanied by a certain nervousness and the result is a tempo that never really settles.

In the last movement, climactic moments go for little, as at bar 381. The music is pushed forward too quickly, and robbed of nobility. In the final *presto*, the tempo is careful where it should be headlong. The timpani suddenly erupt at bars 457-458 then falls back to nothing. What could Solti have had in mind? There is nothing in the score to justify this strange reading. At bar 469 the brass is held down to about *mf* to allow the clarinets and bassoons to emerge with their scale passages. However, the effect comes across as contrived in the final bars of such a symphony. For the sake of textual clarity the piece finishes with a whimper instead of a bang. Solti is so intent on solving the *Eroica*'s technical problems, he utterly fails to give a real performance.

There is not much improvement in the later 1989 recording, except that, if anything, the trumpets and timpani are even more restrained when they should be powerful and heroic.

Symphony No. 4 in B flat major Op. 60

"A slender Greek maiden between two giants." Robert Schumann's poetic description of the Fourth Symphony refers to the fact that both the *Eroica* and the Fifth Symphony are much grander in conception, and possess elements of tragedy not to be found in the Fourth. But this is not to say that the B flat is a lesser work; in some ways it is even more beautiful than its neighbors.

Solti's performance in the first Chicago Symphony cycle is perhaps the most successful in the entire set. Tempi are generally lively and energetic, and not impeded by the rhythmic heaviness prevalent in nearly all the other performances. Solti seems freer in his approach here and it pays off. The flute solo at bar 304 is customarily slowed down with the basses and celli, although there is no marking to allow for a *ritardando* in the score. To his credit, Solti follows tradition in this instance and the passage has a lovely effect.

The tempo for the slow movement is a good one—measured, slightly held back, and only occasionally dangerously slow—and the first violins distinguish themselves with playing of great tonal beauty in the opening bars. At letter A and again from bar 50, Solti coaxes a noble sound from his trumpets that is a joy to hear, and gives them a prominence in these passages just sufficient to create dissonances which one seldom hears brought out so well—a beautifully judged effect.

In the *Scherzo,* Solti goes off the rails several times by being too literal in his approach. His fast tempo is carried straight into the *Trio* each time, even though Beethoven called for *un poco meno allegro.* According to the metronome markings there is to be only a slight difference in tempo, but in Solti's performance there is scarcely any difference at all. And, as happens so often in Solti's Beethoven, the *sforzandi* are greatly overdone at bars 163-166 and again when the passage is repeated. On the other hand, the last movement is played brilliantly, with first-rate performances by each member of the orchestra. One might regret the consistently loud *pianissimos,* particularly in the basses and celli at bar 319, but for the most part Solti's energy and alertness pay great dividends here.

Symphony No. 5 in C minor Op. 67

Solti's 1958 recording of the Fifth with the Vienna Philharmonic, while not letter-perfect, is an exciting and bracing performance. Although it is not a subtle reading—the tempo often borders on the hysterical—the symphony responds well to such treatment, especially when the orchestra is the Vienna Philharmonic. No matter how fast the tempo, or how loud the volume, the players always produce a rich, beautiful tone where others might sound raucous and crude.

By contrast, Solti's Chicago Fifth (first cycle) is an enormous disappointment. Tempi are much slower and even self-consciously held back. In the first movement, not only is the tempo too slow but the climaxes are greatly underpowered. In an apparent effort to avoid the rhetoric of traditional performances of this movement, Solti goes out of his way to maintain the same tempo throughout, despite the logic of the music. The mighty statements of the main theme by brass and timpani really must be slowed down and each note given progressively more weight coming into the *fermatas* before the oboe solo, and again at the end after bar 475. In this last passage Solti does slow up a little and he does not hold the last *fermata* longer than the others; still, it is not enough for a dramatic musical structure on this scale. Moreover, in this same passage, trumpets and timpani should be shattering in their weight and power. Solti, however, keeps them on a very tight rein indeed. The length of the *fermata* is of great importance here too. It must be held long enough to give the impression it will never end; otherwise it is mere repetition without significance. Solti's objective reading is an interesting experiment, perhaps, and Pierre Boulez has made a recording which displays the same kind of detachment, but neither performance should be thought of as idiomatic.

Throughout the second movement the playing is well controlled. Accompaniment figures emerge with pleasing clarity, and the numerous technical problems are admirably sorted out. But the tempo is often too sluggish to be entirely satisfactory, and once again an excessive self-consciousness intrudes upon the performance. It is almost standard for a conductor playing the music for the first time with a new orchestra to say at the first *forte* in the viola and cello tune (bar 7), "No, no, gentlemen, you make a *crescendo* on the E flat when it is *subito forte!*" In other words, the musicians are playing the phrase as becoming gradually louder instead of suddenly louder. How clever of the conductor to correct his lazy musicians. Unfortunately, the "lazy musicians," who anticipate the *forte,* usually play the passage with more musicality than Solti achieves from his Chicago orchestra. The *subito forte* is in the score all right, but an interpretation as extreme as Solti's makes no sense at all; it destroys the line. Played so violently, the *subito forte* becomes, in fact, a *sforzando*.

The tempo Solti chooses for the *Finale* is also a little slow. It can be made to work, but not without masterly control of all the tempo changes, and well-judged climaxes at the end, neither of which conditions Solti meets. Failing to reach a climax is a persistent failing in Solti's Beethoven cycle, and as far as the Fifth Symphony is concerned, a reading without an exciting denouement amounts to a gross distortion of the score.

Symphony No. 6 in F major Op. 68 *(Pastoral)*

The Sixth Symphony is one of the two in the first cycle recorded by Solti and the CSO at the *Sofiensaal* in Vienna. The sound of the orchestra is a great improvement with much warmth in all sections, and generally far less of the forcing of string tone so common in the Chicago recordings. However, the justly celebrated hall was an unfamiliar one to the players and this, coupled with the fact that the recording was made during a hectic European tour, perhaps account for some of the problems in the performance.

The first two movements go reasonably well but then disaster strikes. In the *Scherzo,* the orchestra is curiously untidy, with the horns in particular being chronically late. It is possible that the horns could not hear the rest of the orchestra well enough, and certainly Solti's very fast tempo does not make things any easier; nevertheless, the playing is disgraceful by any standard. The horns blare out like vicious, barking dogs, while trying desperately throughout the whole movement to catch up with the rest of the orchestra. In the horn solo at the beginning of the last movement, Solti asks for such strange phrasing that the player must have turned himself nearly inside out to manage it. And, once again, there is no majesty in the final climax; in fact, there is scarcely any climax at all.

Symphony No. 7 in A major Op. 92

Like the Sixth, Solti's Seventh starts off fine, with a welcome bloom of sound from the *Sofiensaal* on the opening chords. The second movement is particularly well played, with beautiful balances in the lower strings.

The third movement is quite fast, even in the *Trio.* Solti follows Toscanini by being true to the letter of the score here. Beethoven has written *assai meno presto* for the *Trio,* with a metronome marking indicating one to a bar. Still, many conductors believe a much slower tempo makes more sense because it allows the numerous *dolce* hairpins to make their effect. In any case, nearly all conductors are skeptical about the accuracy of Beethoven's metronome markings, and judge each one on its merits in the musical context. Solti's fast tempo for the *Trio* in the Seventh may be textually correct, but it sounds rushed and rather messy.

The *Finale* is fast enough without setting a new speed record, though the accents are heavy to the point of sluggishness. Once more Solti holds the orchestra in check at the climax, so that the ending is a considerable letdown. In both recordings, but especially in the second, I was again puzzled by the fact that the trumpets are rarely allowed to play a real *fortissimo.* There are many places in the Seventh Symphony where Beethoven obviously wants them to be prominent and powerful. Solti seems to have another view. Nor does Solti ever allow the excitement in the last movement to get out of hand or even threaten to get out of hand. But that is surely the point of it all. It is meant to be exciting and almost out of control.

I found it fascinating to compare Solti's second recording of the Seventh with the CSO for Decca, and a live performance given about the same time by Solti with the LSO and issued on DVD. The tempi are virtually the same and the overall conception is almost identical, except that in the CSO studio recordings Solti takes all the repeats but in the live performance he doesn't. Solti said that in making a recording he was obligated to obey the letter of the score, but that in concert taking too many repeats would make the performance too long.

But I was particularly interested in the way Solti balanced the orchestra in the live performance, especially the trumpets. On several occasions they are obviously too loud for Solti and he puts his hand up to tell them to drop back, and they do. But in the coda of the last movement he finally lets them out, far more than in either of the CSO studio recordings. The timpani are also more exciting in this live performance. Clearly, Solti was prepared to allow more freedom and excitement in a live performance than he would in the studio. With respect to trumpets and timpani it is easy to understand what he had in mind. If these instruments are not carefully balanced they can easily overpower the rest of the orchestra, particularly the strings. This is a particular problem in Beethoven. But the key question is this: did Beethoven want perfect balances, or did he want the excitement that powerful trumpets and drums can bring?

One further point about the live performance with the LSO. I have no idea what Solti said to the players in the rehearsals but presumably Solti did admonish the trumpets and timpani about playing too loud. However, in the concert it might be understandable that they would tend to disregard what Solti said in rehearsal because of the way he conducted in the concert. Solti's gestures are extremely aggressive and in some of the climactic episodes he certainly seems to be asking for more. It is not at all surprising that the trumpets tended to give him more.

Symphony No. 8 in F major Op. 93

In conversation with William Mann, Solti observes that the Eighth is probably the easiest Beethoven symphony to conduct but the hardest to play, although no such difficulties exist for the Chicago Symphony. In both CSO recordings, Solti is particularly successful in encouraging his players to articulate every note of every triplet in the last movement. On the other hand, this clarity comes at a price. Surely the passage should be tossed off with a flick of the wrist, yet it would seem that in the first CSO recording Solti worked on the figure to the extent that the players were nearly paralyzed in their bow arms, and so produced a heavier sound without much bounce. The feeling which is exhibited throughout the entire movement is on the ponderous side. At bar 157 one notes that the Chicago Symphony bassoon is no better than his colleagues in most other orchestras in that he fails to plays the octaves in tune. The second recording is much better in nearly every respect.

Also in conversation with William Mann, Solti talks about the problem of getting the same kind of *staccato* from all the winds in the opening bars of the second movement. Solti achieves this uniformity, but in the first recording it is too loud and too heavy; what is needed is a precise and light *staccato,* and in the second recording Solti and his players are much more successful.

The highlight of both versions is the playing of the two horns in the *Trio* of the third movement. The dynamics are beautifully shaped and the sound is out of this world.

Symphony No. 9 in D minor Op. 125 *(Choral)*

Solti's version of the Ninth, recorded in the Krannert Center in Chicago in 1972, yields a transparency of sound not to be found in either the Medinah or the *Sofiensaal* recordings. It is a special pleasure to hear the timpani come through as cleanly and forcefully. For most of the Beethoven recordings the timpani sound is remote and muddy, although this has a good deal to do with Solti's rein on the instrument. In the Ninth, however, the timpani are allowed more prominence. This is particularly important at the recapitulation of the first movement and, of course, in the solo passages in the *Scherzo.*

At the very beginning of the symphony Solti makes the pulse clear in the sextuplet accompaniment while maintaining a true *pianissimo,* and the *sotto voce* entrance of the main theme is perfectly judged. When this same passage is recalled at bar 30 in the *Finale,* one is again struck by how well Solti has captured the serenity of the music. The tempo chosen for the first movement as a whole is moderate, except for a notable episode where Solti dares a much slower pace with excellent results. At bar 506, and again four bars later, a *ritardando* is indicated followed immediately by the marking *a tempo.* The entire passage is played quite slowly with great expression, and features lovely phrasing by the winds and strings together. Yet, while Solti obeys the *ritardando,* he never really returns to the main tempo of the movement during this episode. Here he ignores Beethoven's markings when the spirit of the music seems to require that he obey them.

He also disregards the composer's markings elsewhere in the movement. At bar 194 and at the parallel passage (212), Solti begins the *ritardando* a bar early, but the revision is a very musical one. Another deviation from the score occurs at the recapitulation, where Beethoven has written in *fortissimos* for all instruments, from beginning to end. If the music is played accordingly, it is difficult to make out the return of the main theme in the strings. To allow this figure to emerge, Solti reduces the volume of the accompaniment and makes a *crescendo* toward the thirty-second note attack at the end of bar 304 and again at the end of each bar in which the figure is repeated. While this practice is adopted by many conductors and certainly clarifies what is going on in the passage, to my ears it has always seemed somehow unBeethovenian. When the music is played as written, with all instruments including trumpets and timpani issuing a really powerful, sustained *fortissimo* throughout, the melodic figure has to fight to be heard; yet it does come through and the epic grandeur of the passage is matchless. This seems to be what Beethoven intended. Moreover, there is no comparable instance in Beethoven's other works of the *forte-piano crescendo* sequence adopted by Solti. Solti is here retaining a traditional practice favored by Toscanini and many others, but it bears serious rethinking.

For his CSO remake in 1986, Solti took a tempo for the first movement which is again, on the slow side. Indeed, it is ponderous at times in a way that Klemperer's notoriously late-career slow tempi could be. However, at his best, the slow Klemperer could be monumental and profound in this music.

The rest of the symphony in both CSO versions is well played without offering any special insights. The beginning of the finale is particularly disappointing, especially in the later version. This is apocalyptic music which should engender fear in listeners, before the Ode to Joy theme emerges. In Solti's hands there is no sense of this at all. It is all too careful and unemotional. The cello and bass recitative is one of the most heartfelt passages in all of Beethoven. Here it is merely well played. We get no sense that this music comes from the depths of an agonized soul. Compare Furtwängler or Bernstein in these passages.

In the first Chicago recording Solti's vocal quartet—Pilar Lorengar, Yvonne Minton, Stuart Burrows and Martti Talvela—is not at all suited to the music. The sound of the individual voices is often ugly and the blend is non-existent. For the second recording Solti had a much better group—Jessye Norman, Reinhild Runkel, Robert Schunk and Hans Sotin—although Norman swoops unnecessarily from time to time and contributes an ugly wobble on her F sharp in the fermata at bar 842. Throughout both performances Solti appears to have given too much thought and attention to technical problems and not enough to the spiritual depths of the score.

Every recording of Solti's two Beethoven cycles with the CSO is a testament to how seriously he regarded the technical problems of playing and conducting these works, and in talking with William Mann, Solti referred time and again to such difficulties. It will be reassuring for a young conductor to learn that for all his enormous gifts, Solti admitted to having trouble beginning the Fifth Symphony and the *Scherzo* of the Third. He refers to the same problems again years later in his *Memoirs*.

Solti took great care in these performances to do what he believed to be correct, and, in this respect, he was certainly more deeply influenced by Toscanini's "desperate seriousness," than by Furtwängler's poetic spontaneity. It is obvious that Solti knew what he wanted, and he had two excellent opportunities to get it with his own orchestra in Chicago. Unfortunately, compared to some other conductors who have recorded these works over the years, Solti seems to have had little insight into what the music was about. To be sure, few conductors of his generation allowed themselves to interpret this music in a personal way as Furtwängler had done. The prevailing wisdom was that conductors should be faithful to the score and not let their personal feelings intrude. Leonard Bernstein was an exception among Solti's contemporaries and he has left some remarkably idiosyncratic performances recorded with the Vienna Philharmonic for DG. And then there was the emergence of the original instrument movement whose exponents claimed that most conductors had misunderstood Beethoven because they didn't understand the way the instruments would have been played in his time. Conductors such as Hogwood, Norrington, Gardiner and Harnoncourt all recorded the symphonies either with period instruments or in the case of Harnoncourt, using what they had learned about these instruments. Many of these recordings came as a revelation to listeners who had grown up on Toscanini, Furtwängler and Karajan.

Solti was certainly aware of the original instrument movement and remarks on it in his *Memoirs* (p. 213). But he could not understand why anyone would want to use old and inferior instruments when newer and better ones were available. Solti seems to have missed the point of it all. It is not necessarily better to use old instruments instead of newer ones. Rather, one plays on older instruments in order to understand better what the composer would have had available to him and therefore one might more easily grasp what the composer intended.

One younger mainstream conductor who has been particularly impressed by the original instrument movement is Simon Rattle. He works regularly with the Orchestra of the Age of Enlightenment, a specialist group which performs on period instruments and using period performance practices. When his turn came to record the symphonies with the Vienna Philharmonic (2002), he showed he had absorbed all this new information. More than that, he also showed he was willing to take chances and follow his own course. His Beethoven recordings provided a fresh new beginning to the 21st century.

6

Mahler with Many Orchestras

When the first edition of this book appeared in 1978, this chapter was obviously restricted to Solti's Mahler recordings which had been made up until that time. But in some respects, the best was yet to come. When Solti first recorded the nine Mahler symphonies the recordings were not planned to form a cycle; it just worked out that way. His first recorded Mahler was the Fourth, with the Concertgebouw Orchestra, in 1961. Then came recordings of the First (1964), the Second (1966), the Ninth (1967) and the Third (1968), all with the London Symphony. In 1969 Solti became music director of the Chicago Symphony, and after that most of his recordings were made with the CSO. Recordings of the Mahler Fifth (1970), Sixth (1970), Seventh (1971) and Eighth (1971) were all made with the Chicago Symphony. As the Mahler symphony recordings piled up, Decca obviously had their eye on a complete Solti Mahler Symphonies cycle, and they had it by 1971. And it was a very distinguished one. However, as the years went by and given the growing reputation of Solti and the Chicago Symphony, it made even more sense to try to make it a Solti-Chicago Symphony Mahler cycle. Between 1980 and 1983 Solti remade the symphonies 1,2,3,4 and 9 with the Chicago Symphony. These latter recordings also had the benefit of state of the art digital recording techniques.

Technically and temperamentally, Solti was an excellent Mahler conductor. He solved the enormous problems of coordinating the huge orchestral and vocal forces and, more importantly, managed the numerous tempo changes and the extraordinary dynamic range with great assurance and conviction. Solti's famous impetuosity, although somewhat mellowed by the time of these recordings, suited Mahler very well. The scores contain frequent directions to the conductor to suddenly push forward, and Solti could manage this sort of thing with incomparable energy. Yet the more lyrical and relaxed episodes are handled well too.

In the first edition of this book, I complained that Solti frequently ignored the quiet dynamics in his Mahler performances, and that passages which should sound ethereal and mysterious, emerged as matter of fact because they were too loud. But this was not a problem in Solti's Mahler performances from the 1980's with the Chicago Symphony. Perhaps it was the combination of greater maturity and newer technology.

Symphony No. 1 in D major (*Titan*)

Like all the Mahler symphonies, the First was conceived and has to be understood as a vast organism. At the same time, all the extraordinary and innumerable transformations of the thematic ideas must be given their proper character. The listener should never be in doubt that the music is moving towards a logical and emotionally satisfying conclusion. But that conclusion will be empty if the individuality of each episode has not been experienced along the way. For example, the marches and dances which abound in Mahler's symphonies and which were considered vulgar and cheap before the works were better understood, cannot be downplayed or somehow perfumed without sacrificing the rich human experience Mahler was attempting to depict in the language of music. Precisely because they are trite, the marches and dances express an important side of the human experience, which co-exists alongside the more elevated and noble qualities of mankind. Similarly, the cruelty and senselessness of war is vividly expressed in Mahler's symphonies, no less so than in Tolstoy's *War and Peace*. But how difficult it is, Mahler is saying, and how necessary to transcend the vulgar and the aggressive and find lasting truth and beauty.

This eternal struggle of the human soul to rise above itself, sometimes finding peace in nature, but ultimately seeking something more lasting in eternal life has to be realized in performance. Conductors must not shirk from the mindlessness and cruelty of Mahler's military marches, just as they must resist the temptation to make the country dances too sophisticated. And they must crown the whole with a blazing belief in Mahler's vision of life everlasting.

Already in his First Symphony Mahler sought to burst the bonds of traditional orchestral sonority. In the slow introduction to the first movement Mahler instructs the trumpets to "go some distance away" to play their fanfares. The third movement opens with an eight-bar solo for double bass accompanied only by timpani. Later in the movement we hear a parody of a village band. Towards the end of the symphony, to increase the power of the climax, Mahler asks for another set of four horns to be added to the seven already in the orchestra and, in addition, all the horns and trumpets are instructed to stand up with their bells raised and to try to drown out everybody else! Never before in orchestral literature had a composer been so original, extravagant and precise in his demands

The slow introduction to the first movement of the symphony contains the thematic seeds of the whole work, above all, the interval of a descending fourth. It is heard for the first time in the third bar, played softly and in long notes in the minor by the winds, then a little later, played louder and in short notes like a bird call. Further on, the interval is repeated over and over, finally becoming the first two notes of the main theme of the faster section, in a major key version for basses and celli. At the end of the symphony the interval reappears as part of a triumphal peroration in the major. There is also an important fanfare idea in the slow introduction, first played quietly by the muted trumpets. It too returns brilliantly and triumphantly as part of the climactic outbursts in the *Finale*.

Solti's first recording, made in 1964 with the London Symphony, is excellent. The orchestra plays superbly and the recording quality is unusually good. Solti masters every mood of the work and conveys a feeling of great involvement. In a BBC interview, also from 1964, Solti recalled that when he first conducted the LSO, in 1952 or 1953,

> it was not terribly good. A few years later Fleischmann became general secretary and he invited me to come. I was skeptical but it was marvelous. I have great respect for this orchestra. They work very hard to make it better. The string sound has a bite that I like…they can also sing…(a) crisp, clear tone. There are wonderful soloists in the wind group.

The London Symphony *had* improved, with the acquisition of outstanding players such as hornist Barry Tuckwell and clarinetist Gervase de Peyer, but there was also an extraordinary spirit and pride in the group, attributable, at least in part, to the orchestra's self-governing status. The players themselves chose their own colleagues, their manager, their conductors and their engagements. It was certainly Solti's good fortune to make some of his first Mahler recordings with this newly reinvigorated orchestra.

It is instructive to compare this recording with a later one which Giulini made with Solti's own orchestra, the Chicago Symphony. Giulini takes a consistently lyrical view of the work, often wonderfully expressive, but disappointing in the earthier episodes. His conception seems altogether too elegant for the nature of the music. Solti with the LSO, on the other hand, is muscular and even crude when need be, and the recording supports this conception with a more striking realization of the different instrumental timbres.

Solti's Chicago Symphony recording, made in 1983, nearly twenty years after the version with the LSO, is very good and benefits from the latest in recorded sound. Nonetheless, the older version still stands up very well and one would be hard put to declare the later one a clear winner. Solti's conception is essentially the same.

Symphony No. 2 in C minor (*Resurrection*)

Solti recorded this symphony with the LSO for the first time in 1966. If anything, the sound is even better than his LSO recording of the First Symphony, with a range of dynamics and a depth of perception rivaling the *Ring* recordings which had been completed only a year before. There are musical resemblances between the Mahler and the Wagner in the score too; the searing string *tremolos* and the attack of the basses and celli at the beginning of the *Resurrection* are reminiscent of the opening of *Die Walküre* Act I. And in performances of both pieces part of the excitement is the sensation of hearing the physical contact of bow and string, particularly by the double basses. The force of attack Solti coaxes out of the LSO in the Mahler is staggering. Moreover, he manages to maintain this kind of energy throughout the first movement. Only Abbado's 1977 CSO recording of this movement achieves a comparable level of tension and virtuosity. In his 1980 recording with the CSO Solti does not come close to what he and the Decca engineers accomplished with the LSO in 1966.

In the more subdued, even childlike second movement, Solti was equally impressive with the LSO. The phrasing of the strings is wonderfully varied and subtle, so much so, one could almost mistake the orchestra for the Vienna Philharmonic. The magic continues into the third movement where the tricky interplay between winds and strings is beautifully brought off and at just the right tempo—neither rushed nor self-consciously held back.

The fourth and fifth movements, however, in the LSO recording, are a great letdown. Trumpets and oboe play with admirable artistry in their quiet moments in the fourth movement, but not nearly softly enough: *pp* is the marking repeatedly. The *molto espressivo* sounds rather cold and the *molto ritenuto* near the end of the movement is surely far too fast. To ignore so many important tempo and dynamic markings is to render this sublime movement commonplace. Soloist Helen Watts contributes little except an accurate reading of the notes. The CSO remake is far better with respect to the soft dynamics and the brass playing is wonderful. Mira Zakai sounds a little like Kathleen Ferrier and is a hauntingly beautiful soloist.

As Beethoven did in his Ninth Symphony, Mahler introduces a chorus in the final movement of his Second Symphony, and uses it to create an overwhelming effect. The pain and misery of human existence portrayed earlier in the work are superseded at last by resurrection. *"Auferstehen!"* the chorus cries out. "Rise again!" Mahler's music is absolutely gripping and transporting, as it begins softly and mysteriously in the chorus and then bursts forth triumphantly. But time and again in Solti's LSO performance there is a dangerous loss of tension. At the final climax both Solti and the engineers provide only a glimpse of resurrection. It is a musical and carefully prepared performance, when, instead, a feeling should be engendered that the performers have been entirely swept away with the ideas as well as with the notes. Either Solti was still working towards an understanding of the logic of this part of the score, or he simply failed to get what he wanted under the stop-start conditions of studio recording. What a pity after such an auspicious beginning.

Solti's remake of the *Resurrection* was made at the Medinah Temple in Chicago in 1980, fourteen years after the LSO recording. There is some glorious brass playing in this performance and the last movement hangs together much better than it did in the LSO recording. The Chicago Symphony Chorus is also heard to great effect. But again the recording is ultimately disappointing. The engineers do not come close to capturing the weight of sound of the last few pages, where ten horns, six trumpets and four trombones, are joined by two timpani players, bells, two tam-tams and organ. There is also a hard-edge on the upper strings that was all too characteristic of early digital recordings.

Symphony No. 3 in D minor

Mahler's Third Symphony is a rambling epic with a number of significant musical and philosophical resemblances to the Second Symphony. Both require a chorus and at least one vocal soloist, and both follow a tortuous emotional path towards eternal salvation. The climax in the last movement of the Third recalls the parallel passage in the Second in its triumphal major-key bombast.

Solti's conception of the Third has all the virtues and shortcomings of his performance of the Second; an abundance of energy, great attention to detail, but also a disturbing inability to comprehend the logic of the whole or to deliver the *coup de grâce*.

It is notoriously difficult for any conductor to hold the long first movement together, but it can be done. Compare, for example, Jascha Horenstein's recording made about the same time and with the same orchestra, the London Symphony. In Solti's hands, the score appears to be a series of unrelated episodes.

Horenstein, however, manages to communicate a feeling of integration while still allowing the individual qualities of these episodes their due. Even the seemingly inconsequential drum rolls and trivial tunes have important parts to play in the work as a whole. After letter 11, Horenstein gives the oboe tune a character missed entirely by Solti, yet absolutely faithful to Mahler's markings in the score.

In the last movement, Solti takes too fast a tempo at letter 26, in the passage marked *sehr langsam*. Again, he fails to get inside the music. This is a characteristic and heart-rending sequence for three trumpets and trombone. There is a risk that the music might fall apart if taken too slowly here, and Horenstein's brass players do have trouble with both breath control and intonation, but so do Solti's (the very same players?) at a faster tempo. James Levine and the Chicago Symphony achieve much better results on their recording and with a tempo as slow as Horenstein's.

Solti's 1982 recording with the Chicago Symphony is tremendously well-played and recorded, while lacking the spiritual dimension of the Horenstein recording.

Symphony No. 4 in G major

The G major was the first Mahler symphony Solti recorded, and at that time (1961) there was no suggestion that he would go on to record all nine. The Concertgebouw, Solti's orchestra for this recording, was certainly no stranger to the Fourth. Its first performance of the work was in 1904, just three years after the premiere. The composer himself was on the podium and, in fact, conducted the symphony twice at the same concert! Willem Mengelberg, the orchestra's music director, conducted the work a year later and many times thereafter, most notably in his Mahler Festival of 1921 and in a 1939 recorded performance. Mengelberg and the Concertgebouw were steeped in Mahler and the style and spirit of his music. It is appropriate that Mengelberg's successors, Eduard Van Beinum and Bernard Haitink, have also shown an affinity for Mahler, and that both have recorded the Fourth Symphony with the orchestra. Solti's version made for four recordings over about a thirty-year period of the same work by the same orchestra.

In spite of the fact that the Concertgebouw learned its Mahler from the composer himself, and that the score is meticulously marked with all sorts of detailed instructions concerning tempo and dynamics, the four performances are by no means identical. Mengelberg, of course, had a reputation for being a willful, eccentric conductor. His interpretations were both daringly unique and controversial, but there was no disputing his control over the orchestra, nor the inspired quality of his best performances. The singularity of his style can be heard in his 1939 recording of the Fourth, which is in very good sound and readily available today on compact disc. In the first movement in the third bar there is a marking *un poco ritardando*. When the same figure is repeated fourteen bars later there is no such marking, and no other conductor slows up at this point except Mengelberg. Later in the movement, at letter 7, Mengelberg adds another of his inimitable touches, stretching out the top note of the cello and viola phrase each time. Although Mahler did mark an accent on these notes, Mengelberg's interpretation virtually amounts to a rewriting of the rhythm.

Mahler's Fourth is his least ambitious symphony. The orchestration is almost classical in its modest requirements of two trumpets and no trombones, and there is no heaven-storming, apocalyptic finale. On the contrary, the symphony ends quietly. Nonetheless, there are some highly original touches. In the second movement, for example, the concertmaster must use two instruments tuned differently—one a whole tone higher than the other—to suggest the brazen, rather coarse playing of a street fiddler.

In the last movement there are surprising disagreements among conductors about the proper tempo. Bruno Walter, Mahler's associate for many years and one of the foremost interpreters of his music, took quite a fast tempo. Mengelberg, with an equal claim to know the composer's intentions, conducted the movement far more slowly. Solti decided on a middle course in his Concertgebouw recording and did the same in his remake with the CSO.

Solti's Concertgebouw recording is technically superb, with some characteristically rich and exciting playing. The recording quality is excellent too. All that is lacking is that otherworldly beauty which is so necessary in the last two movements. Mengelberg achieves it, and so too does Haitink with the help of the finest soprano to grace any recording of a Mahler Fourth, Elly Ameling. Solti's soloist was the competent but rather ordinary Sylvia Stahlman. Solti's excellent remake with the CSO had one of his favorite sopranos, Kiri Te Kanawa, as soloist in the last movement.

Symphony No. 5 in C sharp minor

The 1970 recording of the Fifth Symphony was the first of Solti's Mahler recordings to be made with his own orchestra, the Chicago Symphony. While the LSO in the earlier Mahler recordings was in top form, the Chicago Symphony under Solti was a very great orchestra. One generally assumes, and makes allowances for the fact, that brass instruments lack the agility of winds or strings. The Mahler symphonies are filled with tough passages for brass which require not only agility, but security and strength in the upper registers, as well as stamina to sustain such difficult playing over the course of works lasting up to ninety minutes. Of course stamina is not a problem in a recording. If the players should tire, the piece can be finished the next day; or, the strenuous passages can be scheduled early in the session. Also, to some extent, additional strength can be supplied by the engineer. Even so, the brass, and indeed all the instrumentalists in the Chicago Symphony recordings are astounding.

To take only one recording for comparison, Solti and his Chicago players often surpass Karajan and the Berlin Philharmonic on DG in their respective recordings of the Mahler Fifth. Both performances are tremendously powerful in the opening bars of the first and second movements, although the CSO brass is more accurate. On the other hand, Karajan and his strings achieve a more poetic sound at letter 2 in the first movement, and again before letter 12. Solti's *Finale*, however, sets new standards of performance for this movement. He takes an exhilaratingly fast tempo, and yet his horns produce a *staccatissimo* that makes their Berlin counterparts sound sloppy by comparison. And listen to the cellos at letter 2! They far outshine the Berliners in their playing of the *staccato* eighth notes. Overall, Solti's realization brings out more of the humor obviously intended by Mahler with his *allegro giocoso* marking.

The moments one regrets in Solti's reading are few. In the quiet passages, before letter 9 and after letter 27, where Karajan produces a fine inward quality, Solti's sound is too loud. And at the big climax after letter 33, Solti's trumpets almost disappear when, as in Karajan's recording, they should blare forth triumphantly.

In November, 1990 Solti and the CSO toured Europe to great acclaim. In Vienna their program included the Mahler Fifth and the Decca engineers were there to record the event for posterity. It turned out to be an even finer recording than the one they had made in Chicago twenty years before. The virtuosity is on the same high level but there is a depth of feeling, particularly in the Adagietto, that is quite striking. The sound quality is also remarkable, taking advantage of the latest in digital technology. There are numerous subtleties of soft playing only hinted at in the earlier recording. One of Mahler's most original touches of orchestration is the use of a tam-tam in the second movement. It is marked *piano* and in most recordings it is simply not audible. But in this one it has an altogether distinctive presence that colors the whole texture of the music. Wonderful! There are times when one misses the expansiveness of expression that is so moving in the Bernstein or Karajan recordings, but this is nonetheless one of best documentations of Solti and the CSO in their prime together.

Symphony No. 6 in A minor (*Tragic*)

Solti's only recording of the Sixth Symphony, also with the Chicago Symphony, is another virtuosic *tour de force*. His conducting is super-aggressive and dynamic, and the orchestra produces some incredibly fast, loud playing. But again, while this approach suits the music most of the time, one misses some of the tenderness and ethereal softness heard in other versions.

Solti's tempo for the first movement is arguably at odds with the *allegro energico ma non troppo* called for in the score. His fast beginning is impressive until letter 7, which, according to Mahler's instructions, is supposed to be played at the same tempo. The theme here is softer, more expressive and more lyrical. Solti's quick tempo causes it to sound superficial rather than hauntingly beautiful.

The *Finale* contains the most remarkable playing in any of Solti's Mahler recordings. After letter 33, strings, woodwinds and brass alike play their rapid sixteenths with equal agility and with absolute fearlessness, as if technical problems did not exist. And at Solti's ferocious tempo, it is all quite breathtaking.

Symphony No. 7 in E minor (*Song of the Night*)

This too is a Chicago Symphony performance, and it still stands as perhaps the finest Mahler Seventh put on records. In comparison, the others seem hopelessly underrehearsed and incoherent. The most original movement is the third, with its almost Webernesque melodies, irregular rhythms, and odd orchestration (Mahler makes uses of such unlikely orchestral instruments as a guitar and a mandolin!). The rhythm settles into waltz time but it is a demented waltz—a waltz for a society coming apart at the seams, and haunted by its own inadequacy and guilt. Solti brings out this nightmarish quality with great assurance.

An important element in his conducting here is the incisive accenting. Only by stressing every accent can Mahler's unusual rhythmic patterns make their full effect, and Solti gives the music exactly what is needed. This relentless accenting has always been a part of Solti's conducting style, although it has not always been a virtue. The accents in his recording of Wagner's *Tristan und Isolde* are so unremitting, one begins to feel a little seasick after a while. In Mahler, however, where there are often three or four rhythmic patterns going on simultaneously and where the music can so easily become porridge, with neither shape nor clarity of texture, Solti's approach is a great advantage.

Sharp accenting also does wonders for the notoriously problematic last movement of the Seventh, with its frequent complex fugal passages and its tricky alternation of the two main tempos. While Solti takes the second tempo (two bars before letter 234) correctly in terms of Mahler's instructions regarding the relation between the two tempos, it appears to be too fast. He has to slow up a little later on, and quite drastically at the *pesante* passage after letter 237. This trouble shifting gears occurs in a number of places throughout the movement, but the rhythmic life and energy in Solti's conducting are major compensations. He brings more cogency to the music than any other conductor on record. The sound is exemplary, save for the usual lack of truly quiet passages, and the balances are good too except that, as in the recording of the Fifth, the trumpets are consistently cut back in favor of the horns. The Chicago Symphony horn players led by Dale Clevenger are spectacularly good; still, that does not mean they should always be heard at the expense of the trumpets.

Symphony No. 8 in E flat major (*Symphony of a Thousand*)

The Eighth was the last of Solti's first Mahler cycle to be completed, and it was done under rather unusual circumstances. The original plan had been to record the work in Chicago with the magnificent Chicago Symphony Chorus. Unfortunately, it was discovered that the choristers would have to be paid staggering fees, and a cheaper scheme was put together instead. The Chicago Symphony was scheduled to tour Europe in 1971. Why not arrange for the CSO to stop over in Vienna an extra few days and make use of one of Europe's best choirs, the Vienna *Singverein?* In effect, it was much cheaper to send the orchestra to Europe than to record the work at home in Chicago! For Solti it must have been especially attractive to return to the scene of past glories—in the same hall where his highly-acclaimed *Ring* cycle had been recorded—this time with his own orchestra.

Solti's performance contains plenty of his usual energy but he manages some calm and inward moments as well, particularly at *Alles Vergängliche* (All things transitory) in the final section. Also on the plus side in this recording is the presence of several fine soloists (tenor René Kollo as Doctor Marianus and Heather Harper as Magna Peccatrix). And Solti deserves enormous credit for mustering such a robust sound from the Vienna *Singverein,* especially when it is evident that this is really not his kind of choir. He seems to be striving for what he already had in the Chicago Symphony Chorus: a choral ensemble with as much technical virtuosity as his orchestra.

The most serious drawback in the recording is the quality of sound. For a conductor and company with an incomparable *Ring* cycle to their credit—recorded in the same location, the *Sofiensaal*—it is a major disappointment. Part of the trouble may have been due to the lack of rehearsal time, which is always a problem under touring conditions. How else to account for the numerous rough and obvious edits on the original LP release? How else to make sense of the general lack of clarity of sound? At the end of the symphony the extra brass make a considerable effect, but still come nowhere near to equaling the weight and clarity of sound produced by the Vienna Philharmonic in the *Ring*. Admittedly, the basic sound of the Chicago Symphony is different from that of the Vienna Philharmonic. Nonetheless, as a production job, this recording simply cannot be considered alongside the *Ring* achievement. To make matters worse, tenor René Kollo is off-mike virtually throughout the whole first movement. Apparently, much of his part was dubbed in later because of illness and scheduling problems.

Symphony No. 9 in D major

To turn from Solti's flawed recording of the Mahler Eighth to his brilliant recording of the Ninth made in London four years earlier, is to be able to reaffirm the conductor's great qualities as a Mahler interpreter. Compare it to the almost universally-acclaimed 1976 recording of the work by Giulini and the Chicago Symphony for DG, and it is just as rich and detailed, but even more vivid. Surprisingly though, considering the Chicago Symphony is supposed to be unrivaled, especially in the Mahler repertoire, there is not much to choose between the orchestras. In a work with so many horn solos, the quality of the principal horn player can make a big difference, and while both players are superlative, there is something extra provided by the LSO's musician (Barry Tuckwell?). In addition to remarkable technical feats and thrilling power, he produces a rare expressive quality. Solo oboe and violin have their special moments too in the Solti-LSO recording.

    Solti's LSO Mahler Ninth is full of muscle and, for some, might be too aggressive. If one compares Solti and Giulini in the third movement, for example, and is partial to Solti, his drive and rhythmic energy, above all in the hair-raising final *più stretto* and *presto,* will make Giulini appear casual to the point of sloppiness, and absurdly elegant. On the other hand, Giulini supporters will charge Solti with being brutal and insensitive. His relentless *staccato* will seem monotonous to listeners sympathetic to Giulini's more musical kind of articulation. Furthermore, Solti will appear to miss entirely the right feeling for the middle section after letter 36, even though he obeys the letter of the score in not slowing up. Giulini does achieve an undeniably remarkable quiet beauty in this passage, and it is this kind of revelatory interpretative touch, Giulini's admirers insist, which demonstrates precisely what Solti's conducting lacks: only rarely can he make the imaginative leap from the page of a score to the mind of the composer. Solti's critics grant that his work is technically of the highest order, but they feel it lacks distinction. This is a thorny argument at best and will be considered at length in a later chapter. Suffice it to say here that Solti, in his own way, interprets the music as much as Giulini.

In his recording of the Ninth with the LSO, Solti does not charge through the score with all guns blazing, as one might be led to believe from the preceding discussion. The sheer physical excitement and weight of his reading are striking, but other qualities emerge too. The closing pages of the first movement are chamber music, and Solti plays them that way. There is no pushing or pulling here, and no larger-than-life accents. The tonal beauty of the two horns, oboe and solo violin is one of the glories of this performance. The climax of the last movement (Universal Edition, p. 176) is perfectly judged with respect to both tempo and dynamics. In comparison, Giulini's climax is rather ordinary.

Solti also manages most of the tempo contrasts in the second movement with admirable adroitness. His initial tempo is quite slow yet very rhythmic. It makes even more sense at the *poco più mosso subito* (Tempo II), because this section need not go really quickly to sound lively. Solti throttles back with great aplomb for the slow and expressive *ländler* (Tempo III), but he does err thirteen bars later in taking the return of Tempo I so fast. Perhaps he forgot his initial slow tempo. Later still, the extremely long *luftpause* before the return of Tempo III (Universal edition, p. 84) is a questionable touch.

Still, these are relatively minor quibbles within the context of such an exciting and committed performance. Both conductor and orchestra convey a joy of music-making, and the engineers have captured it all in spectacular sound.

Das Lied von der Erde (*The Song of the Earth*)

This song cycle or symphony with two solo voices belongs, as does the Ninth Symphony, to the last period of Mahler's life. Both works reflect the composer's awareness of his own impending death and his preoccupation with its meaning. He did not live to hear either work performed.

For his texts, Mahler chose some Chinese poems which had been recently translated and which perfectly reflected his mood. Each of the poems combines images of joy, usually in nature, with bittersweet visions of death. The basic theme of *The Song of the Earth* is the ephemeral nature of both life and beauty, and the imminence of death. The first of the six songs in the cycle, for example, includes the lines:

> The heavens are ever blue, but you, man how long will you live? Not a hundred years. So take up the wine—dark is life, dark is death.

The symphony therefore begins with an almost demented attempt to live life to the full in the face of its obvious brevity. To perform the first movement, both tenor and orchestra must capture this reckless mood of merry-making. The music should be tossed off with abandon, and it should be almost violent in its passion. Mahler has certainly called for this in the score, with the poor tenor in danger of being overwhelmed by the orchestra on every page. But the performers must also be sensitive to the quieter, more lyrical pages of the song which are full of characteristically Mahlerian sentiment.

Solti's tenor in this performance, René Kollo, recorded the work no fewer than three times in his career: first with Solti in 1972, then with Bernstein during the same year, and finally with Karajan in 1975. The three recordings indicate considerable development on Kollo's part, but also reveal the different approaches of the conductors. Solti is, as one might expect, the most aggressive or muscular. His orchestra plays louder, the accents are sharper and, in general, the tempos are faster.

There is also a difference in recording quality. Solti's engineers prefer to spotlight instruments, as do Columbia's for Bernstein, whereas their DG counterparts opt for a more natural blend of sound for Karajan. Spotlighting is not necessarily unsuitable in Mahler, but what is unacceptable is poor balance between vocal soloists and orchestra. In Solti's recording, both Kollo and Yvonne Minton are too often submerged, and while this is not unlike what one might hear in concert, it is inexcusable in a recording. Here is one way in which studio production can improve on concert hall realism and its limitations.

This choice of balance on Solti's recording destroys an otherwise fine performance. Within DG's ambience, Karajan and Kollo bring out some uncommonly beautiful moments of the score, and Kollo's voice floats more freely. Still, one does miss the earthiness of Solti's conception, so vital to the opening song. Bernstein tends towards the Karajan approach, perhaps because his orchestra, the Israel Philharmonic, has a more mellow, less aggressive sound.

In the final *Abschied*, Karajan's blended sound becomes more of a liability than a virtue. Strangely, for him, he seems unable to sustain such a long and subdued slow movement. Solti is better here thanks to crisper accenting and a more detailed sound quality. But Bernstein is best of all in his unfailing concentration and his command of mood and line. Solti is also handicapped by a competent but far from memorable performance of the solo part by Yvonne Minton. Christa Ludwig does a much finer job for Karajan and perhaps because it is a live performance, she excels even more in the Bernstein recording.

In 1992 Solti gave a performance of *Das Lied von der Erde* with the RCO in Amsterdam and Decca recorded it live. The soloists were Marjana Lipovšek and Thomas Moser. The *Penguin Guide to Compact Discs (1994)* noted that in this recording Solti "takes a clean-cut dry-eyed view," and that while it is "beautifully played in a detached way, the performance lacks mystery even in the final song."

Lovers of Mahler's music will know that, in addition to *Das Lied von der Erde*, he began a Tenth Symphony. He finished the first movement and left extensive sketches for the rest of the work. Deryck Cooke has put together a performing edition of the entire symphony based on these sketches, and others, most notably Clinton Carpenter and Remo Mazzetti Jr., have done the same. Solti finally performed the first movement of the Tenth Symphony, for the first time in his career, in 1996, and had become very interested in going further:

> The English musicologist Deryck Cooke made the first reconstruction of the symphony, but I have not used it, as I think it lacks the contrapuntal element in Mahler's writing. Three further versions of the Tenth Symphony exist or are in preparation, and in the summer of 1999 I would like to work on a solution to the symphony, putting together the different reconstructions that are available and adding points of my own. (*Memoirs*, pp. 200-201)

Sadly, Solti did not live to carry out his plans concerning the Mahler Tenth.

Solti's Mahler cycle, including some remakes of some of the symphonies with the Chicago Symphony, is a remarkably distinguished one. Among the conductors who have recorded all the symphonies—Kubelik, Bernstein, Haitink and Abravanel—Solti must be regarded as one of the most successful. His major contribution has been to show how well much of this music can be played. It was not so long ago that even dedicated Mahlerians complained that certain passages could never be made to "sound," or that the brass or string writing was awkward. With both the Chicago Symphony and the London Symphony, Solti has put an end to this sort of talk once and for all. Moreover, he has demonstrated that Mahler's music can be made to sound like orchestral showpieces. This is really a considerable achievement. His readings may be lacking in mystery as a result, but then no conductor has ever succeeded in encompassing all the riches of both music and ideas in these works, and perhaps none ever will.

Sir Georg Solti conducting *Das Rheingold*, Sofiensaal, Vienna 1958. Photo: Hans Wild, courtesy Decca Music Group.

Sir Georg Solti conducting *Die Walküre*, Sofiensaal, Vienna 1965. Photo: Elfriede Hanak, courtesy Decca Music Group.

The musical brain trust of the Chicago Symphony at Orchestra Hall in April, 1971: Music Director Solti and Principal Guest Conductor Carlo Maria Giulini. Photo: Rosenthal Archives, Chicago Symphony Orchestra (Lightfoot)

Solti and the CSO return in triumph from a European tour with a ticker tape parade down Chicago's LaSalle St. October 14, 1971. Photo: Rosenthal Archives, Chicago Symphony Orchestra (Lightfoot).

Solti conducts Schoenberg's opera *Moses and Aaron* at Orchestra Hall, Chicago, November 13, 1971. Photo: Rosenthal Archives, Chicago Symphony Orchestra.

Solti and the CSO at the Proms, Royal Albert Hall, London in Sept. 1981.
Photo: Rosenthal Archives, Chicago Symphony Orchestra.

"It is his eyes and facial muscles, both of which impart an infectious alertness"
(Robinson on Solti). Solti in rehearsal with the CSO in the 1970s. Photo:
Rosenthal Archives, Chicago Symphony Orchestra.

Solti in rehearsal with the CSO in 1973. Photo: Rosenthal Archives, Chicago Symphony Orchestra.

"I firmly believe that the essential quality of a conductor is, first of all, that power to project your imagination to other people" (Solti). Solti in rehearsal with the CSO in 1976. Photo: Rosenthal Archives, Chicago Symphony Orchestra.

Solti in concert in 1989. Photo: Rosenthal Archives, Chicago Symphony Orchestra (Jim Steere).

Solti acknowledging applause after a performance in 1989. Photo: Rosenthal Archives, Chicago Symphony Orchestra (Jim Steere).

Solti and soprano Birgit Nilsson rehearsing at the piano, December, 1974. Rosenthal Archives, Chicago Symphony Orchestra (Terry's).

Solti in rehearsal with British composer Sir Michael Tippett, on the occasion of the first performance of Tippett's *Symphony No. 4*, at Orchestra Hall, Chicago, October, 1977. Photo: Rosenthal Archives, Chicago Symphony Orchestra (Terry's).

7

The Interpreter in the Opera House

Solti's involvement with opera and opera houses went back to the very beginning of his career in Budapest. Up until 1969, when he was appointed music director of the Chicago Symphony, his professional career was centered in the world of opera. In succession he headed the Munich Opera, the Frankfurt Opera and the Royal Opera House, Covent Garden. When he took over in Chicago he continued to keep his hand in, conducting at least one opera production a year. After he left the Royal Opera House in 1971, Solti planned to spend most of his time henceforth on the concert platform and, for the most part, he stuck to that position while setting aside several months each year for opera. But at one point, it appeared as if he had changed his mind. Within two years of his departure from Covent Garden he accepted the post of music advisor to the Paris Opera. He seemed to be plunging back into all the plotting and turmoil of a major opera house, although he did not see his decision in that light:

> Liebermann asked me to do it and I wanted to give him the credit of my name. So I worked out a program for his first two seasons. But he and I knew this was just to get over the first hurdle. I am a guest conductor, like any other (*Opera News,* September, 1976)

Rolf Liebermann had performed miracles as *Intendant* of the Hamburg Opera and, with Solti's help, believed he could do the same with the Paris Opera. The house had been a notorious basket case for years, with poor management, slack discipline in the orchestra and mostly dismal performances. The French government made a policy decision that the Paris Opera was, in fact, one of the bastions of French culture and must be brought up to international standards. Sufficient funds were made available and the best administrator around—Liebermann—was hired to get things moving. Liebermann knew that firm and experienced musical direction was essential in a major opera house, and so he turned immediately to Solti whose success in building the musical side of the company at Covent Garden paralleled Liebermann's building program in Hamburg. The two would make an unbeatable team of opera directors.

Solti willingly responded to the plea for help from his old and respected friend, and he was no doubt flattered to be called in on such a prestigious project. At the same time, as he himself pointed out, he agreed to make only guest appearances as a conductor. During the years of his involvement with the Paris Opera he barely managed to live up to this commitment, rarely conducting more than one opera each season.

He first mounted the podium for Mozart's *Le Nozze di Figaro* which opened in the spring of 1973. A performance symbolic of the new era of French culture, it was given in Louis XV's *Opéra Royal* at Versailles before an invited audience of 750 guests paying between $200 and $500 each. The production was later moved to the Paris Opera's own house. In the fall of that same year, Solti returned to lead the first performances in France of Schoenberg's *Moses und Aaron,* one of his great triumphs at Covent Garden. For the Paris Opera, the work was done in French with Raymond Gerome producing and also taking the part of Moses. Richard Lewis was Aaron, as he had been for Solti in London. Solti again emerged triumphant:

> Solti's precise, vital direction was everything one could wish for, in turns mysterious, frenzied, triumphant, and the chorus sang magnificently. Surely every recording company must now have its eyes fixed on the Paris Opera Orchestra and Chorus. (Charles Pitt, *Opera,* December, 1973)

In successive years Solti returned to Paris to conduct *Don Giovanni* and *Otello,* and both were well received. Overall, under Liebermann and Solti, the Paris Opera was raised to world-class stature with amazing rapidity. And to ensure that this achievement received due attention, the company took to the road. In the fall of 1976, it sent an orchestra of 104, a chorus of 100, plus vast quantities of sets and costumes to Washington, D.C., and New York. Billed as the French contribution to the American Bicentennial celebrations, the troupe performed three operas: *Le Nozze di Figaro, Otello* and for French content, *Faust.* Each one featured first-class soloists on the order of Edith Mathis, Frederica von Stade and Tom Krause in *Figaro,* Margaret Price and Carlos Cossutta in *Otello* and Mirella Freni and Nicolai Gedda in *Faust;* and each involved stagings which were also far from routine. Max Bignen's iron and crystal sets for *Faust* were highly original.

So too were Joseph Svobada's stark white blocks for *Otello*. And Giorgio Strehler brought out an unusual degree of social and political commentary in his direction of *Figaro*.

Solti was in the pit for *Figaro* and *Otello*, and his firm hand was an important contribution to the success of both productions. Unfortunately, the Metropolitan Opera House in New York is much too large for *Figaro*, and the fine points in the performance went undetected. The unexpected unevenness of the singing was a further misfortune. While von Stade stopped the show as Cherubino, Christiane Eda-Pierre proved a positive embarrassment as the Countess.

Otello was much more successful, with a solid cast and a scale of orchestral sound more appropriate to the house. It is some indication of the former state of artistic direction at the Paris Opera that this work, which is unquestionably one of the masterpieces of the repertoire, had not been produced at the house since 1894. Its long overdue revival had premiered earlier in the year in Paris, where it was enthusiastically received:

> Sir Georg Solti, as one might expect, drew everything together tautly. He is, in addition, learning to relax, to give the lyrical music its head. Not only did he produce effects of remarkable brilliance in places like the opening storm and the Act III *Finale*, he also, for the first time in my experience, got close to the poetical tenderness of the love duet, and to the poignancy of the Quartet in Act II. (Dale Harris, *Music and Musicians,* September, 1976)

In New York, the critics were rapturous in their praise. Solti had become something of a cult figure in the city anyway on the strength of his annual visits with the Chicago Symphony, but his intense, vibrant conducting was deserving of the accolades.

Nineteen seventy-six was undoubtedly the year of Solti's deepest involvement with the Paris Opera. Not only did he prepare *Otello* in July and then take it to the United States along with *Figaro,* he embarked, near the end of the year, on preparations for a new *Ring* cycle. Ingmar Bergman was announced as producer, but for some reason he backed out of the project. In his place, Peter Stein directed *Rheingold* and Klaus Michael Grüber took charge of *Walküre*. Solti conducted performances of both works in December of 1976. But as was mentioned in Chapter 4, Solti had problems with the producers and the musicians and decided to pack it in at the Paris Opera.

Solti continued to conduct opera regularly in his later years. He conducted the *Ring* at Bayreuth in 1983, and returned regularly to Covent Garden where he conducted, among other operas, *Parsifal* (1979), *Die Entführung aus dem Serail* (1987), *Simon Boccanegra* (1991) and *La Traviata* (1994)

When Herbert von Karajan died suddenly in the summer of 1989 Solti received an urgent call from officials at the Salzburg Festival. Solti had never conducted an opera in Salzburg but all of a sudden he was being asked to step in and save Verdi's *Un Ballo in Maschera*. Karajan was supposed to conduct it with a cast headed by Placido Domingo and John Schlesinger directing. On a week's notice Solti stepped in and conducted a work he had not conducted onstage for more than twenty years. It was ironic that Solti was stepping in for Karajan, the man who had probably kept him from conducting opera in Salzburg all these years. However, the previous year Karajan had invited Solti to conduct the Berlin Philharmonic at the Salzburg Easter Festival and the Chicago Symphony had appeared with Solti at the summer festival too.

On the strength of his last-minute rescue of the 1989 Salzburg Festival, Solti became an important figure in Salzburg. He succeeded Karajan as the music director of the Salzburg Easter Festival and conducted *Die Zauberflöte* in 1991, *Die Frau ohne Schatten* in 1992, and *Falstaff* in 1993. Each production was also repeated at the summer festival. Unfortunately, the story did not have a happy ending. There was a complicating factor. A few years after Karajan's death, the Berlin Philharmonic had been taken over by Claudio Abbado. Since Karajan had created the Salzburg Easter Festival and since he had made the Berlin Philharmonic the resident orchestra for all the concert and opera performances, Abbado and the directors of the Easter Festival felt that the music director of the Berlin Philharmonic should also be the music director of the Easter Festival. The result was that Solti was replaced by Abbado as music director of the Easter Festival. Unfortunately, the transition was very poorly handled and Solti felt that he had been used to fill in until Abbado was ready and then chucked out. Solti felt he had been treated badly:

> I am glad to be free of the politics of the Salzburg Festival and to have no more administrative responsibilities, but it saddens me that at the time, none of the people who were my colleagues in the administration had either the courage or the decency to tell me what was going on. Had I been directly and immediately informed, I would have been the first person to understand. (*Memoirs*, pp. 188-189)

On records, as in the opera house, Solti's repertoire was very heavily weighted in favor of Wagner. Since there were many who regarded him as the finest living Wagner conductor, it was not surprising that Decca thought it important to document his work and, in fact, has done so to the extent that Solti recorded more complete Wagner operas than any other conductor in history.

Tristan und Isolde was recorded in 1960, two years after *Rheingold* and before the other three parts of the *Ring*, and the production made use of many of the tetralogy's participants. John Culshaw was the producer, the orchestra was the Vienna Philharmonic, and Birgit Nilsson—the *Ring* cycle Brünnhilde—played Isolde. As part of its boxed set of the complete opera on LP, Decca included a record of rehearsal excerpts. While it was intended primarily as a glimpse behind the scenes of how a complex recording is made, it also offered a revealing portrait of Solti in action. The man's enormous energy and involvement are apparent throughout, whether rehearsing the singers with piano, discussing the recording set-up with Culshaw, or rehearsing the orchestra. Unfortunately, the performance itself is overwrought: climaxes are exciting but frequently noisy and vulgar; accents are often overdone, destroying line and proportion; and the quieter moments lack tenderness. This recording is valuable mainly as a document of Nilsson's Isolde. Although her interpretation of character and text is uninteresting, when she rears back and lets fly she produces a volume of glorious sound the like of which one might only dream of ever hearing from another Isolde. Poor Fritz Uhl as Tristan is overwhelmed by her, in addition to being mercilessly hammered by Solti. But Solti himself was not happy with this recording either:

> I plan to rerecord *Tristan* in Vienna in 1998 and 1999, because I was too inexperienced when I conducted the 1960 version. Besides, the acoustical balance was not good. John Culshaw and Gordon Parry believed, correctly, that Furtwängler's EMI recording of *Tristan* had been badly balanced, with the singers singing directly into the microphones and the orchestra swamped in the background, but our 1960 recording had gone to the opposite extreme, with the orchestra swamping the singers—even Birgit Nilsson. (*Memoirs*, pp. 195-196)

Unfortunately, this was another of Solti's plans that he did not live to realize.

Most of Solti's Wagner opera and music drama recordings have been made with the Vienna Philharmonic. They include the *Ring*, *Tristan und Isolde*, *Tannhäuser*, *Lohengrin*, *Die Meistersinger* and *Lohengrin*. With the Chicago Symphony he recorded *Die fliegende Holländer* and a second version of *Die Meistersinger*. Decca preferred to use the Vienna Philharmonic because of the great success it had had with the *Ring* cycle, and the fact that it had invested a lot of money for recording equipment in the *Sofiensaal* and got superb sound there. The recording rates were also much cheaper in Vienna for both orchestra and chorus. While Solti always had problems with the Vienna Philharmonic—as a matter of tradition they didn't like to play exactly on the beat and this drove him crazy—and he would have preferred to use the Chicago Symphony. After completing the *Ring, Tristan, Parsifal, Die Meistersinger,* and *Tannhäuser* in Vienna, Solti finally persuaded Decca to do the next project in Chicago. They recorded *Die fliegende Holländer* in 1976 after a series of concert performances and it was a dud. The orchestra sounds mechanical and the sound lacks weight and color. The famous Solti Wagner sound is nowhere to be heard. Everyone concerned did a much better job with *Die Meistersinger* in Chicago in 1996.

Solti himself often spoke about the difficulty of finding singers who could sing the great Wagner roles in the opera house, let alone record them for posterity, and several of his recordings were clearly inadequately cast. Norman Bailey was a major liability in the first *Meistersinger;* Jose Van Dam, although a little lightweight, was a big improvement in the second one. Likewise, René Kollo was barely adequate in the first *Meistersinger* recording. Ben Heppner was more like the real thing in the second one.

Lohengrin, recorded in Vienna in 1986, was particularly well cast, with Domingo, Norman, Randova and Nimsgern in the leading roles. One must wonder, however, about the casting of Dietrich Fischer-Dieskau as the Herald. The role calls for a stentorian voice and even on a recording, an aging Fischer-Dieskau doesn't fit that description. But overall this is a wonderful performance with Solti not only making the most of the drama but also finding some ravishing quiet moments. It is to Solti's credit too that the Vienna State Opera Chorus, especially the men, sounds so committed and so precise in its rhythm.

Solti amply repaid the confidence Decca management showed in him early in his career, especially as a Wagner conductor. Except for the *Tristan* debacle he conducted a strong series of performances. No other conductor has ever had the opportunity to record so many Wagner works, but it is difficult to suggest one who might have done them better. In 2003 Decca issued a 21-CD limited edition set containing six complete Wagner operas conducted by Solti under the title, *Wagner: The Opera Collection: Sir Georg Solti*. Even seven years after his death Solti remains unsurpassed as a Wagner conductor.

Solti also enjoys the distinction of having recorded more Richard Strauss operas than any other conductor, and he set a very high standard. He recorded *Salome, Elektra, Der Rosenkavalier, Die Frau ohne Schatten,* and *Arabella,* all with the Vienna Philharmonic, and *Ariadne auf Naxos* with the London Philharmonic.

While each recording has a strong cast and great moments, *Elektra* is the most outstanding. Solti's high-strung temperament is ideal for such a score. There is tremendous tension and sweep in his conducting here, with hair-raising playing by the Vienna Philharmonic. And there is love and relaxation too as, for example, after the recognition of Orest.

Early in his career Solti was categorized as a conductor of German opera. This is not surprising, considering his recorded *Ring* cycle and the continuous stream of excellent Wagner and Strauss discs. Still, Solti worked hard to combat this type-casting by spending a significant portion of his time on Mozart and Verdi. Over the years he conducted and recorded most of the major works of both composers.

Solti's Verdi recordings have been deservedly overshadowed by his Wagner and Strauss. The latter were nearly all made under optimum conditions in Vienna, with the best singers and producers, and with the continuity necessary for consistently high standards. By contrast, only one of the Verdi operas was recorded in Vienna; a documentation of the *Otello* production prepared for the Paris Opera in 1977. The cast was nearly identical, but the Vienna Philharmonic instead of the Paris Opera Orchestra, is a distinct improvement. Carlos Cossutta does not give us a character study to be classed with Vickers, nor is his voice up there with the great ones, yet this recording, is still an exciting and vivid one.

In 1991 Solti got a chance to record *Otello* again and it was a very special occasion. Solti chose to mark his retirement as music director of the Chicago Symphony with concert performances of the opera in Chicago and New York, with an extraordinary cast headed by Luciano Pavarotti, Kiri Te Kanawa and Leo Nucci. Decca was there to record these historic performances for posterity. The festivities almost ended in disaster as both Pavarotti and Solti came down with colds. Luckily, the shows went on and Decca was able to cobble together the best moments from each of the performances.

But it is arguable that an even better Solti *Otello* is the DVD of a 1992 performance from the Royal Opera House, starring Placido Domingo, Kiri Te Kanawa and Sergei Leiferkus. The final scene is particularly beautiful and absolutely heart-rending. It would be hard to choose between the casts Solti had at his disposal in Chicago and London. Pavarotti and Domingo were the greatest tenors of their time and both were authoritative in this role. Kiri Te Kanawa was the ranking Desdemona for many years and never looked or sounded better than in the Covent Garden performance. Nucci and Leiferkus are equally odious and forceful as Iago. This is simply glorious music drama.

Solti's earlier Verdi recordings were made, for the most part, in Rome, with ordinary orchestras and ill-chosen casts. Solti deserved a great deal of credit for encouraging his orchestras to play so alertly and so accurately in these performances—there are some thrilling moments in each one of them—however, the Italian orchestras tend to sound raw and vulgar, and the younger Solti had rather too much of these qualities himself. The combination produces some exceedingly unpleasant episodes in *Falstaff,* redeemed only in part by Solti's unflagging energy. This recording also has a strong cast headed by Geraint Evans and Giulietta Simionato, with Mirella Freni and Alfredo Kraus as a fresh-sounding pair of lovers. But what can one say in defense of *Rigoletto* with Robert Merrill walking through the title role and Anna Moffo scooping and swooning? Overall, this is a performance lacking in the essential ingredients of menace and mystery. This is also true of *Aïda,* although both Leontyne Price and Jon Vickers offer tremendously powerful characterizations.

Verdi's *Don Carlos* was recorded in London in 1965 with forces drawn from the Royal Opera House and, in this respect, was an important milestone indicating the new status of the house under Solti. When he arrived it would not have occurred to anyone to record a Royal Opera production for commercial distribution. Thanks to Solti's initiative and the fine work of his successors Colin Davis and Bernard Haitink, this became a commonplace practice at Covent Garden. Admittedly, the orchestra was not the Vienna Philharmonic and the sound Decca achieved for *Don Carlos* was far inferior to the Vienna recordings, but a unified conception emerges containing some fine performances by Renata Tebaldi, Grace Bumbry, Carlo Bergonzi and Nicolai Ghiaurov. Solti was curiously subdued, particularly in the more spectacular scenes where some of the old fire would have been welcome.

Solti's last Verdi recording, issued both as a CD and as a DVD, was his first-ever recording of *La Traviata.* The recording was based on Covent Garden performances from 1994 with a cast headed by Angela Gheorghiu, Frank Lopardo and Leo Nucci, and it is very good. Gheorghiu was a revelation in her debut as Violetta. But the sound on the DVD is thin on the orchestra, and there is a studied quality about the performance as a whole. There is no applause except at the end of each Act. This suggests that the performance was not really recorded "live." Nonetheless, this was an important documentation of a wonderful collaboration:

> The part of Violetta was sung by Angela Gheorghiu, a comparatively unknown singer from Rumania. I had not originally planned to record the production, but at the first stage rehearsals with orchestra, when I realized how wonderfully Angela sang and played the role, I changed my mind....The schedules on BBC2 were cleared for an entire evening at less than two weeks notice so that there could be a live broadcast. As a result, we

have a permanent visual record of the production, as well as a wonderful CD. (*Memoirs,* p. 194)

Solti did not conduct any Verdi at all under after the war, but then he tried to make up for lost time. Verdi was clearly a composer close to his heart and he studied the operas thoroughly. As an indication of the seriousness with which Solti approached Verdi, there is an article he wrote for *Opera News* in December, 1963 called "The Verdi I Know." This essay, which is part-autobiographical and part-analytical, demonstrates genuine insight into the distinctive requirements of each of Verdi's operas. Solti also added a thoughtful comment about the composer's choice of keys:

> I think that too little importance is attributed to Verdi's key relationships. In *Don Carlos* the dark keys predominate—F sharp minor, C sharp minor—reflecting the mood of the Spanish world. Verdi did not use them frequently in other operas. *Aïda,* on the other hand, is all B flat major, E flat major, and even the minor keys have brighter colors: F minor, E flat minor, B flat minor. It is hard to describe music and its effects, but choice of key does create atmosphere.

In his *Memoirs,* Solti again spoke of his fascination with Verdi's music and with the man himself:

> I adore Verdi's modesty and his concern for his fellow human beings. His correspondence with Arrigo Boïto, his last librettist, remains among the great documents in music history. Even though Verdi became much wealthier than Wagner, his exact contemporary, it is hard to imagine Wagner, under any conditions, building a hospital for local peasants, creating a rest home for old musicians, or taking a keen interest in the running of a farm. (p. 224)

Mozart was another composer to whom Solti was especially drawn throughout his career, but his performances have been variable. One of Solti's greatest assets as a conductor was his ability to extract the maximum rhythmic clarity from any scores he conducted; but one of his greatest deficiencies was his tendency towards heavy accentuation. The combination of these qualities can be fatal in Mozart, where rhythmic clarity must be coupled with lightness. Solti's Mozart moved, but more as a result of the application of external pressure than because the inner tension was realized.

Too frequently in Mozart, conductors get in the way of the music. With a good orchestra, often all one ought to do beyond settling certain mechanical matters about bowing is to determine the right tempo and then stand back, attending to balances as necessary and maintaining the appropriate spirit of the music. Solti's 1974 recording of *Così fan tutte* is a good example; it often lacks wit and sparkle because Solti seems to be too busy, being busy. It did not help that the recording lacked a first-rate Fiordiligi. But the second *Così* recording was excellent. With a cast headed by Renée Fleming and Anne Sofie von Otter, and the sparkling Chamber Orchestra of Europe, the older and wiser Solti got to the heart of the matter. Other fine Mozart opera recordings from his later years include *Don Giovanni* with Fleming and Bryn Terfel, *Die Entführung* with Gruberova and Battle, and *Le Nozze di Figaro* with Te Kanawa, Popp and von Stade.

In 1973 Solti conducted Bizet's *Carmen* at Covent Garden and recorded it two years later with the same principals. This recording is especially noteworthy for the conductor's serious attempts to come to grips with the textual disparities in the score. Any conductor of *Carmen* must first decide whether to use the *opéra-comique* version with spoken dialogue, or the more commonly used, somewhat spurious version with accompanied recitatives. The problem is that while the recitatives are very effective, they were not composed by Bizet but added later by Ernest Guiraud. It is only in recent years that the version with spoken dialogue has gained independent recognition. Since it is this version which Bizet apparently preferred himself, most conductors now feel that his wishes should be respected. Several of the finest recordings—Bernstein (DG), Abbado (DG) and Solti (Decca)—opt for the *opéra-comique* version.

The other textual issues in *Carmen* do not allow for such clear-cut solutions. They involve many minute changes in the score which have been brought to light by recent research. There are significant discrepancies between Bizet's manuscripts for the opera and the printed score (Choudens) which probably reflects what was played at the first performance in 1875. Just after 1960, the earliest manuscript copy of the score was found in a Paris library by Fritz Oeser and published by him in 1964. This new edition has forced conductors to reconsider much of the score.

Solti had been performing the traditional Choudens version for years, but when the Oeser appeared he immediately adopted it. His 1973 Covent Garden production was almost entirely the Oeser version. But then Solti began to reconsider the relative merits of the two versions and by the time of the recording in 1975 he ended up with something in between. As part of his deliberation Solti went to see Oeser and consulted also with the English scholar Winton Dean. The booklet which accompanies the Decca *Carmen* recording, contains Solti's detailed notes as to why he chose one edition rather than the other at particular points in the score. It makes fascinating reading and provides a unique insight into a conductor's preparation. Here is one example concerning a passage in Act I:

> In the Morales/Don José melodrama, the Oeser version includes thirty-two bars in which the dialogue is spoken over an incredibly lovely and original piece of music played by just a few instruments. It is a perfect little minor canon, precisely underlining the words. This was undoubtedly cut before the first night because it is not included in the Choudens vocal score, but I felt it may have been one of the cuts that had been forced on Bizet, and so I decided to keep the passage and follow the Oeser score.

The notes contain eighteen other comments of similar penetration and reasonableness. Solti concludes with a warning that not too much should be made of the disputed material, as only about ten per cent of the entire score is open to this kind of debate, the remainder being identical in both versions. Solti's conducting on this recording, although less fiery than it would have been a decade earlier, is tightly controlled and often quite beautiful. The cast is superb with Tatiana Troyanos, a very musical and compelling Carmen; Placido Domingo, a more interesting figure than usual for Don José; and José van Dam, a tremendously heroic Escamillo. When Abbado's version of the opera appeared in 1978, Alan Blyth compared it to Solti's and regretted the latter's lack of restraint:

> Much as one admired the intelligence, musicality and care of the rival Decca performance under Solti, DG and Abbado have surpassed it by dint of adding the sense of a real and dramatic interpretation...If I could take just one moment to demonstrate the difference between Solti and Abbado it would be the orchestral phrase after José's "*Tu ne m'aimes donc plus?*" in the *Finale*. This is well enough delineated by Solti and the LPO, but Abbado, with a perfect control of the *cresc-ff-dim* asked for by Bizet and with the surge of the string playing of the LSO, ideally characterizes the desperate misery of José's feelings. Indeed, throughout this crucial scene, Abbado time and again gives that extra dimension of intensity, élan and concentration so essential to its proper execution. (*Gramophone,* October, 1978)

Solti was not particularly fond of Puccini. He only recorded two works—*La Bohème and Tosca*—and in the opera house, very little else. During his years at Covent Garden he conducted only *Gianni Schicchi* and before that in Frankfurt he conducted only *Gianni Schicchi* and *Il Tabarro*. At other houses he did conduct a few performances of *Tosca* and *Turandot*. In his *Memoirs* Solti confessed that he did not care for either *Madama Butterfly* or *La Fanciulla del West* (p. 225).

One of Solti's greatest operatic triumphs in the opera house was the British premiere of Schoenberg's *Moses und Aaron,* produced at Covent Garden in 1965. Solti himself described it as

> one of the most difficult tasks I have ever undertaken…I remember feeling depressed as I grappled with the score during my 1964 Christmas holiday: I simply didn't know how to learn the piece, how to get it into my bloodstream…The rehearsals were spread over many weeks. I remember it vividly as the only time in my life when everyone—myself, (director) Peter Hall, and the singers—was afraid of the rehearsals. My approach was nebulous; I just didn't know where to start or how to bring the sounds together. (*Memoirs,* pp. 139-140)

What an extraordinary confession for a great conductor, that with all his talent and experience, he had met his musical match in a piece of overwhelming complexity. But Solti and his colleagues persevered and emerged triumphant. In fact, having put himself through this artistic hell and survived to tell the tale, he took it on again a few years later in Chicago. With the Chicago Symphony he made a recording of the work which must have cost Decca a lot of money and which they will never recover. But it stands as a tribute to Solti's remarkable musical ability, to his commitment to his art, and to his leadership.

Solti was one of the 'old school' conductors, a man who learned his craft primarily by starting as a coach in an opera house, learning the repertoire and then when he was ready, taking the baton for occasional performances. Solti got his start this way in Budapest and then the war intervened, forcing him into retirement almost before his career had really got started. Then came the big break after the war that put him in charge of the Munich Opera, and he was on his way. And in spite of his more than twenty years in Chicago he remained one of the greatest operatic conductors of his generation, up until the very end of his life.

One of the joys of his last years was the American soprano Renée Fleming. They recorded together Mozart's *Così fan tutte* in 1994. This was one of those lucky breaks that seem to fall to every great artist sooner or later. In this case Solti had cast someone else but she had withdrawn when she discovered the role was too heavy for her. Fleming was recommended by Evans Mirageas, Decca's senior vice president of artists and repertoire, but she still had to prove to Solti that she was up to his standards. At short notice she flew from New York to London arriving at 2 a.m. and by 9 she was in Solti's studio and found herself singing through the entire opera from beginning to end. To say the least this kind of experience can be a character-builder and Fleming rose to the occasion:

> I was immediately struck by Solti's intensity—not to mention the record thirty-two Grammys lining the windows of his studio. I felt inspired just being in his presence…My recording contract came about in large part because of Solti's excitement at my voice, which he was to christen "double crème" in Paris. (*The Inner Voice,* p. 95)

Solti got so excited about Fleming she quickly became his favorite Mozart soprano. After the *Così* recording came a recording of *Don Giovanni*. Then came a gesture of incomparable respect and generosity. When the French *Académie du Disque Lyrique* decided to establish an annual prize in Solti's name, he stipulated that it be awarded to an outstanding singer of the younger generation of recording artists. On March 4, 1996, when the new award was announced, Solti was in Paris where three nights before he had reopened the resplendent Palais Garnier with a gala concert performance of Mozart's *Don Giovanni*:

> That day, he called his Donna Anna, asking her to join him at a press event, leaving her in the dark as to its purpose. At the ceremony, she (Renée Fleming) was astonished to learn that she was there to receive the first-ever *Prix Solti*. (Matthew Gurewitsch, liner notes for *Signature,* London 455 760)

Nine months later, Solti paid Renée Fleming an even greater tribute, when he recorded an album of opera arias with her for Decca. Great conductors rarely wish to be relegated to the role of accompanist, especially on records. Solti had done it only once before, on an all-Richard Strauss album with Kiri Te Kanawa, and now on one of his very last recordings he chose to do it with the young Renée Fleming. The album was called *Signature* and included music by Mozart, Dvořák, Tchaikovsky, Verdi, Britten and Richard Strauss. It was a triumph for all concerned and a fitting valedictory operatic album for the maestro. It was a wonderful documentation of his love of opera and of his encouragement of a new generation.

8

The Interpreter on the Concert Platform

When he left Covent Garden in 1971, it was assumed that Solti's life would now be centered on the Chicago Symphony which he had taken over in 1969. And it was. For the next twenty-two years, Solti and the Chicago Symphony became internationally renowned for the high standards of their performances together, in the concert hall and on records. But Solti was a restless and ambitious man. He not only accepted a post with the Paris Opera shortly after leaving the Royal Opera House; in addition, and at almost the same time, he took on the musical direction of the Orchestre de Paris, while continuing his involvement in Chicago. At the Paris Opera Solti contributed to an almost miraculous rejuvenation of the house, but with the Orchestre de Paris, he was not nearly as successful.

The Orchestre de Paris has had a short and troubled history. France has always boasted numerous orchestras, and in Paris alone there have been, at various times, at least four or five in competition with each other. Yet not one has ever become a world-class ensemble. To correct this situation, in 1967 the French government created the Orchestre de Paris and brought back recently-retired Boston Symphony music director Charles Münch from the United States to be its conductor. Just when it seemed that the project might be on the right track, Münch died during a tour with the orchestra. So that the momentum would not be lost, the government appointed one of the most celebrated conductors of the day, Herbert von Karajan, to succeed him. Under Karajan, the orchestra briefly reached even higher levels of achievement. But the conductor-for-life of the Berlin Philharmonic was not available for more than about six weeks each year, and this simply was not enough time to produce any lasting changes. Karajan bowed out and was replaced by Solti. Again, the idea was quick improvement and prestige through the hiring of a top name.

Unfortunately, Solti's time with the orchestra was also limited and ended badly. Solti knew from prior experience that French musicians were notoriously undisciplined and unwilling to submit themselves to strict discipline. Solti vowed to change all that and thought he had a mandate from the government to do what was necessary. But he had little success and spoke publicly about his problems. In an interview, he declared that the French musician was not interested in working with his fellows to create a first-class orchestra:

> He is endowed with a natural quality of insubordination at the highest degree…The professional ambition of the French orchestras is non-existent, and this is a matter of education. If an American musician makes an error during a rehearsal, nobody laughs, and one picks up immediately; in Paris that's funny and there's an uproar. (Interview with Solti in *Harmonie,* September, 1974)

Solti also claimed that he had been misled. He had been given to understand that Münch had held auditions to form the orchestra. In fact, fifty of the players had been hired without audition. If he had known that, Solti said, he would never have accepted the position. But the orchestra members had complaints of their own about the maestro which they made known after Solti's caustic remarks published in *Harmonie.* In October of 1974 *Le Monde* carried the following letter from the musicians:

> We would have liked to work with Maestro Solti more often and in a more organized manner. For that reason we deplore that he could not or thought it not necessary to be physically present at the head of the Orchestre de Paris for on the average no more than five days a month…we would have liked for Maestro Solti to show more interest in the Orchestre de Paris and for this reason, we too regret the misunderstandings, the aborted projects, the interrupted tours, the records made elsewhere, the disappointed hopes and the bitter words, which we hope will not be all that remains of three years.

It had not helped that one Solti concert with the orchestra had been a fiasco and was reported as such in the press. It was a concert performance of Strauss's opera *Salome* with Grace Bumbry in the title role. From the beginning it was obvious that either Bumbry could not cope with the role or she was indisposed. When it came to the *Dance of the Seven Veils,* she left the stage. In view of the taxing vocal passages she would soon have to face it would not have been unusual for her to slip out and refresh herself. However, she simply did not reappear, leaving Solti, the other singers and the Orchestre de Paris with no alternative but to grind to a halt. Solti was furious, the audience was outraged and the press tended to blame the conductor for miscasting Bumbry.

Solti had taken on the Orchestre de Paris for the same reason he had accepted a post with the Paris Opera: he believed he could help create the conditions necessary for first-class music-making. As it happened, Solti and the orchestra got off to a good start with a highly successful tour of Germany and a well-received recording of Liszt tone poems. An American tour was announced but had to be canceled when Solti resigned.

Obviously, Solti had been spoiled by working with orchestras of the caliber of the Chicago Symphony and the Vienna Philharmonic, and he no longer had the patience to bring along a lesser ensemble. Even with a Solti or a Karajan on the podium it takes time to affect lasting improvements in an orchestra, and time is what superstar conductors simply do not possess. Daniel Barenboim succeeded Solti with the Orchestre de Paris—and later with the Chicago Symphony—and at the time it suited him well. He was just beginning a more or less full-time career as a conductor and he welcomed the opportunity. It also provided him a challenging full-time position not far from his wife Jacqueline Du Pré, at a time when the great young British cellist was forced to terminate her career in the face of debilitating illness.

After his troubles with the Orchestre de Paris one might have expected Solti to content himself with the Chicago Symphony. What better orchestra could he head? However, Solti's ambition was too large to keep in check. When Pierre Boulez resigned as music director of the New York Philharmonic, Solti was under very serious consideration. Carlos Moseley, the orchestra's president, flew secretly to Europe in the spring of 1975 to offer Solti the job. Solti was tempted but finally turned it down:

> Don't think it was an easy decision; it wasn't. I love New York and the New York public. So the temptation was a big one—even with all the problems. And I knew them because I had heard the orchestra recently. (*New York Times,* May 9, 1976)

A few years later Solti did accept an offer to become principal conductor of the London Philharmonic. Since Solti had long since made London his main home, and the position had no administrative responsibilities attached, it suited him perfectly. The LPO also became the orchestra used for many of his European recordings.

Solti came to regular concert conducting relatively late in his career. He was trained to be a conductor in the opera house, and opera formed the bulk of his repertoire until he was well into his fifties. He started making orchestral recordings in 1947 but it wasn't until he took over the Chicago Symphony that he began to make such recordings on a regular basis. By the time he was finished he had put together an impressive recorded legacy. It includes the complete symphonies of Beethoven, Brahms, Bruckner, Elgar, Mahler, and Schumann. In addition, he recorded the major orchestral works of Bartók, many of the Haydn and Mozart symphonies, and virtually all the important orchestral music of Richard Strauss. Late in life he also discovered the Shostakovich symphonies and performed seven of the fifteen.

The following discussion of Solti's concert conducting is organized into chronological periods of music history. Since the Beethoven and Mahler cycles have been dealt with at length in earlier chapters, they are not discussed here.

Music Before 1800

Few of the most successful superstar conductors have shown much affinity for music before Mozart and Haydn. This is not surprising since the symphony orchestra scarcely existed before the time of these composers. Moreover, the performance of earlier music requires both unusual orchestral (and choral) forces and often a great deal of expert research on the part of the conductor. Karajan, Stokowski and a few others have presented Monteverdi operas from time to time—usually in questionable editions with modern instruments—but more recently such repertoire has been better served by a new generation of conductors willing to spend years of their lives researching this music. Conductors who have distinguished themselves in this area are, among others, Leppard, Hogwood, Harnoncourt, Pinnock, Norrington and Gardiner. While the music of Bach and Handel poses fewer problems, fundamental ones still exist, and this repertoire too has been increasingly the province of specialist scholar conductors, often using period instruments.

Yet it can be argued that there will always be a place for performances of this repertoire which employ more modern forces, so long as the conductor has done his homework and paid attention to what can be learned from the musicologists and specialist conductors. There is even a case to be made for traditional large-scale oratorio performances with enormous choirs and orchestras in works like *Messiah,* because so many of the essential qualities of the music survive intact. On the other hand, works such as the *Brandenburg* Concertos take on a different character altogether if too many instruments or voices are involved. A further question to be considered is whether it is appropriate to present small-scale baroque and classical period works in enormous modern concert halls.

Over the course of his career Solti conducted very little music by Handel, but he did perform and record *Messiah* in Chicago. The music of Bach was only slightly better represented. He conducted and recorded two of the major choral works, the *St. Matthew Passion* and the Mass in B minor. His conducting of a 1971 performance of the former was thought to be "relaxed, reverent, completely controlled," by Robert C. Marsh (*Chicago Sun-Times,* April, 1971). Listening recently to Solti's recording of the B Minor Mass I was struck by how square and uneventful it was. The further back one goes in the history of music the fewer indications are found by composers as to how the music should be played. That is why older music often requires the services of a scholar-conductor who understands older performance practice and who can more expertly translate the often meager markings in old manuscripts. Conductors such as Nikolaus Harnoncourt and John Eliot Gardiner are such specialists and they have given us wonderfully fresh recordings of the B minor Mass. Turning to Solti after listening to these modern specialists, one is shocked by the plainness of it all. Solti is slavishly bound to the printed score, and in music from this period that is not nearly enough. Where Harnoncourt and Gardiner shape phrases and vary vibrato with wonderful freedom and imagination, Solti simply plods along. Even the instrumental solos sound awkward and lifeless.

In Chicago Solti also programmed three of the *Brandenburgs,* one of the orchestral suites and a few concertos. It should be noted that in the months before he died, Solti was studying Bach's *St. John Passion*, in preparation for performances and recording.

Surprisingly, in view of his later career, the most prominent names in the list of composers whose pieces Solti first recorded are Mozart and Haydn: three Haydn symphonies and two by Mozart stand out in a small group which also includes Beethoven, Mendelssohn and Tchaikovsky symphonies, as well as overtures and short pieces by other composers. Solti had a reputation in his early days for enormous fire and energy in his performances, often to an excessive degree. The excitement he could whip up is amply demonstrated on the album of Suppé overtures from this period. It is an unexpected pleasure, therefore, to find that his early Mozart and Haydn recordings, while exciting, are also beautifully proportioned performances.

Mozart's Symphony No. 25 in g minor, by its very nature, encourages a certain amount of *Sturm und Drang* from a conductor, and one might anticipate that Solti might go overboard. This is not the case. Even though the constant first-beat accents in the first movement are tiresome, the playing on his 1951 recording with the LPO is so well-disciplined there is no major cause for complaint. The slow movement is rather quick but Solti finds time to be expressive. The *Menuetto* is razor-sharp rhythmically and contrasts are well-judged, and the fast tempo taken in the *Finale* is under strict control. The *Prague* Symphony recording made in the same sessions is also excellent. Solti avoids exaggerations and injects the performance with a great deal of life and feeling. Later in his career Solti recorded Mozart symphonies with the Chicago Symphony (Nos. 38-39) and the Chamber Orchestra of Europe (Nos. 40-41), and they are also first-class.

Solti also recorded a very good performance of the Mozart *Requiem* in Vienna for the anniversary of Mozart's death in 1991—issued on both CD and DVD—and there are two performances of the *Mass in C minor,* one with the VPO recorded commercially for Decca, and another which has been issued by the Chicago Symphony in a boxed set of CDs of Solti performances never released commercially. The *Requiem* performance was an historic occasion in several respects. It was a commemoration of Mozart's death but it also became a kind of requiem for one of its soloists. Soprano Arleen Auger was engaged for the performance but on the morning of the concert she lost her voice and was unable to sing. A substitute, Judith Howarth, was rushed by private plane from the north of England to Vienna. In the event, Auger recovered and sang the performance. Sadly, she soon discovered she had cancer and died shortly afterwards.

Of considerable interest too are some recordings of Mozart's piano music with Solti at the keyboard. He appears as soloist in the Piano Concerto No. 20 in d minor K. 466 with the English Chamber Orchestra, with András Schiff in the Concerto for Two Pianos and with Schiff and Barenboim in the Concerto for Three Pianos. There is also an album devoted to the Mozart Piano Quartets with the Melos Quartet. These recordings remind us that Solti was a gifted pianist throughout his life and maintained an excellent technique well into his 80s. Another fine example of his pianistic prowess late in life was a CD devoted to the songs of Richard Strauss and featuring soprano Kiri Te Kanawa. Part of the CD is devoted to the Four Last Songs with the Vienna Philharmonic, but there are also twelve other songs in which Te Kanawa is accompanied by Solti at the piano(Decca 430 511).

Solti's early Haydn symphony recordings also reveal a fine sense of classical style. Solti was still very much under the influence of Toscanini at the time they were made (1949-54) but he made no attempt to emulate Toscanini's often absurdly fast tempi. And again, there is neither exaggeration nor eccentricity.

In his Chicago years Solti programmed and recorded both major Haydn oratorios, *The Creation,* and *The Seasons.* In Chicago he also programmed eleven different Haydn symphonies. With the London Philharmonic, Solti recorded the entire set of London Symphonies (93-104). While these recordings do not have the flair and charm of a Beecham, the fastidiousness of a Colin Davis, or the scholarly imagination of a Harnoncourt, they are nonetheless well-played and respectable performances. It was a sign of the times and the reality of union agreements that these recordings were made in London rather than Chicago. Recording fees in Chicago were not only much higher but U.S. rules would have required Decca to pay all 115 members of the CSO even though only about 50 were required for this repertoire. The London rules were far more flexible and affordable.

The Early Romantic Period

Among Solti's earliest recordings is a performance of Mendelssohn's Symphony No. 3 (*Scottish*). It was recorded with the London Symphony in 1952, and it is disappointing. The slower sections, the opening bars and the quiet episode just before the last movement *coda*, for example, lack poetry, and the final *allegro maestoso* seems to be too fast for the orchestra: the sixteenth notes in the trumpets are a mess. The later recording with the Chicago Symphony is much better. Solti occasionally performed Mendelssohn's *Italian* symphony, a few symphonies by Schubert, and a little Berlioz, but of the composers from the first half of the nineteenth century he has given the most attention to Beethoven and Schumann.

One of the major items in Solti's discography is a complete set of the Schumann symphonies with the Vienna Philharmonic (1967-69). It is also one of his least successful projects. In these performances he appears to equate speed with excitement. Unfortunately what works in Suppé is disastrous in Schumann. Solti's conducting of the Second Symphony is typical of his approach in the entire set. His enthusiasm, his forward motion, his commitment, and the playing of the Vienna Philharmonic, particularly the strings, are all deserving of admiration. Yet the driving tempi taken in every movement are often clearly at variance not only with Schumann's markings in the score, but also with the style and spirit of the music.

After the slow introduction to the first movement there is a section marked *allegro ma non troppo* (fast but not too much). If the *non troppo* is ignored, as is the case in Solti's reading, the tempo is too fast to allow for the kind of phrasing necessary to bring out the distinctive character of each musical idea. Solti sees the movement as dangerously episodic, which it is, and tries to overcome this deficiency with his hurried tempo. For all its faults, however, the music cannot stand to be rushed; it must say what it has to say in its own discursive way. Otherwise, the numerous *crescendos* and *diminuendos* Schumann has marked in the score become incomprehensible. The playing at bar 210 suggests even more strongly than do the tempi that producer, conductor and orchestra alike were in too much of a hurry when they made this recording: the timpani comes in one bar early! At the climax of the movement there is a wonderfully grand peroration in the brass which the Vienna Philharmonic under Solti causes to sound blaring rather than noble. And why on earth is the very last chord so much louder than anything that has gone before?

The second movement *Scherzo* suffers from the same drawbacks. It is too fast, too unyielding and too messy. This movement is notoriously difficult for the violins, and even the Vienna Philharmonic players have trouble at Solti's tempo. The *Finale* is again hard-driven, to the point where the orchestra has trouble maintaining ensemble and the listener has difficulty making sense of the music. Leonard Bernstein also recorded all the Schumann symphonies with the Vienna Philharmonic. At his best, in the Second Symphony, Bernstein shows how a conductor can take time for expression and phrasing without any loss of excitement.

The Later Romantic Period

The favorite stamping ground of every star conductor is the music of the last half of the nineteenth century. The compositions of Brahms, Tchaikovsky, Wagner, Bruckner and Richard Strauss allow a conductor to make full use of the large, modern symphony orchestra, and the style of the music encourages more freedom of expression. Solti recorded some Brahms early in his career and it was not particularly memorable. Later, he recorded all the symphonies and *Ein Deutsches Requiem* with the Chicago Symphony. These are perfectly respectable performances, beautifully played but not very distinctive or compelling. They have neither the fire of a Toscanini nor the spontaneity and insight of a Furtwängler.

Solti recorded four of the Tchaikovsky symphonies over the course of his career. A high-voltage reading of the Symphony No. 2 (*Little Russian*) from 1956 with the Paris Conservatory Orchestra reveals the same super-tense Solti who is so apt to go off the rails in a Schumann symphony. But in Tchaikovsky, Solti's approach is enormously exhilarating. He attacks this repetitious, often uninspired symphony with conviction. Listeners who might be put off in the opening bars by the extreme *vibrato* in the french horn solo should bear in mind that such playing was quite conventional in France at the time, and in the Soviet Union and may, in fact, be a tradition extending back to Tchaikovsky's own time. With the beginning of the *allegro vivo* Solti really comes into his own. The sound may be a little harsh and the orchestra may not be the world's finest; still, Solti gives a compelling performance. In comparison, most other recordings of this work sound mushy and dull.

In later years Solti no longer attacked Tchaikovsky with the same vehemence. His 1975 recording of the Fifth Symphony is intense but heavy-handed and somehow muscle-bound. The combined energies of Solti and the Chicago Symphony cannot seem to break loose, so that the music is constricted and held back where it should be exuberant and free. But there is a live performance of the Sixth Symphony with the Bavarian Radio Symphony, available on DVD as part of a feature called *Solti: The Making of a Maestro*. It is exceptionally good.

Because Solti demonstrated such an extraordinary affinity for the music of Wagner, one might expect him to be equally at home in Bruckner. In fact, he recorded all the Bruckner symphonies but the results were inconsistent.

He made his first recording of a Bruckner symphony—the Seventh—with the Vienna Philharmonic in 1965, as a by-product of his work on the *Ring* cycle. John Culshaw was again the producer, and he brought to the recording the same spectacular sound of the *Ring* productions. It was certainly one of the most vivid recordings of the Seventh ever made; every instrument comes through with wonderful presence and clarity, especially the brass, yet this is not necessarily the ideal sound for Bruckner. DG's recording of the work with Jochum and EMI's with Karajan both favored a quite different sound that was less immediate and more suggestive of the resonance and distance of a great cathedral. Bruckner's music has always been closely associated with the church, and while his symphonies were not necessarily conceived for church performance, the music seems to benefit from such spaciousness.

Another important difference between the Solti and the Jochum performances concerns Solti's higher degree of aggressiveness. In his recording of the Seventh, as well as the Eighth with the same orchestra, Solti encourages the brass at every opportunity; he makes more of every *crescendo;* in other words, he will not let any phrase pass without imbuing it with animation. In this way he upholds the tension and energy of the music, but he often does so at the expense of sections that depend for their effect on relaxation. And he also seriously jeopardizes the continuity of Bruckner's unusually long lines. The most difficult problem in any Bruckner symphony is maintaining the flow; bridging the silent bars, rests, string tremolos, and soft timpani rolls, etc., between different themes and episodes. The tension cannot be allowed to sag in such passages. Jochum, who was recognized as one of the greatest living interpreters of Bruckner, realized that the supposed gaps in the music must be played with as much care as the notes, and thus he demonstrated a better understanding of the shape of Bruckner's long phrases and large movements than Solti did. Jochum was criticized for sometimes altering Bruckner's tempo instructions, but the criticism is highly questionable. Certain tempo adjustments are necessary and many of Jochum's are quite inspired.

Solti later recorded the other Bruckner symphonies in Chicago. These performances lack the dark, burnished beauty of the Vienna recordings but Solti's approach is more expansive and less intense, to the great benefit of the music.

Just as Solti's Wagner does not prepare one for his Bruckner, his conducting of Richard Strauss's tone poems does not measure up to his conducting of *Elektra* and *Salome*.

Solti's recording of *Don Juan* with the Chicago Symphony (1972) begins with his customary energy, and here energy is just what is needed. But Solti renders the love music square and uninflected, and at the end there is not much of a climax. The final bars are too loud to be poignant. It all passes with a quickness that hinders listener involvement. "After all," Solti seems to be saying, "this is only a showpiece for a virtuoso orchestra." There is more character in *Till Eulenspiegel*, even though the heavy accentuation becomes quite tiresome in spite of brilliant playing.

Also sprach Zarathustra recorded in Chicago in 1975, is given an exciting reading that is wonderfully exact rhythmically, and which drives forward impressively. For all Solti's concern with rhythm and clarity, however, he does not bring out the dotted timpani figure at the climax as successfully as Karajan does in his DG recording. And while Karajan's tempo is much slower, he not only manages to be just as spirited as Solti, he also finds more substance in nearly every section of the score. The eloquence of the B major final section in his performance is not even hinted at in Solti's. The Chicago strings lack color and sensitivity, and the bass and celli *pizzicato* notes in the last bars are far too loud. Perhaps the worst failing of the Solti recording is the violin solo. Technically the playing is well below what one would expect from a concertmaster of the Chicago Symphony, and musically it is a non-starter alongside Schwalbé for Karajan. Interestingly, after Karajan's death Solti made a second recording of *Zarathustra*, with the Berlin Philharmonic, Karajan's old orchestra. This second version by Solti was far superior to his first, but it still doesn't hold a candle to the Karajan for drama and poetry.

To my ears, one of Solti's finest Strauss recordings was *An Alpine Symphony*, with the Bavarian Radio Symphony. Both the playing and the recording are wonderfully full and rich, and Solti paints vivid pictures of each episode up and down the mountain.

Given Solti's increasing fondness for England over the course of his career, it was perhaps not surprising that he developed an affection for British music. At Covent Garden he led performances of several Britten operas—*A Midsummer Night's Dream* and *Billy Budd*—and in the concert hall he championed the music of Michael Tippett. Both *Byzantium* and the Symphony No. 4 were composed by Tippett for Solti and the Chicago Symphony. Most of all, he regularly conducted the music of Elgar. British music critics have tended to be patronizing about performances of English music by non-English conductors, and not always without justification. A Boult, a Barbirolli or a Colin Davis does seem to bring to his reading a special quality which eludes a Toscanini, a Karajan or a Bernstein. But while Solti's Elgar performances had their deficiencies too, it would be difficult to argue that the problem was Solti's lack of understanding of British culture. Boult certainly didn't think so (Sir Adrian Boult in conversation with Bernard Jacobson, in *Conductors on Conducting*, p. 193). Nonetheless, in his recording of Elgar's First Symphony, for example, towards the end of the first movement where Barbirolli captures a wonderful wistfulness, Solti merely plays the notes. Similarly, in the beginning of the last movement, Barbirolli achieves a poetic tenderness which has characteristically eluded Solti, not only in Elgar's music but in the works of other composers as well.

Solti said that he listened to Elgar's recordings in preparing his own, and generally speaking the broad outlines of both are the same. But Sir Adrian Boult among others felt that Elgar's recordings were not necessarily reliable, especially with respect to tempo and relaxation. Boult felt that the circumstances of recording forced Elgar to take faster and more unyielding tempi than he might have otherwise:

> I would say that actually I'm quite sure that, in my career, the worst performance I ever gave of an Elgar work was when I did the First Symphony a day or two after I had played his recording. I can't explain it very well, but I do know that he was always in a hurry in the recording studio, because, of course, he was still imbued with that awful four-minutes-per-side business, and the result was that he did hurry things. (*Conductors and Conducting*, p. 194)

Boult also noted that Elgar often changed his mind about particular details after the scores were printed. This means that conductors who treat the score as holy writ can be misled. For instance, in the First Symphony, Elgar has not written a *ritardando* in the score just before 108 in the last movement introduction, yet he himself reduces speed markedly on the last two notes, and he does so again before 110. Solti adheres to the letter of the score, unlike the composer, thereby forfeiting a very pleasing effect. It is touches of this sort that individualize a performance and give the music more character. Further, Solti's loud and intense *grandioso* final section lacks breadth. And before 148, where Elgar had carefully worked out the dynamics so that the right voices emerged at the right time—a scheme which works to perfection in his own recording, with trumpets and trombones giving way to the horns, and then reasserting themselves—Solti decided to virtually ignore the composer's instructions.

On the other hand, there is a great deal to enjoy in Solti's recording of the First Symphony. Most memorable of all, perhaps, is the way he tears into the *allegro* of the last movement. Also, the standard of playing is exceptionally high.

Solti made two recordings of the *Enigma Variations*. The first, with the Chicago Symphony (1974), is undoubtedly one of the best the work has ever had. The trumpets are always dead-on in rhythm and intonation, the clarity of the timpani in the lightning-fast variation 7 is incredible, and the solo cello in variation 12 is the work of a great artist. From the opening bars Solti conveys a feeling of deep involvement with the music, and the impression is maintained throughout. I would prefer to hear more of the organ in the *Finale* and more G-string tone from the violins, but the engineers may be at fault there.

One of Solti's last recordings (1996) was a second version of the *Enigma Variations*, this time with the Vienna Philharmonic. It does not have the virtuosity of the earlier CSO version but it does have sumptuous warmth of tone, and the *Finale* is played and recorded with much greater success. This CD (Decca 452 853) is also of special interest for its imaginative programming: it is an all-variation album, with the Elgar joined by Kodály's Peacock Variations and Blacher's Paganini Variations. The performances were recorded live.

Music of the Twentieth Century

As was noted in an earlier chapter, Solti programmed more contemporary music than some of his critics were prepared to admit. When Solti was a student in Budapest he met Bartók and learned some of his music from the composer himself. Solti went on to become an authoritative interpreter of Bartók's music in the concert hall and on records. Solti conducted Bartók well, not simply because he knew the composer nor because they shared a common nationality, but because Solti had a genuine affinity for the music. It would be hard to imagine a better recording of the Music for Strings, Percussion and Celesta with the Chicago Symphony. Technically, it is simply beyond outstanding and Solti makes the music exciting and hauntingly beautiful in all the right places.

Solti recorded most of the major Bartók works, in near-definitive performances, and his very last recording, made in Hungary, includes Solti's first-ever recording of the *Cantata Profana* (Decca 458 929). Of special interest is a recording of Bartók's Sonata for Two Pianos and Percussion with Solti and Murray Perahia at the two keyboards (Sony 42625). Solti was present at the first performance of this work in Budapest in 1938 when it was played by the composer and his wife, indeed, Solti was not only present but turned pages for Ditta Pásztory (Mrs. Bartók)!

Solti made a recording of Bartók's major orchestral work, the Concerto for Orchestra with the LSO in 1965, and another one later with the CSO—both are excellent—but a performance of unusual interest is the one recorded live in Geneva in 1995 by the World Orchestra for Peace. It was released as both a CD and a DVD. This was part of a concert to celebrate the 50th anniversary of the United Nations. For the occasion, many of the world's leading orchestras sent representatives to take part, a kind of mini-UN itself. It was a superb ensemble with the likes of Rainer Küchl from the Vienna Philharmonic as concertmaster, Marylou Speaker Churchill of the Boston Symphony leading the second violins, Robert Vernon from the Cleveland Orchestra leading the violas, Richard Woodhams of the Philadelphia Orchestra as principal oboe, Larry Combs of the Chicago Symphony as principal clarinet, Dale Clevenger from the Chicago Symphony as principal horn, Thomas Stevens from the Los Angeles Philharmonic as principal trumpet, David Corkhill from the Philharmonia as timpanist, and so on.

Solti conducted a fair number of Stravinsky's works over the years and made a stunning recording of *Le Sacre du Printemps* with the Chicago Symphony in 1974. Solti's nervous energy and his obsession with rhythmic control were important assets. With the Chicago Symphony to play the notes and the Decca engineers to handle recording duties, all the elements existed to make Solti's recording of this ballet score first-class. Some of the subtle coloration may be missing but none of the raw power of the piece. Solti also recorded *Oedipus Rex, Jeu de Cartes,* the Symphony in C, the Symphony in Three Movements, *Petrouchka,* and the Symphony of Psalms.

Due to Solti's great success with Schoenberg's opera *Moses und Aaron,* one might have expected him to play more of Schoenberg's music and the music of Berg and Webern. In fact, his only other recording of a work by any of these composers was Schoenberg's Variations Op. 31, with the Chicago Symphony in 1974. Unfortunately, while there are passages of remarkable virtuosity in Solti's recording, the players are not at their best. Perhaps there was insufficient rehearsal time. Also, Solti does not really penetrate beneath the surface of the music. The theme is hauntingly expressive in its first statement in the cellos, and is no less so near the end in the solo violin, but each time Solti and his musicians are simply content to play the notes. Compare Karajan with the Berlin Philharmonic. He finds a whole range of dynamic inflections and tonal colors not even suggested in the Solti recording. Even though the trumpets of the Berlin Philharmonic do not play with the security of their Chicago counterparts, one gains a far greater sense of the character of each variation and of the logic of the whole from the Karajan recording.

As music director of the Chicago Symphony Solti was expected to champion music by American composers, but it was not one of his favorite obligations. He did program it from time to time but without much enthusiasm, and recorded almost nothing by American composers. A notable exception was the David Del Tredici piece *Final Alice*. Solti's recording of this imaginative work with soprano Barbara Hendricks was exceptionally good. Unfortunately, it is also one of the very few Solti-Chicago Symphony recordings Decca has never issued on CD.

Finally, one must note Solti's discovery of the Shostakovich symphonies late in his career. He had avoided Shostakovich all his life, primarily for political reasons. As a Hungarian expatriate Solti was outraged by the Soviet Union's occupation of his homeland after the Second World War, and in Solti's mind Shostakovich was part of that odious regime.

> I came very late in my life to Shostakovich—for a very simple, political reason. I didn't know much about his life, I didn't realize how much he was oppressed under the Stalinist or Khrushchev regime. I didn't trust what I heard and so everything that was Stalinism was suspect; so I didn't want to touch it. (from liner notes for Shostakovich Symphony No. 13 Decca 444 791, 1995)

In his *Memoirs* (p. 228) Solti says it was the book by Solomon Volkov based on conversations with Shostakovich that changed his mind. Solti realized he had been wrong about Shostakovich and returned to his music with new insight and understanding.

In Chicago, he performed the symphonies Nos. 1, 5, 8-10, 13 and 15, and he recorded all seven of them, but not all with the CSO: Symphony No. 1 (Royal Concertgebouw Orchestra); Symphony No. 5 (Vienna Philharmonic); Symphony No. 8 (CSO); Symphony No. 9 (Vienna Philharmonic and Solti Orchestra Project at Carnegie Hall in 1994); Symphony No. 10 (CSO CD and a DVD with the Bavarian Radio Symphony); Symphony No. 13 (*Babi Yar*) (CSO); Symphony No. 15 (CSO).

The 1995 recording of the *Babi Yar* is unusual and imaginative in including readings in English of the Yevtushenko poems by Sir Anthony Hopkins, before Shostakovich's settings of the same text.

The Symphony No. 15 was recorded in Chicago in March, 1997, just six months before Solti died. It shows the conductor at the height of his powers, with playing of incomparable intensity. The Symphony No. 15 is a puzzling work, with its quotations from Rossini and Wagner, but in Solti's performance there is no doubt about the quality of the music. The major companion piece on the CD is an equally fine performance of Shostakovich's orchestration of Mussorgsky's Songs and Dances of Death. Bass Sergei Aleksashkin is the outstanding soloist.

9

A Summing Up

I firmly believe that the essential quality of a conductor is, first of all, that power to project your imagination to other people. (Solti, in conversation with Norman Pelligrini for the WFMT program *Profiles of Greatness,* November 28, 1974)

Whatever criticisms one might have about Solti's handling of particular pieces, there is no doubt that he himself possessed all the attributes required of a fine conductor. His preparation for the podium was solid in the old-fashioned European way: he became highly proficient at the keyboard and learned to read orchestral scores; he coached in an opera house and so learned the repertoire and how to work with singers and how to coordinate vocal soloists, chorus and orchestra in performance; and he was exposed to, and thereby learned from some outstanding conductors during his formative years. Furthermore, he had an excellent ear, a reliable if unorthodox baton technique, and he was equally at home in almost any part of the standard orchestral and operatic literature. But as he himself pointed out, his most valuable asset was his ability to project his imagination to others. The greatest conductors have this last quality to an exceptional degree, and Solti was indeed exceptional.

As a physical presence, Solti was a compelling figure. He exuded energy and authority through his bearing: jaw set, eyes blazing, body coiled and restless. Toscanini had a legendary magnetism. Players said that when you looked at him you could not help but give him what he wanted; he was a leader and you had to follow him. Solti had the same power over musicians, and like Toscanini, he had the good fortune to retain this power well into his eighties. Solti's enormous communicative powers were evident in all his performances, whether in concert, in the pit of an opera house or in a recording session. But while the fact of this ability was undeniable, there was by no means general agreement concerning the quality of the musical product. Over the years Solti had his prominent and persistent detractors. One of them was the conductor and writer Robert Lawrence, who disliked even the most widely-admired Solti recordings:

> The negative reaction stems largely from his recordings of the *Ring, Salome, Elektra,* with their abdication of the right to mold sonorities of his [*sic*] own, balance instruments and voices perceptively, work for organic tone. Studio forces have taken over instead with crude, blow-up insistence. Nor have I been overwhelmed in the flesh by an adroit but undistinguished *Tannhäuser,* and *Don Carlos.* (*A Rage for Opera,* 1971)

The *New York Times'* senior music critic, Harold C. Schonberg, echoed this view with reference to Solti's recordings of the Beethoven symphonies:

> Even Mr. Solti's set, for all the instrumental glamour and occasional punchy excitement, seems to lack a distinctive overall point of view. (*New York Times,* May 7, 1978)

If Lawrence and Schonberg found Solti often superficial and uninteresting, other critics have taken issue with his aggressiveness. Adrian Jack, covering a performance of the Mahler Sixth with the London Philharmonic, had this to report:

> In the first movement he invariably gave predominance to brass themes, even though some of them are secondary: too often the horns let rip so that the woodwind and strings were smothered. The whole of the first subject-group was played as if by a brass band composed of thugs. (*Music and Musicians,* July, 1974)

Harold Schonberg also complained about this aspect of Solti's conducting. Reviewing a Carnegie Hall performance of *Die Fliegende Holländer,* he registered a strong complaint about the decibel level:

> Can Georg Solti have forgotten that the difference between heavy volume and sheer noise can sometimes be a hairline distinction? He conducted the orchestra with such enthusiasm that the results occasionally approached aural pain. He has one of the most powerful orchestras in the business—those brasses!—and is himself an ardent, impetuous musician. All that, together with Carnegie Hall sound, made for some very noisy happenings during the evening. (*New York Times,* May 16, 1976)

The editor of the *Musical Newsletter* was even more vehement in his remarks about the same concert:

> Solti had mercilessly stomped on a work that deserved far different handling, and had produced a crude and vulgar slam-bang rather than a musical performance. (Vol. VI, No. 2, Spring, 1976)

Nicholas Kenyon had a similar reaction to most performances given by Solti with the London Philharmonic in an extended series of concerts at the Festival Hall in February and March of 1977. Kenyon was particularly impatient with a reading of Walton's *Belshazzar's Feast:*

> Once again going for the dramatic effect and once again ignoring moments of lyricism and bulldozing his way through the score, he seemed concerned only to generate thrills, and instead produced a brash and nasty rush across the surface of the music which was anything but thrilling. (*Music and Musicians,* May, 1977, p. 47)

Such comments dogged Solti almost from the earliest stages of his career. On the other hand, in all the same places where Solti has been dealt with harshly, he has also been extravagantly praised by other critics, and audiences have often cheered him for as much as half an hour after a performance.

When Solti conducted Brahms *Ein Deutsches Requiem* in New York—and this is a work which demands the utmost sensitivity and taste to perform—Raymond Ericson declared that it was the best performance of the work he had ever heard:

> Mr. Solti, with a superb orchestra and chorus at his command, seemed to do everything exactly right. What many consider to be flaws in his performances, the slick, high-powered drive, the theatricalization of detail, were absent. Yet there was enough sense of calculation left to keep the music poised and flowing. The tempos were perfectly set to establish the indicated mood and then never allowed to sag. The few liberties that were taken, broad *ritards* at the end of a couple of movements, were logical. (*New York Times,* May 14, 1978*)*

Discussing a 1971 concert performance of *Das Rheingold* by Solti and the Chicago Symphony, Roger Dettmer likewise reached for the most extreme compliments:

> The stars were Solti—in an unusually expansive mood—and the orchestra played for him with a splendor unequaled in my experience of any *Ring*

opera, on whatever continent, whether live or recorded, in an opera house or on a concert stage. (*Opera,* December, 1971)

Even Harold Schonberg was often lavish in his praise of Solti. He was on record as preferring Solti's *Ring* cycle—"monumental in conception" (*New York Times,* November 28, 1976)—to Karajan's, and in 1963 he was most enthusiastic about a performance of *Aïda* at the Metropolitan Opera:

> There were some remarkably fine things in the musical end. Chief among these…Georg Solti. His conducting was all fire, lyricism and imagination…By touching up a tempo here, by inserting a few *ritards* and *fermatas,* by adjusting the balances so that Verdi's orchestration could come through, by not being afraid to let loose when necessary, Mr. Solti provided almost a new light on the opera. (*New York Times,* October 15, 1963)

Harold Schonberg wrote on one occasion that "Solti never makes a rhythmic mistake" (*New York Times,* November 28, 1976). It was certainly true that Solti was almost pathologically concerned that rhythmic patterns be played correctly and that the metric pulse of every score be realized. But the result was often overemphasis on rhythmic accentuation, which, in turn, led to an unpleasant heaviness. Even where no accent is written—at the beginning of a bar or on strong beats in general—Solti usually supplied one. He did this so often it became a mannerism, even a trademark. Ironically, the conductor most concerned with rhythmic accuracy was the conductor who so frequently distorted it.

Solti's general lack of expansiveness in his phrasing—his unwillingness to produce a singing line, particularly in loud and heavily-scored passages—was another of his shortcomings. There was a tightness, unpleasantly military in its feeling, which robbed much of the music he conducted of its nobility. I also lamented his inability to unify scores organically. He had the energy and the concentration, but seldom the willingness to make all the details relate to a conception of the whole. I often came away from a Solti performance feeling that I had heard every note of the piece, extremely well played, yet somehow missed hearing the work as a whole.

I always believed that Solti's sheer force of personality was both his greatest strength and his greatest weakness. This powerful personality was made manifest not only in his demeanor but in his conducting style. He was so incisive in his movements that his musicians were compelled to respond in spite of themselves. That was the good part. The downside was that they tended to respond the way he conducted, by overdoing it.

The reader will note that many of the critical comments cited thus far in the present chapter were also contained in the first edition of this book which appeared in 1979. And at this point, I suggested that Solti was in the prime of his career and that "there are signs he is continuing to grow." Happily, that comment turned out to be prophetic. Over the next eighteen years Solti did indeed continue to grow and to mature as a conductor. He steadily became a good deal less brash and masculine in his conducting. The obsession with precision and rhythmic accuracy never went away but it was coupled with a new interest in realizing the poetic moments in the scores he conducted. Solti became far less of a black and white conductor and more subtle in his approach. Unlike many aging conductors who tend to narrow their repertoire to the pieces they know best, Solti was still expanding his repertoire when he died. Into his eighties he was learning Shostakovich symphonies one by one and intended to perform all fifteen before he died. Sadly, he didn't quite make it. Another major work in his sights was Debussy's opera *Pelléas et Melisande*, and still another was Bach's *St. John Passion*. But he ran out of time before getting to perform either one.

And if Solti sometimes fell short as an interpreter—a frustrating fact of life for even the greatest conductors—he nonetheless achieved a great deal over the course of his long career. Many musical institutions are healthier today because he was in charge of them: the Royal Opera House, Covent Garden, the Paris Opera, and, above all, the Chicago Symphony are deeply in his debt. His success with any one of these organizations would be enough to warrant his eminent reputation. He was twenty-two years with the Chicago Symphony and towards the end there was a fairly widespread feeling that he had stayed a little too long and that it was time for a change. But in 2006, fifteen years after his departure, there are many who look back on the Solti years as a Golden Age which will probably never be matched again.

As for his legacy, Solti left a huge number of extraordinarily fine recordings and films, many of which have already been discussed in detail in these pages. He also started the World Orchestra for Peace in 1995—a kind of United Nations of top orchestral players—which is brought together every few years on special commemorative occasions to promote peace. Charles Kaye, Solti's former assistant is now the director of the WOP and Valery Gergiev has conducted all of its concerts since Solti's death. Finally, there is the *Solti Accademia di Bel Canto*, a world-class singing school which takes place every year in Castiglione in Tuscany, near Solti's beloved summer home Roccomare. The vocal coach Jonathan Papp organizes most of the activities of the school with Solti's widow Valerie as one of the guiding lights. One of Solti's favorite sopranos, Kiri Te Kanawa, gives master classes. Even after his death Solti's life-long obsession with opera and fine singing continues to bear fruit.

As a man and a musician Solti was a force of nature and musicians everywhere were affected by him as if struck by lightning. Kiri Te Kanawa remembers him as a dynamo:

> He was always rushing, rushing into the next hour. Wherever he was, the walls would rattle with his presence. He taught me sheer dedication: he was entirely focused to the duty of classical music. No compromise, no popularization, no commercialization. (*BBC Music Magazine,* January, 2005)

Peter Hall recalls an invitation from Solti so forceful he could hardly withstand it. His comments provide a fitting epitaph for a great musical leader:

> Solti yelled at me with his engaging mixture of Hungarian charm and hysteria…I was flattered, and also captivated by the sheer exuberance of the man. He spoke of music as if he was eating it…He was a man of formidable energy and concentration; and his determination to get the best out of the people working with him creates an electricity, a tension, which can have the most extraordinary results. It is hard to be indifferent to a Solti performance. Even at its worst, when it is tight and overemphatic, it produces a tingling anxiety. At its best, it is genius. (*Making an Exhibition of Myself,* p. 230)

SELECTED BIBLIOGRAPHY

Bloomfield, Arthur J., *The San Francisco Opera 1923-1961*. New York: Appleton-Century-Crofts, 1961

Chesterman, Robert, editor, *Conductors in Conversation*. London: Robson Books, 1990.

Culshaw, John, *Ring Resounding*. New York: Viking, 1967.

David, Ronald, *Opera in Chicago*. New York: Appleton-Century-Crofts, 1966.

Fay, Stephen, *The Ring: Anatomy of an Opera*. Dover, New Hampshire: Longwood Press, 1984.

Fleming, Renée, *The Inner Voice: The Making of a Singer*. London: Penguin Books, 2005.

Furlong, William Barry, *Season with Solti: A Year in the Life of the Chicago Symphony*. New York: Macmillan, 1974.

Hall, Peter, *Making an Exhibition of Myself*. London: Oberon Books, 2000.

Haltrecht, Montague, *The Quiet Showman*. London: Collins, 1975.

Lawrence, Robert, *A Rage for Opera*. New York: Dodd, Mead, 1971.

Lebrecht, Norman, *The Maestro Myth: Great Conductors in Pursuit of Power*. New York: Birch Land Press, 1991.

Osborne, Richard, *Herbert von Karajan: a Life in Music*. Boston: Northeastern University Press, 1998.

Schneider, David, *The San Francisco Symphony: Music, Maestros and Musicians*. Novato, CA: Presidio Press, 1983.

Schulman, Laurie, *The Myerson Symphony Center: Building a Dream*. Denton: University of North Texas Press, 2000.

Solti, Sir Georg, *Memoirs*. New York: Knopf, 1997.

Spotts, Frederic, *Bayreuth: A History of the Bayreuth Festival*. New Haven and London: Yale University Press, 1994.

DISCOGRAPHY

Sir Georg Solti's recording career extended from 1947 until a few months before his death in 1997. For that entire period he was under contract to one company: Decca ("London" in North America). All the recordings listed below were made for Decca unless otherwise indicated. Some notable exceptions are the boxed sets of live performances issued by the Chicago Symphony Orchestra. These sets contain many compositions which Solti never recorded commercially. The purpose of this Discography is to provide a reference list for every work played or conducted by Solti and issued for public sale. All recordings listed are compact discs unless otherwise indicated. No attempt has been made to list all possible compilations and reissues. For currently available Solti recordings readers may wish to consult websites such as www.iclassics.com and www.deccaclassics.com. The official Solti website, www.georgsolti.com, and the Chicago Symphony website, www.cso.org, and the author's website—www.theartoftheconductor.com—may also be useful

Abbreviations

1. Choirs

ASCC	Chorus of the Accademia di Santa Cecilia, Rome
BRC	Berlin Radio Chorus
CSOC	Chicago Symphony Orchestra Chorus
CCC	Chichester Cathedral Chorus
CRC	Cologne Radio Chorus
FOMC	Frankfurt Opera and Museum Chorus
GSC	Gumpoldskirchner Spätzen Chorus
CHS	Haberdasher's School Chorus, Elstree
HRTVC	Hungarian Radio and TV Choir
JAC	John Alldis Chorus

LSC	Chorus of La Scala
LSOC	London Symphony Orchestra Chorus
LV	London Voices
RCAC	RCA Italian Opera Chorus
ROC	Rome Opera Chorus
ROHC	Royal Opera House Chorus, Covent Garden
SCC	Salisbury Cathedral Choir
VBC	Vienna Boys' Choir
VGM	Vienna Gesellschaft Chorus
VS	Vienna Singverein
VSOC	Vienna State Opera Chorus
WBC	Wandsworth Boys' Choir
WCC	Winchester Cathedral Chorus

2. Orchestras

ASCO	Accademia di Santa Cecilia, Rome
BFO	Budapest Festival Orchestra
BRS	Bavarian Radio Symphony Orchestra
BSO	Bavarian State Opera Orchestra
BPO	Berlin Philharmonic Orchestra
COA	Concertgebouw Orchestra, Amsterdam
COE	Chamber Orchestra of Europe
CLOO	Chicago Lyric Opera Orchestra
CSO	Chicago Symphony Orchestra
CRS	Cologne Radio Symphony
FOMO	Frankfurt Opera and Museum Orchestra
IPO	Israel Philharmonic Orchestra
LPO	London Philharmonic Orchestra

LSO	London Symphony Orchestra
LSOO	La Scala Opera Orchestra
NP	National Philharmonic
NYPS	New York Philharmonic-Symphony
OP	Orchestre de Paris
PCO	Paris Conservatory Orchestra
RCAO	RCA Italiana Orchestra
RCOA	Royal Concertgebouw Orchestra, Amsterdam
ROO	Rome Opera Orchestra
ROHO	Royal Opera House Orchestra, Covent Garden
SHFO	Schleswig-Holstein Festival Orchestra
SOP	Solti Orchestral Project at Carnegie Hall
RSPO	Royal Stockholm Philharmonic Orchestra
TOZ	Tonhalle Orchestra, Zurich
VPO	Vienna Philharmonic Orchestra
WOP	World Orchestra for Peace

A. Recordings as Pianist

BARTÓK, Béla (1881-1945)

Music for Two Pianos and Percussion
   Murray Perahia/Solti, pianos
   David Corkhill/Evelyn Glennie,
   Percussion   1988   Sony 42625

BEETHOVEN, Ludwig van (1770-1827)

Violin Sonata in A major Op. 47 (*Kreutzer*)

| Georg Kulenkampff/Solti | 6/47 | Decca 473 272 |

BRAHMS, Johannes (1833-1897)

Variations on a Theme by Haydn Op. 56a for Two Pianos
| Perahia/Solti | 1988 | Sony 42625 |

Variations on a Theme by Haydn Op. 56a for Two Pianos: Variations 5 and 7
| Dudley Moore/Solti | 6/90 | Decca 430 838 |

Variations on a Theme of Schumann for piano 4-hands
| András Schiff/Solti | 4/88 | Decca 425 110 |

Violin Sonata No. 1 in G major Op. 78
| Kulenkampff/Solti | 2/47 | Decca 473 272 |

Violin Sonata No. 2 in A major Op. 100
| Kulenkampff/Solti | 7/48 | Decca 473 272 |

Violin Sonata No. 3 in D minor Op. 108
| Kulenkampff/Solti | 7/48 | Decca 473 272 |

MOZART, Wolfgang Amadeus (1756-1791)

Piano Concerto No. 7 for Three Pianos in F major K. 242
| Barenboim/Schiff/Solti/ECO | 6/89 | Decca 430 232 |

Piano Concerto No. 10 for Two Pianos in E flat major K. 365
| Barenboim/Solti/ECO | 6/89 | Decca 430 232 |

Piano Concerto No. 20 in D minor K. 466
| Solti/ECO | 6/89 | Decca 430 232 |

Piano Quartet No. 1 in G minor K. 478
| Solti/Melos Quartet members | 6/84 | Decca 417 190 |

Piano Quartet No. 2 in E flat major K. 493

| Solti/Melos Quartet members | 6/85 | Decca 417 190 |

STRAUSS, Richard (1864-1949)

Lieder (13)
   Kiri Te Kanawa, soprano
| Solti, piano | 6/90 | Decca 455 760 |

B. Recordings as Conductor

BACH, Johann Sebastian (1685-1750)

Brandenburg Concerto No. 1 in F major BWV 1046
| CSO | 1980 | Decca (never released) |

Brandenburg Concerto No. 2 in F major BWV 1047
| CSO | 1980 | Decca (never released) |

Brandenburg Concerto No. 3 in G major BWV 1048 (3rd movement)
| SHFO | 6/90 | Decca 430 838 |

Mass in B minor
   Lott/von Otter/Blockwitz/Howell
| CSOC/CSO | 1/90 | Decca 430 353 |

St. Matthew Passion
   Te Kanawa/von Otter/Krause/Rolfe-Johnson
| CSOC/CSO | 3/87 | Decca 421 177 |

Suite No. 3 in D major BWV 1068: Air
| CSO | 1974 | RCA DPM1-0444 (CSO-M5) |

BARBER, Samuel (1910-1981)

Essay No. 1
    Royal Albert Hall, London
    CSO (live)   9/81   CSO CD99-2

BARTÓK, Béla (1881-1945)

Bluebeard's Castle
    Kovats/Sass/Sztankay/LPO   3/79   Decca 433 082
Cantata Profana
    Tamás Daróczy/Alexandru/
    Agache/HRTVC/BFO   6/97   Decca 458 929
Concerto for Orchestra
    LSO   2/65   Decca 467 686
    CSO   1/80   Decca 417 754
    WOP (live)   7/95   Decca 448 901
Dance Suite
    LPO   11/52   Decca 473 272
    LSO   2/65   Decca 467 686
    CSO (live)   1965   CSO 89/2
    CSO   1/81   Decca 417 754
Divertimento for Strings
    CSO   1/90   Decca 430 352
Hungarian Sketches
    CSO   11/93   Decca 443 444
The Miraculous Mandarin Suite Op. 19

LSO	12/63	Decca 467 686
CSO	2/90	Decca 430 352

Music for Strings Percussion and Celesta
LPO	4/55	Decca 473 272
CSO	2/90	Decca 430 352

Music for Strings Percussion and Celesta (2nd movement excerpt)
SHFO	6/90	Decca 430 838

Piano Concerto No. 1
Ashkenazy/LPO	4/81	Decca 473 271

Piano Concerto No. 2
Ashkenazy/LPO	3/79	Decca 473 271

Piano Concerto No. 3
A. Fischer/VPO (live)	1964	Orfeo C628 041B
Ashkenazy/LPO	3/79	Decca 473 271

Roumanian Dances
CSO	11/93	Decca 443 444

Two Portraits
CSO (live)	1987	CSO CD00-10-9

Violin Concerto No. 1
Chung/CSO	10/83	Decca 411 804

Violin Concerto No. 2
Chung/LPO	2/76	Decca 411 804

BEETHOVEN, Ludwig van (1770-1827)

Coriolan Overture
CSO	9/74	Decca 421 675

Egmont Overture

TOZ	1948	London LL 49 (lp only)
CSO	5/72	Decca 421 675
CSO	11/89	Decca 430 087

Fidelio (complete)
    Behrens/Ghazarian/Hofmann/Adam/Howells/Sotin

CSOC/CSO	9/79	Decca 410 227

Fidelio (Finale Act II)
    Kohn/Dohmen/Andersen
    Herlitzius/Tschammer/Ziesak

Lippert/LV/WOP (live)	7/95	Decca 448 901

Leonore No. 3 Overture

TOZ	1948	London LL 49 (lp only)
CSO	5/72	Decca 421 678
CSO	5/88	Decca 421 773

Missa Solemnis Op. 123
    Popp/Minton/Walker/Howell

CSOC/CSO	5/77	Decca 411 842

    Varady/Vermillion/Cole/Pape

BRC/BPO	3/94	Decca 444 337

Piano Concertos (complete)

Ashkenazy/CSO	1972	Decca 425 582

Piano Concerto No. 1 in C major Op. 15

Ashkenazy/CSO	5/72	Decca 425 582

Piano Concerto No. 2 in B flat major Op. 19

Ashkenazy/CSO	5/72	Decca 417 703

Piano Concerto No. 3 in C minor Op. 37

Ashkenazy/CSO	5/72	Decca 417 740

Piano Concerto No. 4 in G major Op. 58

    Ashkenazy/CSO   5/72   Decca 417 740

Piano Concerto No. 5 in E flat major Op. 73 (*Emperor*)

    Ashkenazy/CSO   5/72   Decca 417 703

Symphonies 1-9 (complete)

    CSO   1972-74   Decca 430 792

    CSO   1986-90   Decca 430 400

Symphony No. 1 in C major Op. 21

    CSO   5/74   Decca 421 677

    CSO   11/89   Decca 430 320

Symphony No. 2 in D major Op. 36

    CSO   5/74   Decca 421 674

    CSO   1 and 2/90   Decca 430 320

Symphony No. 3 in E flat major Op. 55 (*Eroica*)

    VPO   5/59   Decca 467 679

    CSO   11/73   Decca 421 675

    CSO   5/89   Decca 430 087

Symphony No. 4 in B flat major Op. 60

    LPO   11/50   London LL 319 (lp only)

    CSO   5/74   Decca 421 678

    CSO   9/87   Decca 421 580

Symphony No. 5 in C minor Op. 67

    VPO   9/58   Decca 467 679

    CSO   11/74   Decca 421 674

    CSO   10/86   Decca 421 580

    VPO   5/90   Decca 430 505

Symphony No. 6 in F major Op. 68 (*Pastoral*)

    CSO   10/74   Decca 421 676

CSO	5 and 10/88	Decca 421 773
Symphony No. 7 in A major Op. 92		
VPO	9/58	Decca 467 679
CSO	10/74	Decca 421 677
CSO	5/88	Decca 425 525
Symphony No. 8 in F major Op. 93		
CSO	11/73	Decca 421 676
CSO	10/88	Decca 425 525
Symphony No. 9 in D minor Op. 125 (*Choral*)		
Lorengar/Minton/Burrows/Talvela		
CSOC/CSO	5/72	Decca 421 678
Norman/Runkel/Schunk/Sotin		
CSOC/CSO	10/86	Decca 417 800
Symphony No. 9 in D minor Op. 125 (*Choral*) (4th movement excerpt)		
SHFO	6/90	Decca 430 838
Violin Concerto in D major Op. 61		
Elman/LPO	4/55	Decca 473 272
Gerhard Tashner/BPO	?	Musicproduction Dabringhaus und Grimm 6062311132

BERG, Alban (1885-1935)

Violin Concerto
    Chung/CSO   1/83   Decca 411 804

BERLIOZ, Hector (1803-1869)

Le Damnation de Faust Op. 24

Von Stade/Riegel/Van Dam/King		
CSOC/CSO	5/81	Decca 414 680
Les Francs-Juges Overture Op. 3		
CSO	5/72	Decca 430 441
Symphonie Fantastique Op. 14		
CSO	5/72	Decca 414 307
CSO (live in Salzburg)	6/92	Decca 436 839
Symphonie Fantastique Op. 14 (March to the Scaffold)		
SHFO	6/90	Decca 430 838

BIZET, Georges (1838-1875)

Carmen (complete)		
Te Kanawa/Troyanos/Domingo/Van Dam		
LPO	7/75	Decca 414 489
Carmen: Prelude to Act I		
ROHO	3/68	London OSA 1276
		(lp only)

BLACHER, Boris (1903-1975)

Variations on a Theme of Paganini Op. 26		
VPO (live)	4/96	Decca 452 853

BOÏTO, Arrigo (1842-1918)

Mefistofele: "l'altre notte"		
Tebaldi/CLOO	1956	Decca 448 154

BORODIN, Alexander (1833-1887)

Prince Igor: Overture
    BPO   6/59   London CS 6944 (lp only)
    LSO   2/66   Decca 460 977

Prince Igor: Polovtsian Dances
    LSOC/LSO   5/66   Decca 460 977

BRAHMS. Johannes (1833-1897)

Academic Festival Overture Op. 80
    CSO   5/78   Decca 414 488

Ein Deutsches Requiem Op. 45
    Adam/Wismann
    FOMC/FOMO   1954   Capitol PRB 8300 lp only)

    Te Kanawa/Weikl
    CSOC/CSO   5/78   Decca 414 627

Piano Concerto No. 1 in D minor Op. 15
    Schiff/VPO   4/88   Decca 425 110

Symphonies 1-4 (complete)
    CSO   1978-79   Decca 421 074

Symphony No. 1 in C minor Op. 68
    CSO   1/79   Decca 414 458

Symphony no. 2 in D major Op. 73
    CSO   1/79   Decca 414 487

Symphony No. 3 in F major Op. 90

CSO	5/78	Decca 414 488
Symphony No. 4 in E minor Op. 98		
CSO	5/78	Decca 414 563
Tragic Overture Op. 81		
CSO	5/78	Decca 414 487
Variations on a Theme by Haydn Op. 56a		
CSO	5/77	Decca 414 627
SOP (live)	6/94	Decca 444 458
Variations on a Theme by Haydn Op. 56a: Variation 5		
SHFO	6/90	Decca 430 838

BRITTEN, Benjamin (1913-1976)

Billy Budd: Act 1 "O beauty, a Handsomeness, goodness"		
Robinson/ROHO	3-7/68	London OSA 1276 (lp only)
A Midsummer Night's Dream: Act 3 "Helena!…Hermia"		
Bryn-Jones/McDonald/Robson/Howells		
ROHO	3-7/68	London OSA 1276 (lp only)
Peter Grimes: "Peter seems to have disappeared"		
Fleming/LSO	12/96	Decca 455 760
Young Person's Guide to the Orchestra		
CSO	1979	Decca (never released)

BRUCKNER, Anton (1824-1896)

Symphonies 0-9 (complete)

CSO	1979-95	Decca 448 910
Symphony No. 0 in D minor		
CSO	10/95	Decca 452 160
Symphony No. 1 in C minor		
CSO	2/95	Decca 448 898
Symphony No. 2 in C minor		
CSO	10/91	Decca 436 844
Symphony No. 3 in D minor		
CSO	11/92	Decca 440 312
Symphony No. 4 in E flat major (*Romantic*)		
CSO	1/81	Decca 410 550
Symphony No. 5 in B flat major		
CSO	1/80	Decca 425 008
Symphony No. 6 in A major		
CSO	6/79	Decca 417 389
Symphony No. 7 in E major		
VPO	10/65	London 323-4 (lp only)
CSO	10/86	Decca 417 631
Symphony No. 8 in C minor		
VPO	12/66	Decca 448 124
CSO (live in St. Petersburg)	11/90	Decca 430 228
Symphony No. 9 in D minor		
CSO	10/85	Decca 417 295

CARTER, Elliott (1908-)

Variations
CSO (live)	1982	CSO CD00-10-9

CORIGLIANO, John (1938-)

Tournaments Overture
CSO (live)   1984   CSO 90/12-12

CRESTON, Paul (1906-1985)

Fantasy for Trombone and Orchestra
    Jay Friedman/CSO (live)   1976   CSO 87/2

DEBUSSY, Claude (1862-1918)

La Mer
    CSO   5/76   Decca 417 704
    CSO   10/91   Decca 436 468
Nocturnes
    CSOC/CSO   1/90   Decca 436 468
Prélude à l'après-midi d'un faune
    CSO   5/76   Decca 430 444
    CSO   10/90   Decca 436 468

DEL TREDECI, David (1937-)

Final Alice
    Barbara Hendricks/CSO   10/79   London LDR-71018 (lp)
                                   and 1/80   London POCL 3380 (Japan)

DOHNÁNYI, Ernst von (1877-1960)

Variations on a Nursery Theme
    Schiff/CSO   10/85   Decca 417 294

DOWNS, Jerry

Bear Down, Chicago Bears
    CSO   1986   Decca 417 397
    CSO (live)   1986   CSO CD 98-2

DUKAS, Paul (1865-1935)

The Sorcerer's Apprentice
    IPO   4/57   Decca 443 033

DVOŘÁK, Antonin (1841-1904)

Rusalka: "O silver moon"
    Fleming/LSO   12/96   Decca 455 760
Symphony No. 9 in E minor Op. 95 (*From the New World*)
    CSO   1/83   Decca 410 116

ELGAR, Edward (1857-1934)

Cockaigne Overture Op. 40
    LPO   2/76   Decca 443 856
Enigma Variations Op. 36

CSO	5/74	Decca 417 719
VPO (live)	4/96	Decca 452 853

Falstaff Op. 68
| LPO | 12/79 | Decca 440 326 |

God Save the King (arr. Elgar)
| LPO | 2/77 | Decca 440 317 |

In the South Op. 50
| LPO | 12/79 | Decca 443 856 |

Pomp and Circumstance Marches 1-5 Op. 39
| LPO | 2/77 | Decca 440 317 |

Symphony No. 1 in A flat major Op. 55
| LPO | 2/72 | Decca 443 856 |

Symphony No. 2 in E flat major Op. 63
| LPO | 2/75 | Decca 443 856 |

Violin Concerto in B minor Op. 61
| Chung/LPO | 2/77 | Decca 473 249 |

GERSHWIN, George (1898-1937)

Lullaby (arr. Gould)
Larry Adler, harmonica
| CSO (live) | 10/77 | CSO CD99-2 |

GIORDANO, Umberto (1867-1948)

Andrea Chenier: "Nemico della patria"
| Bastianini/CLOO | 1956 | Decca 448 154 |

GLINKA, Michael Ivanovitch (1804-1857)

Ruslan and Ludmilla: Overture

BPO	6/59	London CS6944 (lp only)
LSO	2/66	Decca 460 977
CSO (live)	1976	CSO 89/2

GLUCK, Christoph Willibald (1714-1787)

Orfeo ed Euridice (complete)
   Horne/Lorengar/Donath

ROHC/ROHO	7/69	Decca 417 410

GOUNOD, Charles (1818-1893)

Faust: Ballet Music

ROHO	5/60	Decca 448 942

HANDEL, George Frideric (1685-1759)

Concerto Grosso Op. 3/2

CSO (live)	1/79	CSO CD99-2

Concerto Grosso Op. 6/11: 2nd movement only

SHFO	6/90	Decca 430 838

Messiah
   Te Kanawa/Gjevang/Lewis/Howell

CSOC/CSO	10/84	Decca 414 396

HAYDN, Franz Joseph (1732-1809)

The Creation (highlights)
    Burrowes/Wohlers/Morris/Greenberg/Nimsgern
    CSOC/CSO | 1981 | Decca 430 739

The Creation (complete)
    Ziesak/Lippert/Pape/Scharinger
    CSOC/CSO | 10 and 11/93 | Decca 443 445

The Seasons
    Ziesak/Heilmann/Pape
    CSOC/CSO | 5/92 | Decca 436 840

Symphonies 93-104 (*London*)
    LPO | 1981-91 | Decca 436 290

Symphony No. 93 in D major
    LPO | 5/87 | Decca 417 620

Symphony No. 96 in G major (*Surprise*)
    LPO | 10/83 | Decca 416 617

Symphony No. 95 in C minor
    LPO | 10/85 | Decca 417 330

Symphony No. 96 in D major (*Miracle*)
    LPO | 3/81 | Decca 436 290

Symphony No. 97 in C major
    LPO | 10/89 | Decca 433 396

Symphony No. 98 in B flat major
    LPO | 2/91 | Decca 433 396

Symphony No. 99 in E flat major
    LPO | 11/86 | Decca 417 620

Symphony No. 99 in E flat major (2nd movement excerpt)

SHFO	6/90	Decca 430 838
Symphony No. 100 in G major (*Military*)		
LPO	4/54	London CM 9106 (lp only)
LPO	10/83	Decca 416 617
Symphony No. 101 in D major (*Clock*)		
LPO	3/81	Decca 436 290
Symphony No. 102 in B flat major		
LPO	11/51	London CM 9106 (lp only)
LPO	12/81	Decca 436 290
Symphony No. 103 in E flat major (*Drumroll*)		
LPO	8/49	London LL 557 (lp only)
LPO	12/81	Decca 436 290
Symphony No. 104 in D major (*London*)		
LPO	10/85	Decca 417 330

HOLST, Gustav (1874-1934)

The Planets Op. 32		
LPO	2/78	Decca 430 447

HUMMEL, Johann Nepomuk (1778-1837)

Trumpet Concerto in E major		
Adolph Herseth, trumpet		
CSO (live)	1983	CSO CD01-2

HUMPERDINCK, Engelbert (1854-1921)

Hänsel und Gretel (complete)
  Popp/Fassbaender/Berry/Hamari
  Schlemm/Burrows/Gruberova
  VBC/VPO   2-3-6/78   Decca 455 063

KODÁLY, Zoltán (1882-1967)

Dances of Galanta
  LPO   11/52   Decca 425 969
Háry János: Suite
  BSO   1948   Decca 473 272
  LPO   4/55   Decca 425 969
  CSO   1993   Decca 443 444
Peacock Variations
  LPO   4/54   Decca 425 969
  VPO (live)   4/96   Decca 452 853
Psalmus Hungaricus Op. 13
  McAlpine/LPC/LPO   5/54   London LL 1020 (lp only)
  Bailey
  GECC/CSOC/CSO (live)   1982   CSO 90/12-11
  T. Daróczy
  HRTVC/SCB/BFO   6/97   Decca 458 929

LISZT, Franz (1811-1886)

A Faust Symphony

Jerusalem/CSOC/CSO	1/86	Decca 417 399
Festklänge		
LPO	4-6/77	London CS 7084 (lp only)
		Decca 440 265 (Germany)
CSO (live)	1977	CSO 89/2
From the Cradle to the Grave		
OP	6/74	London CS 6925 (lp only)
		Decca 440 265 (Germany)
Hungarian Rhapsody No. 2		
CSO	11/93	Decca 443 444
Les Préludes		
LPO	4-6/77	Decca 417 513
CSO (live)	6/92	Decca 436 839
Mephisto Waltz No. 1		
OP	6/74	Decca 417 513
CSO	11/93	Decca 443 444
Prometheus		
LPO	4-6/77	Decca 417 513
Tasso		
OP	6/74	Decca 417 513

LUTOSLAWSKI, Witold (1913-1994)

Symphony No. 3		
CSO (live)	1983	CSO 90/12/-12
Symphony No. 3 (excerpt)		

SHFO	6/90	Decca 430 838

MAHLER, Gustav (1860-1911)

Des Knaben Wunderhorn (2/5/7/9)		
Minton/CSO	2-4/70	Decca 414 675
Das Lied von der Erde		
Minton/Kollo/CSO	5/72	Decca 414 066
Lipovšek/Moser/RCO (live)	12/92	Decca 440 314
Lieder eines fahrenden Gesellen		
Minton/CSO	3-4/70	Decca 414 674
Symphonies 1-9 (complete)		
CSO	1970-83	Decca 430 804
Symphony No. 1 in D major		
LSO	1-2/64	Decca 448 921
VPO (live)	1964	Orfeo C628 041B
CSO	10/83	Decca 411 731
Symphony No. 2 in C minor (*Resurrection*)		
Harper/Watts		
LSOC/LSO	5/66	Decca 448 921
Buchanan/Zakai		
CSOC/CSO	5/80	Decca 410 202
Symphony No. 3 in D minor		
Watts/LSOC/LSO	1/68	Decca 414 254
Dernesch GECC/CSOC/CSO	11/82	Decca 414 268
Symphony No. 4 in G major		
Stahlman/COA	2/61	Decca 458 383
Seefried/NYPS (live)	1/13/62	NY Phil: The Mahler

		Broadcasts 1948-82
		12-cd set
Te Kanawa/CSO	3/83	Decca 410 188
Symphony No. 5 in C sharp minor		
CSO	4/70	Decca 414 321
CSO (live in Vienna)	11/90	Decca 433 329
Symphony No. 6 in A minor		
CSO	4/70	Decca 414 674
Symphony No. 7 in E minor		
CSO	5/71	Decca 414 675
Symphony No. 8 in E flat major (*Symphony of a Thousand*)		
Harper/Popp/Auger/Minton/Watts		
Kollo/Shirley-Quirk/Talvela		
VSC/CSO	9/71	Decca 414 493
Symphony No. 9 in D major		
LSO	4-5/67	Decca 430 247
CSO	5/82	Decca 410 012

MENDELSSOHN, Felix (1809-1847)

A Midsummer Night's Dream: Incidental Music		
CSO	1976	Decca (never released)
A Midsummer Night's Dream: Overture		
CSO (live)	1976	CSO 89/2
Symphony No. 3 in A minor Op. 56 (*Scottish*)		
LSO	11/52	London LL 708 (lp only)
CSO	4/85	Decca 414 665

Symphony No. 4 in A major Op. 90 (*Italian*)

IPO	5/58	Decca 433 023
CSO	4/85	Decca 414 665
VPO	2/93	Decca 440 476

MOZART, Wolfgang Amadeus (1756-1791)

Abduction from the Seraglio (complete)
    Gruberova/Battle/Winbergh/Zednik

VPO	3/87	Decca 417 402

Adagio and Fugue in C minor K. 546

CSO (live)	1976	CSO 89/2

Così fan tutte K. 588 (complete)
    Lorengar/Berganza/Davies
    Bacquier/Krause/Berbié

ROHC/LPO	7/73 and 2/74	Decca 473 354

    Fleming/von Otter/Lopardo/Baer

COE	5/94	Decca 444 174

Don Giovanni K. 527 (complete)
    M. Price/Sass/Popp/Weikl/Moll/Bacquier

LOC/LPO	11/78	Decca 470 427

    Fleming/Murray/Terfel/Pertusi

LPO	10/96	Decca 455 500

Magic Flute K. 620 (complete)
    Lorengar/Deutekom/Burrows
    Talvela/Prey/Plumacher/Sotin
    Fischer-Dieskau/Equiluz
    Van Bork/Minton/Stolze/Kollo

Lachner/VBC/VSOC/VPO	9-10/69	Decca 414 568
Ziesak/Heilmann/Kraus/Moll		
VPO	12/90	Decca 433 210

Marriage of Figaro K. 492 (complete)

Te Kanawa/Popp/von Stade		
Allen/Ramey/LPO	11/83	Decca 410 150

Marriage of Figaro K. 492: Overture

SHFO	6/90	Decca 430 838

Marriage of Figaro K. 492: "Voi che sapete"

Simionato/CLOO	1956	London A 5320 (lp only)

Marriage of Figaro K. 492: "Dove sono"

Carlyle/ROHO	3-7/68	London OSA 1276 (lp only)

Marriage of Figaro K. 492: "Porgi amor"

Fleming/LSO	12/96	Decca 455 760

Marriage of Figaro K. 492: "Deh vieni"

Fleming/LSO	12/96	Decca 455 760

Mass in C minor K. 427

Martin/Otter/Hadley/King		
CSOC/CSO (live)		10/85 (including orchestral inserts from 1978) CSO CD99-2
Norberg-Schulz/Otter/Heilmann/Pape		
VSOC/VPO	12/90	Decca 433 749

Requiem K. 626

Auger/Bartoli/Cole/Pape		
VPO (live)	12/91	Decca 433 688

Piano Concerto No. 7 in F major for Three Pianos K. 242

Barenboim/Schiff/Solti/ECO	6/89	Decca 430 232
Piano Concerto No. 10 in E flat major for Two Pianos K. 365		
Barenboim/Solti/ECO	6/89	Decca 430 232
Piano Concerto No. 20 in D minor K. 466		
Solti/ECO	6/89	Decca 430 232
Piano Concerto No. 25 in C major K. 503		
De Larrocha/LPO	12/77	Decca 461 346
Piano Concerto No. 27 in B flat major		
De Larrocha/LPO	12/77	Decca 461 346
Serenade No. 13 in G major K. 525 (*Eine Kleine Nachtmusik*)		
IPO	10/58	London STS 15141 (lp only)
Symphony No. 25 in G minor K. 183		
LPO	4/51	London LL 1034 (lp only)
CSO (live)	1984	CSO 90/12-12
Symphonies 38-41		
CSO/COE	1982-84	Decca 448 924
Symphony No. 38 in D major K. 504 (*Prague*)		
LPO	4/51	London LL 1034 (lp only)
CSO	4/82	Decca 417 782
Symphony No. 39 in E flat major K. 543		
CSO	4/82	Decca 417 782
Symphony No. 40 in G minor K. 550		
COE	6/84	Decca 448 924
Symphony No. 41 in C major K. 551 (*Jupiter*)		
COE	6/84	Decca 448 924
CSO (live)	1978	CSO CD91-2

MUSSORGSKY, Modeste Ptrovich (1839-1881)

Khovanschina: Prelude (orch. Rimsky-Korsakov)
    BPO   6/59   London CS 6944 (lp only)
    LSO   2/66   Decca 460 977
    CSO   3/97   Decca 458 919

Khovanschina: Dance of the Persian Slaves
    BPO   6/59   Decca 448 942

A Night on Bare Mountain
    BPO   6/59   London CS6944 (lp only)
    LSO   2/66   Decca 460 977

Pictures at an Exhibition (arr. Ravel)
    CSO   5/80   Decca 400 051

Songs and Dances of Death (orch. Shostakovich)
    S. Aleksashkin/CSO   3/97   Decca 458 919

NIELSEN, Carl (1865-1931)

Symphony No. 1 in G minor Op. 7
    CSO (live)   1976   CSO 89/2

OFFENBACH, Jacques (1819-1880)

Gaité Parisienne (arr. Rosenthal)
    ROHO   2/61   Decca 448 942

Tales of Hoffman: Barcarolle

ROHO	6/58	London CS 6753 (lp only)

ORFF, Carl (1895-1982)

Antigone
    Barth/Böhme/Goltz/Haefliger

BSOC/BSOO	1/51	Orfeo 407952

PANUFNIK, Andrzej (1914-1991)

Sinfonia Sacra

CSO (live)	11/81	CSO CD99-2

PONCHIELLI, Amilcare (1834-1886)

La Gioconda: "l'amo come il fulgor"

Simionato/Tebaldi/CLOO	1956	London A5320 (lp only)

La Gioconda: Dance of the Hours

ROHO	6/58	Decca 448 942

PROKOFIEV, Sergei (1891-1953)

Romeo and Juliet (excerpts)

CSO	1982	Decca 410 200

Symphony No. 1 "Classical"

CSO	1982	Decca 410 200

PUCCINI, Giacomo (1858-1924)

La Bohème (complete)
    Caballé/Domingo/Milnes/Raimondi/Blegen
    JAC/WBC/LPO　　　　　　　　　1973　　　　　　　　RCA 432 1394962
Tosca (complete)
    Te Kanawa/Nucci/Aragall
    NPO　　　　　　　　　　　　　　5/84　　　　　　　　Decca 414 597
Turandot (complete)
    Goltz/Schiebener/Schirp/Forster/Hopf
    Stich-Randall/CRC/CRS　　　　　6/58　　　　　　　　Gala 7575450222

RACHMANINOFF, Sergei (1873-1943)

Piano Concerto No. 2 in C minor Op. 18
    Katchen/LSO　　　　　　　　　　6/58　　　　　　　　Decca 448 604

RAVEL, Maurice (1875-1937)

Bolero
    CSO　　　　　　　　　　　　　　5/76　　　　　　　　Decca 417 704
Daphnis et Chloé: Suite No. 2
    CSO (live)　　　　　　　　　　　1987　　　　　　　　CSO 90/12-12
Le Tombeau de Couperin
    CSO　　　　　　　　　　　　　　5/80　　　　　　　　Decca 400 051
La Valse
    CSO (live)　　　　　　　　　　　1976　　　　　　　　CSO 89/2
La Valse (excerpt)

SHFO	6/90	Decca 430 838

RESPIGHI, Ottorino (1879-1936)

La Boutique Fantasque
IPO	4/57	Decca 448 942

ROSSINI, Gioacchino (1792-1868)

Barber of Seville: Overture
LPO	4/55	London LW 5207 (lp only)
CSO	5/72	Decca 460 982

L'Italiana in Algeri: Overture
LPO	2/55	London LW 5207 (lp only)
ROHO	6/58	London CS 6753 (lp only)

Semiramide: Overture
ROHO	6/58	London CS 6753 (lp only)

William Tell: Overture
WOP (live)	7/95	Decca 448 901

SAINT-SAËNS, Camille (1835-1921)

Samson et Dalila: "Mon Coeur s'ouvre à ta voix"
Simionato/CLOO	1956	London A 5320 (lp only)

SCHOENBERG, Arnold (1874-1951)

Moses and Aaron (complete)
    Mazura/Langridge/Haugland/Bonney/Zakai

CSOC/CSO	3 and 4/84	Decca 414 264

Variations for orchestra Op. 31

CSO	5/74	Decca 425 008

SCHUBERT, Franz (1797-1828)

Symphony No. 5 in B flat major

IPO	5/58	Decca 473 272
VPO	9/84	Decca 448 927

Symphony No. 8 in B minor "Unfinished"

VPO	9/84	Decca 448 927

Symphony No. 9 in C major "Great"

VPO	6/81	Decca 448 927

Wanderer Fantasy (arr. Liszt)

Bolet/LPO	7/86	Decca 425 689

SCHUMANN, Robert (1810-1856)

Julius Caesar Overture Op. 128

VPO	9/69	Decca 448 930

Piano Concerto in A minor Op. 54 (1st movement excerpt)

Moore/SHFO	6/90	Decca 430 838

Konzertstück for Four Horns and Orchestra Op. 86
    Williams/Oldberg/Schweikert/Gingrich

CSO (live)	5/89	CSO CD99-2
Overture, Scherzo and Finale Op. 52		
VPO	9/69	Decca 448 930
Symphonies 1-4 (complete)		
VPO	1967-69	Decca 448 930
Symphony No. 1 in B flat major Op. 38 (*Spring*)		
VPO	9/69	Decca 448 930
Symphony No. 2 in C major Op. 61		
VPO	9/69	Decca 448 930
Symphony No. 3 in E flat major Op. 97 (*Rhenish*)		
VPO	11/67	Decca 448 930
Symphony No. 4 in D minor Op. 120		
VPO	11/67	Decca 448 930

SHOSTAKOVICH, Dimitri (1906-1975)

Symphony No. 1 in F minor Op. 10		
RCOA	9/91	Decca 436 469
Symphony No. 5 in D minor Op. 47		
VPO	2/93	Decca 440 476
Symphony No. 8 in C minor Op. 65		
CSO	2/89	Decca 425 675
Symphony No. 9 in E flat major Op. 70		
VPO	5/90	Decca 430 505
SOP (live)	6/94	Decca 444 458
Symphony No. 10 in E minor Op. 93		
CSO (live)	10/90	Decca 433 073
Symphony No. 13 in B flat minor Op. 113 (*Babi Yar*)		

Aleksashkin/Hopkins
CSOC/CSO   2/95   Decca 444 791
Symphony No. 15 in A major Op. 141
CSO   3/97   Decca 458 919

SMETANA, Bedřich (1824-1884)

The Bartered Bride: Overture
SOP (live)   6/94   Decca 444 458

SMITH, John Stafford (1750-1836)

Star-Spangled Banner
CSOC/CSO   1986   Decca 417 397

SOUSA, John Philip (1895-1968)

Stars and Stripes Forever
CSO   1986   Decca 417 397

STRAUSS, Richard (1864-1949)

An Alpine Symphony Op. 64
BRS   9/79   Decca 440 618
Also sprach Zarathustra Op. 30
CSO   5/75   Decca 414 043
BPO (live)   1/96   Decca 452 603
Arabella Op. 79(complete)

Della Casa/London/Edelmann		
Güden/Dermota/Malaniuk/		
Kmentt/Wächter/Proglhof/Cortse		
Hellwig/VSOC/VPO	8/57	Decca 460 230
Ariadne auf Naxos Op. 60 (complete)		
L. Price/Troyanos/Kollo/Kunz/		
Gruberova/Berry/LPO	11/77	Decca 460 233
Daphne Op. 82: "Transformation Scene"		
Fleming/LSO	12/96	Decca 455 760
Don Juan Op. 20		
CSO	5/72	Decca 414 043
SHFO	6/90	Decca 430 838
SOP (live)	6/94	Decca 444 458
Elektra Op. 58 (complete)		
Nilsson/Resnik/Krause/Collier/		
Stolze/VPO	9/67	Decca 417 345
Elektra Op. 58 (excerpts)		
Goltz/BSO	8/52	Decca 473 272
Ein Heldenleben Op. 40		
Küchl/VPO	3/77	Decca 440 618
Four Last Songs		
Te Kanawa/VPO	6/90	Decca 430 511
Die Frau ohne Schatten (complete)		
Varady/Behrens/Runkel/Domingo		
VPO	10/91	Decca 436 243
Der Rosenkavalier Op. 59 (complete)		
Crespin/Minton/Jungwirth/Wiener/		
Donath/Loose/Dickie/Howells/		

Lachner/Prikopa/Equiluz/Jerger/		
Dermota/Pavarotti/Schwaiger/Terkal		
VSOC/VPO	11/68	Decca 417 493
Der Rosenkavalier Op. 59: "Herr Kavalier"		
Langdon/Minton/ROHO	7/78	London OSA 1276 (lp only)
		ABC Classics (Australia)
		470 241
Salome Op. 54 (complete)		
Nilsson/Stolze/Hoffman/Wächter/		
Kmentt/Veasey/Kuen/Schwer/		
Equiluz/Gestner/Proebstl/Krause		
VPO	10/61	Decca 414 414
Salome Op. 54: Dance of the Seven Veils		
BPO (live)	1/96	Decca 452 603
Till Eulenspiegel Op. 28		
CSO	5/75	Decca 414 043
BPO (live)	1/96	Decca 452 603
Tod und Verklärung Op. 24		
CSO (live)	1977	CSO 89/2

STRAVINSKY, Igor (1882-1971)

Jeu de cartes		
CSO	11/93	Decca 443 775
Oedipus Rex		
Pears/Meyer/McIntyre/McCowen		
Dean/JAC/LPO	3/76	Decca 430 001

Petrushka

CSO	11/93	Decca 443 775
LSO (live)	8/7/94	Andante AN4100

Le Sacre du Printemps

CSO	5/74	Decca 417 704
RCOA	9/91	Decca 436 469

Le Sacre du Printemps (excerpt)

SHFO	6/90	Decca 430 838

Symphony in C

CSO	3/97	Decca 458 898

Symphony of Psalms

CSOC/CSO	3/97	Decca 458 898

Symphony in Three Movements

CSO	11/93	Decca 458 898

SUPPÉ, Franz von (1819-1895)

Overtures: Light Cavalry/Poet and Peasant/Morning, Noon and Night
In Vienna/Pique Dame

LPO	4/51	London LL 352 (lp only)
VPO	5/59	Decca 460 982

Pique Dame: Overture

CSO (live)	1/80	CSO CD99-2

TCHAIKOVSKY, Piotr Ilich (1840-1893)

Eugen Onegin (complete)
    Kubiak/Hamari/Weikl/Burrows/

Ghiaurov/JAC/ROHO	7/74	Decca 417 413

Eugen Onegin: "Letter Scene"

Tebaldi/CLOO	1956	London A 5320 (lp only)
Fleming/LSO	12/96	Decca 455 760

Nutcracker Suite Op. 71a

CSO	2/86	Decca 417 400

Overture (*1812*) Op. 49

CSO	2/86	Decca 417 400

Piano Concerto No. 1 in B flat minor Op. 23

Curzon/VPO	10/58	Decca 448 604
Cherkassky/LSO (live)	1/68	BBCL 4160
Schiff/CSO	10/85	Decca 417 294

Piano Concerto No. 1 in B flat minor Op. 23 (lst movement excerpt)

Moore/SHFO	6/90	Decca 430 838

Romeo and Juliet Fantasy Overture

CSO	2/86	Decca 417 400

Serenade for Strings in C major Op. 48

IPO	11/58	London STS 15141 (lp only)

Symphony No. 2 in C minor Op. 17 (*Little Russian*)

PCO	5/56	Decca 460 977

Symphony No. 4 in F minor Op. 36

CSO	5/84	Decca 414 192

Symphony No. 5 in E minor Op. 64

PCO	5/56	London STS 15060 (lp only)
CSO	5/75	Decca 417 723
CSO	9/87	Decca 425 516

LSO (live)	8/7/94	Andante AN4100

Symphony No. 6 in B minor Op. 74 (*Pathétique*)
CSO	5/76	Decca 417 708

Swan Lake: Ballet Suite Op. 20a
CSO	10/88	Decca 425 516

TIPPETT, Sir Michael (1905-1998)

Byzantium
Faye Robinson/CSO (live)	4/91	Decca 433 668

Suite in D (A Suite for the Birthday of Prince Charles)
CSO	5/81	Decca 425 646

Symphony No. 4
CSO	10/79	Decca 425 646

VERDI, Giuseppe (1813-1901)

Aïda (complete)
  L. Price/Vickers/Gorr/Merrill/
  Tozzi/Clabassi/Racciardi/Sighele
ROC/ROO	7/61	Decca 460 765

Aïda: "Gloria all'Egitto"
CSOC/CSO	11/89	Decca 430 226

Un Ballo in Maschera (complete)
  Bergonzi/MacNeil/Nilsson/
  Simionato/Stahlman/Krause/
  Corena/Arbace/De Palma
ASCC/ASCO	7/60 and 7/61	Decca 425 655

Pavarotti/Battle/M. Price/Lloyd
LOC/NPO   5/83   Decca 410 210

Un Ballo in Maschera: "Posa in pace"
CSOC/CSO   11/89   Decca 430 226

Don Carlo (complete)
Tebaldi/Bumbry/Bergonzi/Merrill/
Ghiaurov/Talvela
ROHC/ROHO   7/65   Decca 421 114

Don Carlo: "Spuntato ecco il di d'esultanza"
CSOC/CSO   11/89   Decca 430 226

Falstaff (complete)
Evans/Simionato/Ligabue/Merrill
Freni/Krause
RCAC/RCAO   7/63   Decca 417 168
Van Dam/Serra/Coni/Norberg-Schulz
BRC/BPO (live)   3/93   Decca 440 650

La Forza del Destino (complete)
Veasey/Bergonzi/Cavalli/Ghiaurov
ROHO   (live)   Myto 3224
                                                       Opera d'Oro 1325

La Forza del Destino: Overture
LPO   8/49   London LL 200 (lp only)

Four Sacred Pieces
Pickens/CSOC/CSO   5/77 and 5/78   Decca 425 844

I Lombardi: "Gerusalem"
CSOC/CSO   11/89   Decca 430 226

I Lombardi: "O signore, dal tetto ratio"
CSOC/CSO   11/89   Decca 430 226

Macbeth: "Tre volte miagola"		
CSOC/CSO	11/89	Decca 430 226
Macbeth: "Patria oppressa"		
CSOC/CSO	11/89	Decca 430 226
I Masnadieri: "Le rube, gli stupri"		
CSOC/CSO	11/89	Decca 430 226
Nabucco: "Gli arredi festivi"		
CSOC/CSO	11/89	Decca 430 226
Nabucco: "Va, pensiero"		
CSOC/CSO	11/89	Decca 430 226
Otello (complete)		
M. Price/Cossutta/Bacquier/		
Dvorsky/Berbié/Moll/Equiluz/		
Dean/Helm		
VBC/VSOC/VPO	9/77	Decca 440 045
Te Kanawa/Pavarotti/Nucci		
CSO (live)	4/91	Decca 433 669
Otello: "Ave maria"		
Fleming/LSO	12/96	Decca 455 760
Otello: "Fuoco di gioia"		
CSOC/CSO	11/89	Decca 430 226
Opera Choruses		
CSOC/CSO	11/89	Decca 430 226
Requiem		
Sutherland/Horne/Pavarotti/Talvela		
VSOC/VPO	10/67	Decca 411 944
L. Price/Baker/Luchetti/Van Dam		
CSOC/CSO	6/77	RCA RCD2-2476

Requiem: "Sanctus"
CSOC/CSO	11/89	Decca 430 226

Rigoletto (complete)
    Moffo/Merrill/Kraus/Elias/Flagello
RCAC/RCAO	6/63	RCA 6506-2-RG

Rigoletto: "Zitti, zitti"
CSOC/CSO	11/89	Decca 430 226

Simon Boccanegra (complete)
    Te Kanawa/Nucci/Aragall/Burchuladze
LSC/LSOO	12/88	Decca 425 628

La Traviata (complete)
    Gheorgiu/Lopardi/Nucci
ROHC/ROHO	12/94	Decca 448 119

La Traviata: Preludes to Acts 1 and 3
ROHO	6/58	London CS 6753 (lp only)
		Decca 460 982 (CD contains Act 1 Prelude only)

La Traviata: "Noi siamo zingarelle"
CSOC/CSO	11/89	Decca 430 226

Il Trovatore: "Vedi! Le fosche notturne spoglie"
CSOC/CSO	11/89	Decca 430 226

Il Trovatore: "Squilli, echeggi la tromba"
CSOC/CSO	11/89	Decca 430 226

WAGNER, Richard (1813-1883)

Der fliegende Holländer (complete)

DISCOGRAPHY

Bailey/Martin/Kollo/Talvela/Krenn

CSOC/CSO 5/76 Decca 414 551

Der fliegende Holländer: Overture

VPO 10/61 Decca 440 606

Götterdämmerung (complete)

    Nilsson/Ludwig/Neidlinger/Popp/

    Jones/Guy/Watts/Hoffman/

    Välkki/Windgassen/Frick/

    Fischer-Dieskau/Watson

    VSOC/VPO 5-11/64 Decca 455 569

Kinderkatechismus

    VPO 3/68 London RDNS1 (lp only)

Lohengrin (complete)

    Norman/Randova/Domingo/

    Fischer-Dieskau/Nimsgern/Sotin

    VSOC/VPO 6/86 Decca 421 053

Die Meistersinger (complete)

    Bailey/Moll/Kraus/Engel/Weikl/

    Nienstedt/Schomberg/Appel/

    Sénéchal/Berger/Tuna/Rydl/

    Hartmann/Kollo/Dallapozza/

    Bode/Hamari/Klumlikboldt

    VSOC/VPO 9-10/75 Decca 417 497

    Mattila/Vermillion/Heppner/Lippert/

    Van Dam/Pape

    CSOC/CSO (live) 9/95 Decca 452 606

Die Meistersinger: Prelude to Act 1

    CSO 5/72 Decca 411 951

SHFO	6/90	Decca 430 838
SOP (live)	6/94	Decca 444 458

Parsifal (complete)
    Kollo/Fischer-Dieskau/Hotter/Frick/
    Kéléman/Ludwig/Tear/Lackner/
    Hansliann/Schiml/Zednik/
    Aichberger/Popp/Hargan/Howells/
    Te Kanawa/Knight/Lilowa/Finnila

VBC/VSOC/VPO	12/71-3/72	Decca 470 805

Das Rheingold (complete)
    London/Flagstad/Neidlinger/
    Svanholm/Wächter/Kmentt/
    Wohlfahrt/Kreppel/Böhme/
    Watson/Madeira/Balsborg/

Plumacher/Malaniuk/VPO	5-10/58	Decca 455 556

Das Rheingold: Final Scene
    Schnaut/Jerusalem/Nimsgern/
    Golden/Bailey/Cheek

CSO (live)	4/83	CSO CD99-2

Rienzi: Overture

VPO	10/61	Decca 440 606

Der Ring des Nibelungen (complete)

Soloists/VPO	1958-64	Decca 455 555

Siegfried (complete)
    Windgassen/Nilsson/Stolze/
    Neidlinger/Böhme/Höffgen/

Sutherland/VPO	5-10/62	Decca 455 564

Siegfried Idyll

VPO	11/65	Decca 440 606
Tannhäuser (complete)		
Sotin/Kollo/Braum/Hollweg/Jungwirth/		
Equiluz/Bailey/Dernesch/Ludwig		
BVC/VSOC/VPO	10/70	Decca 414 581
Tannhäuser: Overture and Venusberg Music		
VPO	10/61	Decca 440 606
Tannhäuser: Overture		
CSO	5/77	Decca 411 951
Tannhäuser: "Dich teure halle"		
Leontyne Price, soprano		
CSO (live)	1980	CSO 90/12-12
Tristan und Isolde (complete)		
Uhl/Nilsson/Resnik/Van Mill		
Krause/Kmentt/Klein/Kozub/		
Kirschbichler		
VGM/VPO	9/60	Decca 470 814
Tristan und Isolde: Prelude and Liebestod		
CSO	5/77	Decca 411 951
Die Walküre (complete)		
Nilsson/Hotter/Crespin/King/		
Ludwig/Frick/Schlosser/		
Fassbänder/Lindholm/Tyler/		
Dernesch/Watts/Little/Hellman		
VPO	10-11/65	Decca 455 559
Die Walküre: Act 1		
M. Schech/F. Dalberg/F. Volker		
BRS	5/47	Orfeo 7575413062

Die Walküre: Act 2 "Todesverkundigung" and Act 3
  Flagstad/Svanholm/Edelmann/Schech/
  Balsborg/Steingruber/Hoffmann/
  Bence/Watson/Rösler/VPO   5/57   Decca 467 124

WALTON, Sir William (1902-1983)

Belshazzar's Feast
  Luxon/JAC/LPO   3/77   Decca 425 154
Coronation Te Deum
  SCC/WCC/CCC/LPO   3/77   Decca 425 154

WEBER, Carl Maria von (1786-1826)

Euryanthe: Overture
  CSO (live)   3/86   CSO CD99-2
Oberon: Overture
  CSO   11/73   Decca COOL-00030

WEINER, Leo (1885-1960)

Prinz Csongor und die Kobolde (Prince Csongor and the Goblins):
Introduction and Scherzo
  CSO   11/93   Decca 443 444
Serenade for Small Orchestra Op. 3
  BFO   6/97   Decca 289 458 929

C. **Solti in Rehearsal and Conversation**

BEETHOVEN: Ludwig van (1770-1827)

Symphonies 1-9 (complete)
 CSO   1975   Decca CSP9

When this set was first issued on LP in the UK in 1975 by English Decca it contained a discussion of the Beethoven Symphonies between Solti and music critic William Mann.

WAGNER, Richard (1813-1883)

An Introduction to Der Ring des Nibelungen
 VPO   1967   Decca 443 581 (2 cds)

An analysis of the Ring prepared and presented by Deryck Cooke with musical excerpts played by Solti and the VPO.

Tristan und Isolde (complete)
 Uhl/Nilsson/Resnik, etc.
 VPO   1961   Decca 470 600
                                                          (21-cd set)

When this recording was first issued in 1961 on LP it included several rehearsal excerpts featuring Solti. This material is currently available now under the title "Birth of an Opera" and only as part of a 21-cd set titled "Wagner: The Solti Opera Collection" containing six complete Wagner operas conducted by Solti.

D. Collections

1. Renée Fleming: "Signatures: Great Opera Scenes"

Mozart: le Nozze di Figaro "Porgi amor" and "Dove sono"
 Tchaikovsky: Eugen Onegin "Letter Scene"
 Dvořák: Rusalka "O Silver Moon"

Britten: Peter Grimes "Peter seems to have disappeared"
Verdi: Otello "Willow Song...Ave Maria"
Richard Strauss: Daphne "Transformation Scene"

Renée Fleming, soprano
LSO/Solti (assisting singers are L. Diadkova and J. Summers)
Recorded: December 16-21, 1996
Decca 455 760

2. Immortal Beloved (1994)

A film about Beethoven starring Gary Oldham in the title role and directed by Bernard Rose. Solti was the music director and conductor for the project. The soundtrack was issued by Sony and includes excerpts from Symphonies 3/5/6/9 (an excerpt from the 4th movement featuring tenor Vinson Cole), Violin Concerto (Gidon Kremer, violin), Piano Concerto No. 5 (Murray Perahia, piano), and the Missa Solemnis (Fleming/Murray/Cole/Pape). Solti conducts the LSO.

Recorded: 1994
Sony 066301

3. Tolstoy's Anna Karenina (1996)

A film based on the Tolstoy novel starring Sophie Marceau, Sean Bean and James Fox, directed by Bernard Rose. For this film Solti was music director and conducted music by Tchaikovsky (excerpts from the Symphony No. 6, Eugen Onegin and the Violin Concerto) and Prokofiev (Alexander Nevsky). Soloists were violinist Maxim Vengerov and soprano Galina Gorchakova, with Solti and the St. Petersburg Philharmonic. The soundtrack was issued by Icon Records on the Atlantic label.

Recorded: 1996
Atlantic 92759

4. Orchestra!

In June, 1990, Solti and the actor-pianist Dudley Moore were asked to put together an introduction to orchestral music for Channel 4 Television in England. The result was Orchestra! In the television programs–later issued on VHS–there is a lot of amusing and informative discussion between Solti and

Moore. Solti conducts the Schleswig-Holstein Festival Orchestra–an ensemble of gifted young musicians from all over the world–in mostly excerpts from a whole range of works by Handel, Bach, Mozart, Beethoven, Schubert, Schumann, Berlioz, Brahms, Ravel, Bartók, Stravinsky and Lutoslawski. There are complete performances of the Prelude to Act 1 of Wagner's Die Meistersinger, the Overture to Mozart's le Nozze di Figaro and Richard Strauss' Don Juan. Dudley Moore plays the solo piano part in excerpts from Piano Concertos by Schumann and Tchaikovsky, and harpsichord in the Handel and Bach pieces. Solti and Moore also play excerpts from Brahms's Variations on a Theme by Haydn in the piano duet version. The CD includes all the musical excerpts featured in the series.

Recorded: 6/90
Decca 430 838

VIDEOGRAPHY

This is a list of all known films featuring Sir Georg Solti. Many of the concert performances were originally produced for television or sold to television and never released to the public in any other form. In 2005 Universal Music announced that it intended to bring out the entire Unitel catalogue on DVD, among them a number of Solti opera and concert performances. For the key to abbreviations used for choruses and orchestras see *DISCOGRAPHY*. "Laser Disc" is abbreviated as "LD".

1965

THE GOLDEN RING
A black and white documentary originally produced by Humphrey Burton for the BBC, featuring excerpts from recording sessions for Wagner's *Ring* cycle in Vienna, with the VPO and Decca producer John Culshaw.
DECCA: 071 153-9 (DVD)

1966

SOLTI IN REHEARSAL
A black and white documentary of Solti rehearsing and performing Wagner's *Tannhäuser Overture* with the Stuttgart Radio Symphony Orchestra. This DVD also includes a rehearsal and performance of Berlioz's Hungarian March from *Le Damnation de Faust* with the same orchestra from 1968.
ARTHAUS MUSIK 07280 10699 (DVD)

1976

MENDELSSOHN: Midsummer Night's Dream: Overture
CSO
LONDON: LD (never released)

MENDELSSOHN: Symphony No. 4 in A major Op. 90 (*Italian*)
CSO
LONDON: 071 110-1LH (LD)

WAGNER: Der fliegende Holländer: Overture/Tannhäuser: Overture/Tristan und Isolde: Prelude und Liebestod/Die Meistersinger: Prelude to Act I
CSO
Dir: Humphrey Burton
LONDON: 071 201-1lh (LD); W48V 4509 (VHS)

1977

BERLIOZ: Romeo and Juliet, Dramatic Symphony Op. 17
CSO
LONDON: 071 201-1lh (LD); W48V 4509 (VHS)

MUSSORGSKY: Khovanshchina: Prelude
SHOSTAKOVICH: Symphony No. 1 Op. 10
PROKOFIEV: Symphony No. 1 in D major Op. 25 (*Classical*)
CSO
Dir: Humphrey Burton
LONDON: LD (never released)

STRAUSS: Till Eulenspiegel/Death and Transfiguration/Four Last Songs
Lucia Popp, soprano
CSO
Dir: Humphrey Burton
LONDON: LD (never released)

STRAUSS: Arabella (complete)
Janowitz/Ghazarian/Weikl/Gruberova/Kollo
VPO
Stage Dir: Otto Schenk
DG: 072-505-1 (LD); 072-505-3 (VHS)

1978

BEETHOVEN: Symphony No. 1 in C major Op. 21
BRUCKNER: Symphony No. 7 in E major
CSO
Royal Albert Hall, London, England
LONDON: 071 205-1LH (LD); 071 205-3LH (VHS)

ROSSINI: Il barbiere di Siviglia: Overture/La gazza ladra: Overture/L'Italiana in Algeri: Overture/La scala di seta: Overture/Semiramide: Overture
CSO
LONDON: 071 207-1LH (LD); 071 207-3LH (VHS)

ROSSINI: Le siège de Corinthe: Overture
CSO
LONDON: LD (never released)

SCHUBERT: Symphony No. 6 in C major D. 589/Symphony No. 8 in B minor D. 759 (*Unfinished*)
CSO
LONDON: LD (never released)

1979

BRUCKNER: Symphony No. 6 in A major
CSO
Dir: Humphrey Burton
LONDON: LD (never released)

MENDELSSOHN: Violin Concerto in E minor Op. 64/Symphony No. 3 in A minor Op. 58 (*Scottish*)
Kyung Wha-Chung, violin
CSO
LONDON: 071 110-1LH (LD)

VERDI: Falstaff (complete)
Bacquier/K. Armstrong/Stilwell/Cosotti/Lanigan
VPO
Stage Dir: Götz Friedrich
LONDON: 071 503-1 (LD);
DG 073 408 (DVD)(2005)

NEW YEAR'S CONCERT 1979
BRAHMS: Hungarian Dance No. 5/DELIBES: Coppélia (excerpts)/ELGAR: Pomp and Circumstance March No. 1/OFFENBACH: Gaité Parisienne (excerpts)/PONCHIELLI: La Gioconda: Dance of the Hours/SUPPÉ: Pique

Dame: Overture/STRAUSS: Der Rosenkavalier: Waltzes/TCHAIKOVSKY: Nutcracker Suite
LPO
Dir: Humphrey Burton
UNITEL: (never released)

1980

BARTÓK: Bluebeard's Castle
S. Sass/K. Kováts
LPO
Dir: Miklos Szinetár
LONDON: 071 247-1 (LD); 071 247-3 (VHS)

NEW YEAR'S CONCERT 1980
LISZT: Les Préludes/LISZT: Mephisto Waltz/SMETANA: The Moldau/STRAUSS: Don Juan/SUPPÉ: Poet and Peasant: Overture
LPO
Dir: Rodney Greenberg
LONDON: 071-207-1 (LD)

1981

HUMPERDINCK: Hänsel und Gretel (complete)
Gruberova/Fassbänder/Prey/Dernesch/Jurinac
VPO
Stage Dir: August Everding
LONDON: 071 202-1 (LD); 071 202-3 (VHS);
DG: 073 411 (DVD)

1982

BORODIN: Prince Igor: Overture
TCHAIKOVSKY: Piano Concerto No. 1 in B flat minor Op. 23
STRAUSS: Also sprach Zarathustra
Cecile Licad, piano
CSO
CLARION: LP-101 (VHS)

1984

STRAUSS: Der Rosenkavalier (complete)
Te Kanawa/Howells/Bonney/Haugland
ROHC/ROHO
Stage Dir: John Schlesinger
KULTUR: D2029 (DVD)

1986

MOZART: Symphony No. 35 in D major K. 385 (*Haffner*)
MAHLER: Symphony No. 5
CSO
Bunkakaikan, Tokyo, Japan
SONY: SLV-46377 (LD); SHV-46377 (VHS)

MUSSORGSKY-RAVEL: Pictures at an Exhibition
CSO
Suntory Hall, Tokyo, Japan
SONY: SLV-46377 (LD); SHV-46377 (VHS)

1987

BEETHOVEN: Coriolan Overture/Piano Concerto No. 1 in C major Op. 15/ Symphony No. 7 in A major Op. 92
Murray Perahia, piano
LSO
Dir: Humphrey Burton
IMAGE ENTERTAINMENT: ID9289RADVD (DVD)

MOZART: Die Entführung aus dem Serail (complete)
Nielsen/Watson/van der Walt
ROHC/ROHO
KULTUR: D2098(DVD)

1989

BEETHOVEN: Symphony No. 5 in C minor Op. 67
CSO
LONDON: (LD never released)

BERLIOZ: Le Damnation de Faust Op. 24 (complete)
Otter/Lewis/Van Dam/Rose
Choristers of Westminster Cathedral
CSOC/CSO
Royal Albert Hall, London, England
Dir: Rodney Greenberg
LONDON: 071 410-1LH (LD); 071 410-3LH (VHS)
ARTHAUS-MUSIK: 102023 (DVD)

1990

SHOSTAKOVICH: Symphony No. 9 in E flat major Op. 70
TCHAIKOVSKY: Symphony No. 6 in B minor Op. 74 (*Pathétique*)
BRS
ARTHAUS MUSIK 100 302

ORCHESTRA!
A 3-part series originally produced for television and later released by Decca as a Polygram Music Video. It features Dudley Moore as host with Solti as music director and conductor with the Schleswig-Holstein Festival orchestra.
DECCA: 071 228-3 (VHS)

BARTÓK: Dance Suite/Piano Concerto No. 3/Concerto for Orchestra
András Schiff, piano
CSO
Budapest Convention Centre, Budapest, Hungary
LONDON: 071 277-1LH (LD); 071 277-3LH (VHS)

BEETHOVEN: Symphony No. 5 in C minor Op. 67
BERLIOZ: Le Damnation de Faust Op. 24: Rákóczy March
CSO
Suntory Hall, Tokyo, Japan
CBS/SONY: CSLM 915 (LD)

Salzburg Festival Production
VERDI: Un Ballo in Maschera
Barstow/Nucci/Domingo/Jo
VPO
TDK DV-CLOPUBIM (DVD)

1991

VERDI; Simon Boccanegra (complete)
Te Kanawa/Sylvester/Agache
ROHC/ROHO
Stage Dir: Elijah Moshinsky
DECCA: 071 423-3 (VHS)

NOBEL JUBILEE CONCERT
MOZART: Arias (5)
BRAHMS: Symphony No. 1 in C minor Op. 68
Kiri Te Kanawa, soprano
Royal Stockholm Philharmonic
KULTUR: D1340 (VHS)

MOZART: Requiem in D minor K. 626
Auger/Bartoli/Cole/Pape
VSOC/VPO
St. Stephen's Cathedral, Vienna, Austria
Dir: Humphrey Burton
DECCA: B0002506-09 (DVD); 071 139-3 (DVD)

1992

VERDI: Otello (complete)
Te Kanawa/Domingo/Leiferkus
ROHC/ROHO
Dir: Brian Large
KULTUR: D1492 (DVD)

STRAUSS: Die Frau ohne Schatten (complete)
Studer/Marton/Moser/Hale/Terfel
VPO
Salzburg Festival Production
DECCA: 071 425 (DVD)

THE MAESTRO AND THE DIVA
STRAUSS: Four Last Songs/Lieder
Kiri Te Kanawa, soprano

BBC Philharmonic
SONY: (VHS)

MENDELSSOHN: Symphony No. 4 in A major Op. 90 (*Italian*)
SHOSTAKOVICH: Symphony No. 10 Op. 93
BRS
Dir: Klaus Lindemann
IMAGE ENTERTAINMENT: ID5812RADVD (DVD)

1993

BRUCKNER: Symphony No. 3
STRAVINSKY: Symphony in 3 Movements
BRS
ARTHAUS-MUSIK: 100320 (available in PAL format only)

1994

VERDI: La Traviata (complete)
Gheorgiu/Lopardo/Nucci
ROHC/ROHO
Stage Dir: Richard Eyre
Dir: Humphrey Burton/Peter Maniura
DECCA: 071 431-9 (DVD)

1995

World Orchestra for Peace: UN 50th Anniversary Concert
ROSSINI: William Tell: Overture
BARTÓK: Concerto for Orchestra
BEETHOVEN: Fidelio: Act II Finale
Herlitzius/Andersen/Kohn/Dohmen/Ziesak/Tschammer
LV/WOP
(DVD includes an interview with Solti and rehearsal excerpts)
Dir: Michel Dami
Victoria Hall, Geneva, Switzerland
PHILIPS/DECCA: B0005187-10 (DVD)

HAYDN: Die Schöpfung
Ziesak/Lippert/Scharinger/Hagen

BRC/BRSO
Dir: Peter Maniura
DIGITAL CLASSICS DC 10005 (DVD)

BARTÓK: Rumanian Folk Dances/KODALY: Hary Janos Suite/WEINER: Prince Csongor: Scherzo/BERLIOZ: le Damnation de Faust: Rákóczy March/ BEETHOVEN: Symphony No. 7 in A major Op. 92
VPO
Dir: Horant H. Hohlfeld
UNITEL: (never released)

1997

SOLTI: THE MAKING OF A MAESTRO
A BBC documentary made in the last year of Solti's life, and directed by Peter Maniura. When this documentary was first issued on VHS it also included a complete performance of Tchaikovsky's Symphony No. 6 in B minor Op. 74 (*Pathétique*) with the Bavarian Radio Symphony Orchestra.
IMAGE ENTERTAINMENT: ID9288RADVD (DVD)

SIR GEORG SOLTI, CONDUCTOR—A PORTRAIT
With Isaac Stern, Hildegard Behrens and Wolfgang Wagner.
Dir: Valerie Pitts Solti
UNITEL: (never released)

Index

Abbado, Claudio 35, 45, 107
Aleksashkin, Sergei 131
Ameling, Elly 88

Bailey, Norman 109
Barenboim, Daniel 45, 119
Bartók, Béla 1
Bastianini, Ettore 12
Bergman, Ingmar 106
Bernstein, Leonard 5, 80, 124
Bignen, Max 105
Björling, Jussi 12
Blyth, Alan 114
Böhme, Kurt 10
Borkh, Inge 11, 12
Boulez, Pierre 75, 119
Boult, Sir Adrian x, 127
Britten, Benjamin 19
Bumbry, Grace 111, 118
Burrows, Stuart 79

Cantelli, Guido 13
Cassidy, Claudia 41
Cavalli, Floriana 22
Chandler, Mrs. Norman B. 17
Churchill, Marylou Speaker 129
Clevenger, Dale 91, 129
Combs, Larry 129
Cooke, Deryck 95, 187
Corkhill, David 129, 143
Cossutta, Carlos 105, 110
Culshaw, John x, 8, 50, 51, 56, 108, 125, 191

De Peyer, Gervase 84
Dean, Winton 113
Defauw, Désiré 30
Della Casa, Lisa 26
Dettmer, Roger 134
Dohnányi, Ernst von 1, 46
Domingo, Placido 107, 110, 114
Dorati, Antal 1
Drogheda, Lord 19
Du Pré, Jacqueline 119
Dutoit, Charles 36
Dvoráková, Ludmilla 27

Eda-Pierre, Christiane 106
Edwards, John 32, 33, 43, 44
Ericson, Raymond 39, 134

Ferrier, Kathleen 85
Fischer-Dieskau, Dietrich 26, 56, 109
Fischer, Edwin 7
Flagstad, Kirsten 50
Fleming, Renée 113, 115, 116, 188
Fogel, Henry 43, 44
Frankenstein, Alfred 11
Freni, Mirella 105, 111
Frick, Gottlob 7, 56
Fricsay, Ferenc 1
Furtwängler, Wilhelm 3, 41

Gardiner, John Eliot 121
Gedda, Nicolai 105
Gheorghiu, Angela 111

Ghiaurov, Nicolai 111
Giulini, Carlo Maria 34, 98
Glossop, Peter 28
Glotz, Michel 33
Gorner, Peter 31, 32
Gorr, Rita 20
Greenfield, Edward 56
Greenhalgh, John 24, 58
Grüber, Klaus Michael 106
Grümmer, Elisabeth 7
Guttoso, Renato 21

Haitink, Bernard 87, 111
Haltrecht, Montague 22
Harper, Heather 91
Harris, Dale 106
Hartmann, Rudolf 26
Heath, Edward 27
Heppner, Ben 109
Herseth, Adolph Bud 43
Heyworth, Peter 9
Higgins, John 28
Hillis, Margaret 43
Hines, Jerome 14
Hirzel, Max 4
Hopf, Hans 6, 14
Horenstein, Jascha 86
Hotter, Hans 20, 55, 56

Jack, Adrian 133
Jones, Gwyneth 28
Jurinac, Sena 6

Karajan, Herbert von x, 33, 35, 39, 53, 65, 107, 117, 139
Kawazuka, Junichiro 38
Kenyon, Nicholas 134
Kern, Herbert 20
Kertesz, Istvan 1
Kilenyi, Edward 5

King, James 56
Kleiber, Erich 1
Klemperer, Otto x
Klose, Margarete 11
Knappertsbusch, Hans 6, 51, 52
Kodály, Zoltán 1
Kokoschka, Oskar 7
Kollo, René 91, 92, 94, 109
Köth, Erika 7
Krause, Tom 105
Kraus, Alfredo 111
Kubelik, Rafael 19, 30, 41
Küchl, Rainer 129
Kulenkampff, Georg 144

Langdon, Michael 20
Lawrence, Robert 133
Lebrecht, Norman 45
Legge, Walter 54
Levine, James 87
Lewis, Richard 105
Liebermann, Rolf 104
Lipman, Samuel 58
Lipp, Wilma 6
London, George 56
Lopardo, Frank 111
Lorengar, Pilar 79
Ludwig, Christa 7, 10, 12, 94

Mann, William 2, 6, 65, 69, 77, 78, 80, 187
Martinon, Jean 30
Mathis, Edith 105
Mazer, Henry 34
Mehta, Zubin 5, 17
Mengelberg, Willem 87
Merrill, Robert 111
Miller, Sarah Bryan 45
Minton, Yvonne 79, 94
Mirageas, Evans 115
Mitropoulos, Dimitri x

Moffo, Anna 111
Monson, Karen 41
Monteux, Pierre 11
Moseley, Carlos 119
Münch, Charles 117

Neher, Caspar 15
Neidlinger, Gustav 55
Nikisch, Artur x
Nilsson, Birgit 12, 27, 55, 56, 103, 108
Norman, Jessye 79
Nucci, Leo 110, 111

Oeser, Fritz 113
Ormandy, Eugene 1
Osborne, Conrad L. 58
Osborne, Richard 33
Ozawa, Seiji 5, 35

Parry, Gordon 56, 57, 108
Pásztory, Ditta 129
Peck, Donald 31, 43
Pelligrini, Norman viii, 132
Perahia, Murray 129, 143, 188, 195
Peyer, Gervase de 84
Pitt, Charles 105
Popp, Lucia 192
Porter, Andrew 7
Preauer, Curt 9
Prey, Hermann 14
Price, Leontyne 22, 111, 185
Price, Margaret 105

Raeburn, Christopher 7
Reiner, Fritz 1, 17, 30
Reining, Maria 6, 10
Repass, Richard 14
Rescigno, Nicola 12
Rice, Peter 26

Rodzinski, Artur 30
Rosengarten, Maurice 52
Rosenthal, Harold 19, 21, 23, 26, 27, 28
Rossi-Lemeni, Nicola 12
Rysanek, Leonie 14

Sargeant, Winthrop 39
Schiff, András 122, 144, 196
Schlesinger, John 107, 195
Schöffler, Paul 12
Schonberg, Harold C. x, 3, 13, 14, 133
Simionato, Giulietta 12, 111
Simoneau, Leopold 12
Smith, Cecil 11
Stade, Frederica von 105
Stahlman, Sylvia 88
Steffek, Hanny 10
Stein, Peter 61, 106
Stevens, Thomas 129
Steyer, Ralf 10
Still, Ray 31, 32, 43
Stock, Frederick 30
Stolze, Gerhard 55
Strehler, Giorgio 106
Sudler, Louis 32
Sutcliffe, Tom 27
Szell, George 1, 38, 40

Talley, Howard 12
Talvela, Martti 79
Taubman, Howard 13
Te Kanawa, Kiri 43, 88, 110, 116, 122, 136, 137, 145, 197
Tebaldi, Renata 12, 111
Terfel, Bryn 113
Thomas, Ernst 9
Thomas, Jess 27
Thomas, Theodore 30
Toller, Owen 47
Toscanini, Arturo 2

Troyanos, Tatiana 114
Tucker, Richard 12
Tuckwell, Barry 84, 92

Uebel, Ruth 10
Uhl, Fritz 108
Ustinov, Peter 21

Van Beinum, Eduard 87
Van Dam, José 114
Veasey, Josephine 20
Vernon, Robert 129
Vickers, Jon xi, 20, 56, 111

Wagner, Wolfgang 61, 62, 199

Walter, Bruno 5, 19, 88
Wanamaker, Sam 21
Ward, David 28
Warrack, John 22
Watson, Claire 20
Watts, Helen 85
Webster, Sir David 19, 21, 22
Wilford, Ronald 33
Willis, Thomas 41
Windgassen, Wolfgang 54, 55
Witte, Erich 15
Woodhams, Richard 129

Zakai, Mira 85
Zapf, Rosl 8

978-0-595-39953-6
0-595-39953-3